D1091636

Yale Studies in English
Richard S. Sylvester, Editor
Volume 174

DRYDEN AND THE ABYSS OF LIGHT

A Study of *Religio Laici* and
The Hind and the Panther

SANFORD BUDICK

New Haven and London, Yale University Press, 1970

Published with assistance from the foundation established in memory
of Philip Hamilton McMillan of the class of 1894, Yale College.

Library of Congress catalog card number: 73–115367
International standard book number: 0–300–01338–8

Designed by John O. C. McCrillis,
set in Baskerville type,
and printed in the United States of America by
The Colonial Press Inc., Clinton, Massachusetts.

Distributed in Great Britain, Europe, Asia, and
Africa by Yale University Press Ltd., London; in
Canada by McGill-Queen's University Press, Montreal;
in Mexico by Centro Interamericano de Libros
Académicos, Mexico City; in Australasia by Australia
and New Zealand Book Co., Pty., Ltd., Artarmon,
New South Wales; in India by UBS Publishers'
Distributors Pvt., Ltd., Delhi; in Japan
by John Weatherhill, Inc., Tokyo.

FOR MY PARENTS

If any of so happy a genius be now living, or any future age can produce a man . . . conversant in the philosophy of Plato, as it is now accommodated to Christian use . . . he may build a nobler, a more beautiful, and more perfect poem than any yet extant since the Ancients.

DRYDEN, *A Discourse concerning the Original and Progress of Satire* (1693)

Contents

Preface

The modern revaluation of Augustan poetry has learned to ask one question supremely well: what is the real scope of the artist's subject and achievement? Is it only personal and occasional or does it also have timeless, universal concerns to which local details are, in the end, made subordinate? Dryden's poetry has been late in benefiting from this kind of question, but even in the last decade it has become common to speak of his satires in terms of the same issues that occupy our attention in *Paradise Lost*. The question of scope must now be raised in relation to *Religio Laici* and *The Hind and the Panther*. Readers have always felt that these poems are among Dryden's most important works, but the reasons for their feelings have never been clear. Is *Religio Laici*, in fact, a work of art which attempts to formulate some universal and enduring truth about man and life? Is *The Hind and the Panther*, for all its beast-fable machinery, more than (as Swift would have it) "a compleat Abstract of sixteen thousand Schoolmen from Scotus to Bellarmin"? [1]

Geoffrey Tillotson has remarked that the "eighteenth century liked a restriction which operated before the poem was begun, which operated as a condition of the 'inspiration.' " [2] The answers to our questions await us, first, in describing (with the reader's patience) the "conditions"—in this case, the attitudes of the muse as well as the impinging contexts—that are predicated in these poems; and, second, in demonstrating the poetic wholes that Dryden worked to create. The integrity of Dryden's religious thought is not to be redeemed by arguing

1. Jonathan Swift, *A Tale of a Tub,* ed. A. C. Guthkelch and D. Nichol Smith (Oxford, 1958), p. 69.
2. Geoffrey Tillotson, *Augustan Poetic Diction* (London, 1964), p. 19.

for early, subtle signs of Roman Catholic tendencies in *Religio Laici* or by suggesting that his religious poems are only versified doctrinal treatises of one persuasion or another. There is an overarching, powerful coherence to his religious views which can be discovered by examining all his opinions closely and, what is most important yet most difficult for modern criticism, by treating him, according to his own wish, as a poet.

It is with no thought of making present payment that I attempt to record here some of my many debts. Kindness and affection are, in fact, the only recompense for kindness and affection. My greatest debt is to my parents, to my two brothers, and to my wife. Professor Maynard Mack directed my dissertation on *Religio Laici* at Yale. Everything of value in the following pages has benefited from his kindness and knowledge. He will always serve me as a model of intellectual grace and integrity.

My debt to previous commentators is, I hope, made sufficiently clear in the text and notes. Phillip Harth's recent study of the background of Dryden's religious poems, *Contexts of Dryden's Thought* (Chicago, 1968), appeared after most of this book was written, but I have profited from his work even while I have disagreed with many of his arguments and interpretations of evidence. For aid, encouragement, and enlightening conversation, I wish to thank Emmanuel Bloom of New York City; David Haley, my tutor at Harvard; Steven Hochstein of Jerusalem; Douglas Archibald, Morris R. Brownell, Scott Elledge, James Hutton, David Novarr, and Winthrop Wetherbee, III of Cornell University; John Hollander, James M. Osborn, and Richard S. Sylvester of Yale University; Jerome McGann of the University of Chicago; Ruth Nevo of the Hebrew University; Barbara W. Folsom and Wayland W. Schmitt of Yale University Press; and Samuel Middlebrook, Dean of the City College of New York. All the faults in the book are mine alone.

Thomas H. Clancy, S.J., of Loyola University in New Orleans kindly sent me a copy of his unpublished catalogue,

"English Catholic Books, 1666–1700" (compiled with the aid of David Rogers, Oxford University). I owe a special debt of gratitude to Stuart M. Brown, formerly Dean of the College of Arts and Sciences of Cornell University, and to Ephim G. Fogel, Chairman of the Department of English, whose assistance through the Humanities Faculty Research Grants Committee and the Clark Grant-in-Aid Fund, made possible crucial journeys to British libraries. For able assistance in preparing the index, I wish to thank Gary Wood, my student aide. The librarians of Yale, Cornell, the Union Theological Seminary of New York, the University of Edinburgh, the British Museum, Cambridge, and Oxford responded to my requests graciously and fully. A version of Appendix B has previously appeared in *Notes and Queries,* and some of the materials in chapters 8, 9, and 10 have been published in the *Times Literary Supplement.*

A full acknowledgment of my debt to my wife Emily would require a separate volume. Through the course of my labors, she has provided unstinting assistance, invaluable information, and brimming joy.

S. B.

Ithaca, New York
January 1969

Note on Citations and Abbreviations

All citations from Dryden's poetry are, unless otherwise indicated, to *The Poems of John Dryden,* ed. James Kinsley, 4 vols. (Oxford, 1958).

The following abbreviations have been used throughout the notes:

ES	*English Studies*
HTR	*Harvard Theological Review*
JEGP	*Journal of English and Germanic Philology*
JWCI	*Journal of the Warburg and Courtauld Institutes*
MLN	*Modern Language Notes*
MLR	*Modern Language Review*
N&Q	*Notes and Queries*
PMLA	*Publications of the Modern Language Association of America*
PQ	*Philological Quarterly*
PhR	*Philosophical Review*
RES	*Review of English Studies*
TLS	[London] *Times Literary Supplement*

Where the italics of quoted matter convey no special emphasis I have printed them in roman type within my text. In block quotations I have reproduced all original italics.

1

Challenges to Religious Poetry
in the Restoration

"Theology and Poesy have in all ages of the World gone hand in hand, nor is there really such a disparity between their Natures, as is generally, though without any reason, imagined. . . . I must confess at this day, but by what ill Fate I know not, they are looked upon without the least relation to each other." So wrote Samuel Woodford in 1667 in the preface to his *Paraphrase upon the Psalms.*[1] This was one of the books a man named Dryden purchased on 15 May 1682.[2] We can be sure that even if the poet Dryden did not read Woodford's preface, he was sadly familiar with such sentiments.

Poetry and Metaphor

One kind of "ill Fate" that had separated poetry and theology in the Restoration was well known. In fact, Woodford's preface innocently refers to one of the loudest prognosticators of poetry's impending doom: this was his "very judicious friend Mr. Thomas Sprat."[3] Sprat and Woodford are useful gnomons of poetry's status in the Restoration. They were not enemies of poetry per se. Both wrote verse and both hoped for the "improvement" of modern poetry. Yet they reflect the widespread devaluation of poetry which had been threatening

1. *A Paraphrase upon the Psalms of David* (London, 1667), sigs. a2r–a3r.
2. See T. A. Birrell, "John Dryden's Purchases at Two Book Auctions, 1680 and 1682," *ES*, XLII (1961), 215, and the review of this article by James M. Osborn, *PQ*, XLI (1962), 580. Cf. Appendix B, n. 3.
3. Woodford, *Paraphrase upon the Psalms*, sig. b4v.

since Bacon and now promised to deny poetry any connection
with truth.

Sprat was only echoing *his* good friend Abraham Cowley,
the "darling" of Dryden's youth,[4] when he complained that
"the Fables and Religions of the Ancient World"

> have already serv'd the *Poets* long enough; and it is now
> high time to dismiss them; especially seing [*sic*] they
> have this peculiar *imperfection,* that they were only *Fic-*
> *tions* at first: whereas *Truth* is never so well express'd or
> amplify'd, as by those Ornaments which are *Tru* and *Real*
> in themselves.

We are unfair to Sprat and we misrepresent his age when we
forget that he hoped a solid "Foundation for Wit" would be
found by deriving "true" images from "the Civil Histories of
all Countries, the Customs of Nations, the Bible, the Sciences,
and Manners of Men, the several Arts of their hands, and the
works of Nature." [5]

But in their present state the "Ornaments" of language,
Sprat argued in 1667, are "much degenerated from their original usefulness."

> They were at first, no doubt, an admirable Instrument in
> the hands of *Wise Men:* when they were onely employ'd
> to describe *Goodness, Honesty, Obedience;* in larger,
> fairer, and more moving Images: to represent *Truth,*
> cloth'd with Bodies; and to bring *Knowledg* back again

4. John Dryden, *Of Dramatic Poesy and Other Critical Essays,* ed.
George Watson (London, 1962), II, 150. For Cowley's Spratlike opinions
see his *Poetry and Prose,* ed. L. C. Martin (Oxford, 1949), p. 72.

5. Thomas Sprat, *The History of the Royal Society of London* (London,
1667), pp. 413–14. For correctives to Basil Willey's account of Sprat in
*The Seventeenth Century Background: Studies in the Thought of the
Age in Relation to Poetry and Religion* (New York, 1953), see Donald
Bond, " 'Distrust' of Imagination in English Neo-Classicism," *PQ,* XIV
(1935), 69, and Albert Rosenberg, "Bishop Sprat on Science and Imagery,"
Isis, XLIII (1952), 220–22.

to our very senses, from whence it was at first deriv'd to our understandings. But now they are generally chang'd to worse uses: They make the *Fancy* disgust the best things, if they come sound, and unadorn'd: they are in open defiance against *Reason;* professing, not to hold much correspondence with that; but with its Slaves, *the Passions.*[6]

Sprat's assertions are part of the general distrust of imagination during the Restoration. Metaphor, especially, came to be seriously suspect: science-minded men of the burgeoning Enlightenment objected, as R. F. Jones has explained, to "a word's possessing many meanings or the same meaning as another word. . . . The desire to make the word match the thing, to be in a strict sense a description of a thing or action, explains their exaggerated antipathy to metaphors and such figures of speech." [7] Typical of the contemporary concern with words and things was William Petty's attempt to draw up a "Dictionary of Sensible Words" which would show "what sensible Matter, Thing, Motion or Action, every word therein doth meane and signify." [8] From many quarters came programs for the rehabilitation of the language so that it might "return" to the communication of truth. John Wilkins's *Essay Towards a Real Character, And a Philosophical Language* (London, 1668), for example, argued that "though the varieties of Phrases in Language may seem to contribute to the elegance and ornament of Speech; yet, like other affected ornaments, they prejudice the native simplicity of it, and contribute to the disguising of it with false appearances" (p. 18). Cowley's last poem, the panegyric ode included in Sprat's

6. Sprat, pp. 111–12.

7. "Science and Language in England of the Mid-Seventeenth Century," in *The Seventeenth Century: Studies in the History of English Thought and Literature from Bacon to Pope,* by Richard Foster Jones and others writing in his honor (Stanford, 1951), p. 155.

8. William Petty, *The Petty Papers,* ed. Marquis of Lansdowne (London, 1927), I, 150–51.

History of the Royal Society (1667), contains agonized evidence of the dilemma which such strictures imposed on the poet. In praising Bacon's achievement, Cowley becomes embroiled in a self-contradictory rhetorical position.

> From Words, which are but Pictures of the Thought,
> (Though we our Thoughts from them perversely drew)
> To Things, the Minds right Object, he it brought,
> Like foolish Birds to painted Grapes we flew;
> He sought and gather'd for our use the True;
> And when on heaps the chosen Bunches lay,
> He prest them wisely the Mechanick way,
> Till all their juyce did in one Vessel joyn,
> Ferment into a Nourishment Divine,
> The thirsty Souls refreshing Wine.[9]

It is difficult, if not impossible, to consider the last two lines as anything but "painted Grapes." It is not surprising to find Dryden warning us, in *The Author's Apology for Heroic Poetry and Poetic Licence* (1677), to be "pleased with the image, without being cozened by the fiction." [10] The embarrassment of using the imagination to describe truth in an Age of Reason is manifest in his views on rhyme. Rhyme is useful, he says, because it "most regulates the fancy" or "lawless imagination." [11] Even when he took a brief holiday from rhyme, in the last heroic plays, it was only because he considered rhyme inappropriate for expressing the irrational: "Passion's too fierce," he tells us, "to be in Fetters bound." [12]

Theology and Imagination

When it came to the most crucial area of linguistic endeavor —the communicating of God's abstract Word—the critics of poetic language often became hysterical. In 1670, Samuel

9. Cowley, *Poetry and Prose*, p. 56.
10. *Of Dramatic Poesy*, I, 202.
11. Ibid., I, 9 and 91.
12. Prologue to *Aureng-Zebe* (1676), l. 9.

Parker asked for an act of Parliament "to abridge Preachers the use of fulsom and lushious Metaphors" because, as he believed, tropes bred faction and fanaticism.[13] That Dryden sympathized with the general attack on pulpit eloquence is evident from his remarks, in 1672, on the practice of "playing" with words in the age of Sir Philip Sidney: "In his time, I believe, it ascended first into the pulpit, where (if you will give me leave to clench too) it yet finds the benefit of its clergy. For they are commonly the first corrupters of eloquence, and the last reformed from vicious oratory." [14] Parker protested that "All those Theories in Philosophie which are expressed only in metaphorical Termes, are not real Truths, but the meer Products of Imagination, dress'd up (like Childrens babies) in a few spangled empty words." [15] Spiritual truth, it was felt by many, can never be discovered by the material imagination which deals in pictures and distracts us from the abstract. Glanvill speaks of the "evil conduct of our Imaginations; whose irregular strength and importunity doth almost perpetually abuse us." To reach "spirituals" we must "denudate them of all material Phantasmes" so that they may be apprehended by our "Intellects." [16] Even the Cambridge Platonists, who were perhaps the most poetically inclined theologians and philosophers of the period, spoke with contempt of this "materious Disease" with its "Symptoms of a mind desperately sick of this Corporeal Malady of Imagination." [17]

13. Samuel Parker, *A Discourse of Ecclesiastical Politie* (London, 1670), p. 76. Cf. R. F. Jones, "The Attack on Pulpit Eloquence in the Restoration: An Episode in the Development of the Neo-Classical Standard for Prose," in *The Seventeenth Century*, pp. 111–42.

14. *Of Dramatic Poesy*, I, 179; cf. Jones, *The Seventeenth Century*, p. 141.

15. Samuel Parker, *A Free and Impartial Censure of the Platonick Philosophie* (Oxford, 1667), p. 79.

16. Joseph Glanvill, *The Vanity of Dogmatizing* (London, 1661), pp. 95–97.

17. Henry More, "The easie true, and genuine Notion, and consistent Explication of the Nature of a Spirit," appended to Glanvill's *Saducismus Triumphatus* (London, 1681), pp. 149 and 156.

In a work like *Religio Laici* (1682), where "Sacred Truth" is the object, even the use of rhymes like Hopkins's or Shadwell's (l. 456) is better, Dryden suggests, than leaving the imagination unbridled. Imagination and passion, as the last sentence of the Preface to *Religio Laici* informs us, are antithetical to reason and truth.

Skepticism

Another aspect of the awkward position of the religious poet in the Restoration was the growing belief that truth could only be discovered through skeptical "method." "I could name you authors," Culverwel objected, "of good worth and credit, who tell you that Homer, and Archilochus, and Euripides, and the wise men of Greece, were all sceptics; yet those proofs which they bring to evidence and evince it, are not so pregnant and satisfying, but that you may very lawfully doubt of it, and yet be no sceptics neither." [18] The *scepsis scientifica* of the researcher was too often taken on as "personated Scepticism" [19]—a pose—by writers who wished to be identified as modern men. Dryden was adopting just such a pose, for reasons of rhetorical strategy, when he described the essay *Of Dramatic Poesy* as "a dialogue sustained by persons of several opinions, all of them left doubtful, to be determined by the readers in general." [20] Elizabeth Merrill's examination of the *Essay* revealed that "its main purpose is to set forth Dryden's views" and that it is "almost equivalent in value to three essays, in each of which is represented a prevailing view and its refutation." [21] Dryden proudly tells us in the Preface to *Religio Laici* that, "Being naturally inclin'd to Scepticism

18. Nathanael Culverwel, *Of the Light of Nature, A Discourse*, ed. John Brown (Edinburgh, 1857), p. 196.

19. Glanvill, *Vanity of Dogmatizing*, p. 222–23.

20. *Of Dramatic Poesy*, I, 123.

21. Elizabeth Merrill, *The Dialogue in English Literature* (New York, 1911), p. 72.

in Philosophy, I have no reason to impose my Opinions, in a Subject which is above it" (ll. 22–24). This too is a functional pose or mask. Dryden's condemnation of Athanasius, to take just one example, is surely an opinion expressed with the obvious intent of persuading. To build his avowal of "scepticism" into a theological Pyrrhonism is erroneous, both because the premise—that Dryden is announcing a thoroughgoing skeptical attitude—is mistaken, and because the conclusion—that *Religio Laici* is constructed on skeptical principles—is insupportable in terms of the evidence in the poem.[22] No Pyrrhonist who was in the process of leaping into the arms of the Roman Catholic faith would ever assert the independence and the adequacy of his reason in matters of salvation, as Dryden does:

> If *others* in the *same Glass better* see
> 'Tis for *Themselves* they look, but not for *me:*
> For *MY* Salvation must its Doom receive
> Not from what *OTHERS,* but what *I* believe.
>
> [ll. 301–04]

As an intellectual attitude, Dryden's skepticism betokens, at most, a modest degree of tentativeness and open-mindedness which was regarded as necessary to stating truth. As a poetic

22. Louis I. Bredvold, *The Intellectual Milieu of John Dryden: Studies in Some Aspects of Seventeenth-Century Thought* (Ann Arbor, Mich., 1959; first published in 1934) attempted to explain Dryden's intellectual development and the coherence of his poetry in terms of his Pyrrhonistic tendencies. Bredvold's theory has been effectively refuted and replaced by a more accurate conception of Dryden's *scepsis scientifica* in a long series of studies, beginning with early incisive reviews of Bredvold's book by George Williamson, *MLN*, LI (1936), 195–96, and M. E. Prior, *MP*, XXXII (1935), 324–9, and including the articles "Dryden's Apparent Scepticism in *Religio Laici,*" *HTR*, LIV (1961), 207–21, by Elias J. Chiasson and "Dryden's *Religio Laici*: An Anglican Poem," *PMLA*, LXXVI (1961), 205–17, by Thomas H. Fujimura. Phillip Harth's recent chapter on Dryden "The Sceptical Critic" in *Contexts of Dryden's Thought* (Chicago, 1968), pp. 1–31, has admirably summed up and added to earlier investigations.

procedure, it signifies, as we shall see, a concessive, multivocal inquiry artfully managed to produce not only a planned resolution but also a special mood and context.

Poetry of Reason

The situation of the religious poet in the Restoration was, I think, very close to impossible. He was attempting to tell "Sacred Truth" (l. 455) using what the world told him—and he half-admitted to himself—was an instrument of "delightful deceit." [23] "Who can behold, without indignation," asked Sprat, "how many mists and uncertainties, these specious Tropes and Figures have brought on our Knowledg?" [24] Where truth abstract is the only kind of truth, where *Ornari res ipsa negat* (to quote the epigraph of *Religio Laici*) and dialectic has divorced rhetoric in anticipation of a logical positivism, there is not much left for poetry. The implication of Sprat's outlook is that poetry in its present state has no business treating subjects where important truths are at stake. Truth belongs to objective prose, to "a close, naked, natural way of speaking; positive expressions; clear senses; a native easiness: bringing all things as near the Mathematical plainness" as possible.[25] It was partly because Dryden accepted the validity of such a claim that he chose "unpolish'd, rugged Verse, . . . / As fittest for Discourse, and nearest Prose" (ll. 453–54). Only then could his words attempt to communicate "Sacred Truth."

Dryden's consciousness of his task, as I understand it, is made explicit in the Preface. Sprat's protest—that the devices of poetic utterance "are in open defiance against Reason; professing, not to hold much correspondence with that; but with its Slaves, the Passions"—finds a clear echo in Dryden's defense of *Religio Laici*: "The Florid, Elevated, and Figurative

23. Sprat, p. 62.
24. Sprat, p. 112.
25. Sprat, p. 113.

way is for the Passions; for Love and Hatred, Fear and Anger, are begotten in the Soul by shewing their Objects out of their true proportion; either greater than the Life, or less; but Instruction is to be given by shewing them what they naturally are. A Man is to be cheated into Passion, but to be reason'd into Truth" (ll. 350–55). The "Smoothness, the Numbers and the Turn of Heroick Poetry" must be avoided in order to approach the *Ding-an-sich,* the real truth with which "Discourse" (l. 454) is concerned. Dryden invokes Horace's *Epistles* as a precedential argument for the bare possibility of telling practical truth in poetry. Nor can we hope that the religious poet's situation was much improved by 1686, the year in which Dryden sat down to write *The Hind and the Panther.* Dryden's puzzling desire to employ a combination of "Majestick," "perspicuous," and "familiar" verse reflects continued uneasiness about the appropriateness of poetic expression to theological subjects.[26]

For those who believed that a poetry of reason had a responsibility in stating religious truth, the only way open was to create a seemingly impossible commodity: a true abstract image. Dryden's two responses to this challenge were, I believe, quite spectacular; but, by their very nature, they can only be broached to the understanding by the somewhat devious, fact-bound methods of "discourse." The answers to the largest questions, as Dryden himself realized and reflected in his choice of occasional media, must be held patiently in abeyance until they can emerge naturally from the alphabet of being—from the conflicts and doubts and beliefs which are the stuff of life and of a living poetry.

26. Prefatory note to *The Hind and the Panther,* ll. 94–99.

2

Facts and Problems: *Religio Laici*

It was once thought that Dryden's contemporaries received *Religio Laici* without interest. We know now, however, that three issues of the first edition and a second edition (possibly a reprint) were run off in 1682, and that a third edition was soon called for in 1683.[1] The first edition was accompanied by two commendatory poems: one anonymous (probably by John Vaughan)[2] and the other by Thomas Creech. The third edition prefixed additional verses by Roscommon. The poem was not reprinted again, presumably in accordance with Dryden's personal injunction, until 1701, when Tonson brought out the posthumous folio edition of Dryden's poems.[3]

Dryden and Simon's *Histoire critique du Vieux Testament*

But the circumstances of the poem's composition remain clouded. Dryden tells us in the Preface that

> the Verses were written for an ingenious young Gentle-
> man my Friend; upon his Translation of *The Critical
> History of the Old Testament*, compos'd by the learned

1. See Hugh Macdonald, *John Dryden: A Bibliography of Early Editions and of Drydeniana* (Oxford, 1939), pp. 33–35.
2. See Richard H. Perkinson, "A Note on Dryden's *Religio Laici*," *PQ*, XXVIII (1949), 517–18.
3. Dryden's earliest announced reason for preventing further publication of the poem was apparently not related to a change in religious conviction. In 1684 he agreed with Tonson that *Religio Laici* should not be included in the forthcoming Miscellanies, which was to be an entirely new volume: "Your opinion of the Miscellanyes is likewise mine: I will for once lay by the Religio Laici, till another time"—see *The Letters of John Dryden*, ed. Charles E. Ward (Durham, N.C., 1942), p. 23.

Father *Simon:* The Verses therefore are address'd to the
Translatour of that Work, and the style of them is, what
it ought to be, Epistolary.[4] [ll. 338–42]

4. The identity of the "ingenious young Gentleman" was, for a long
time, a problem, but persuasive evidence has now left no doubt that
the man in question was one Henry Dickinson. We know almost nothing
definite about Dickinson's life. Why Dryden calls him "my Friend,"
three times (once in the Preface, l. 339, and twice in the poem, ll. 228
and 398) is not clear. The closest connection between Dickinson and
Dryden which has been discovered to date is that Dickinson's translation
and the second part of *Absalom and Achitophel* were both going
through Tonson's hands at the same time: the two men may have met
through Tonson, or possibly, while reading proof. Scott suggested that
Henry Dickinson (or Dickenson) was "probably a son of Edmund
Dickinson, a physician, and author of *Delphi Phenicizantes* and other
learned pieces": see *The Works of John Dryden,* edited by Sir Walter
Scott and revised by George Saintsbury (Edinburgh, 1885), x, 32 n.
(Hereafter cited as *Works of John Dryden.*)

It should also be noted, I think, that there is a superficial similarity
between the elder Dickinson's works and some of the subjects treated in
Dryden's Preface. *Delphi Phœnicizantes* (Oxford, 1665) argues the continuity of religious knowledge from Noah through the Greeks. Dryden
makes a similar point in the Preface, ll. 44–82 (these views are discussed
in detail in chap. 5). Most of Edmund Dickinson's scholarly activities
were centered around the preparation of *Physica vetus et vera* (London,
1702) in which he attempted to establish a philosophy on principles
gathered from the Pentateuch. This too is a subject which is relevant
to *Religio Laici.* He was appointed physician in ordinary and physician
to the household by Charles II. It is possible that Dryden knew him
and through the father met the son. In a bill of complaint against
Henry Dickinson, Tonson says that Henry Dickinson told him that "he
had obtained the principal end he aimed at in the translation which
was the pleasing of his father." This bill of complaint is reproduced,
in part, by Charles E. Ward in his article, "*Religio Laici* and Father
Simon's *History,*" *MLN,* LXI (1946), 407–12. (Ward does not suggest any connection between **Tonson's** remark and Scott's identification.) It must
be pointed out, however, that W. N. Blomberg's *An Account of the
Life and Writings of Edmund Dickinson* (London, 1737) makes no
mention of any sons, although it does record the birth of a daughter by
Dickinson's first wife (p. 62). Unless additional information comes to
light, it must be said that Ward's suggestion that the appellation was
only the effect of Dryden's usual kindness to young literary men is
most plausible (p. 407).

That the translation of Simon's *Histoire critique du Vieux Testament* was in some sense, as Kinsley puts it, the "occasion"[5] of *Religio Laici* is certain. Dryden explicitly tells us so in the Preface and commends the work in the body of the poem. But that the *Critical History* is not the main subject of *Religio Laici* is equally certain. At line 224, Dryden turns to his addressee, Dickinson, for the first time, and says,

> Thus far my Charity this path has try'd;
> (A much unskilfull, but well meaning guide:)
> Yet what they are, ev'n these crude thoughts were bred
> By reading that, which better thou hast read,
> Thy Matchless Author's work.

This is somewhat puzzling if interpreted rigidly, because Dryden has just been arguing for the salvation of heathens against Athanasius: this is not one of the concerns of Simon's *Critical History*. In fact, there can be no doubt that Simon would have been made unhappy to learn that his book "bred" an attack on the Athanasian Creed. Louis I. Bredvold, who has been the primary advocate of the significance of Simon's *Critical History* for the meaning of the poem and who has gone so far as to say that "Dryden's acquaintance with it was perhaps the most critical event in his intellectual life,"[6] has offered no explanation for this difficulty. It is misleading to intimate that, at this time, Dryden saw (much less accepted) any of the implications of Catholic fideism which Bredvold argues are the inevitable consequences of Simon's work. It is true that Evelyn penned a frantic letter to Dr. Fell, Bishop of Oxford, on the "great danger and fatal consequences" of Simon's work: "For the love of God, let our Universities, my Lord, no longer remain thus silent; it is the cause of God, and of our Church!"[7] But the universities did

5. *The Poems of John Dryden*, ed. James Kinsley, IV, 1932.
6. *The Intellectual Milieu of John Dryden*, p. 106.
7. Quoted by Bredvold, pp. 104–05.

remain thus silent. In fact only one Englishman published
any kind of rebuttal to Dickinson's translation.[8] The verses
which Richard Duke addressed to Dickinson should serve, as
they were intended, to minimize the importance of reactions
like Evelyn's. Duke's lines account for Evelyn's alarm as well
as the calmer reaction of Dryden and most of the nation:

> *No less a Piece than this could make amends*
> *For all the trump'ry France amongst us sends.*
> *Nor let ill-grounded, superstitious fear*
> *Fright any but the fools from reading here.*
> *The sacred Oracles may well endure*
> *Th' exactest search, of their own truth secure;*
> *Though at this Piece some noisy Zelots bawl,*
> *And to their aid a numerous Faction call*
> *With stretch'd out arms, as if the Ark could fall;*
> *Yet wiser heads will think so firm it stands,*
> *That, were it shook, 'twould need no mortal hands.*[9]

8. William Lorimer, *An Examination of a considerable part of Pere
Simon's Critical History of the Old Testament, wherein all his Objections,
with the Weightiest of Spinoza's against Moses's being the Author of
the first Five Books of the Bible, are Answered, and some difficult places
of Holy Scripture are Explained* (London, 1682). Lorimer's treatise was
published as the "Second Part" of *An Excellent Discourse Proving the
Divine Original, and Authority of the Five Books of Moses. Written
Originally in French by Monsieur Du Bois de la Cour, And Approved
by six Doctors of the Sorbon.* Cf. Bredvold, p. 105, n. 64. Bredvold gives
the name of the author as it appears on the title page as "W.L."; the
copy at Yale may be of another edition, for here the name "William
Lorimer" is printed in full.

9. "To his Friend the Translatour of Father *Simon*." Duke's commendatory verses first appeared in the second issue of Dickinson's translation
(London, 1682). Given the paucity of published reaction to the *Critical
History*—in an age when the polemical pen seldom lay idle—it is difficult to credit Harth's theory that the commendatory poems to Dickinson
(including *Religio Laici*) were written as a business favor to Tonson who
hoped to allay widespread fear concerning the heretical nature of the
book so that it would sell well (*Contexts of Dryden's Thought,* p. 187 ff.).
There is no reason to dismiss as simply "fictitious" (Harth, p. 196)
Dryden's explicit account of the intellectual genesis of *Religio Laici* or

The Title of the Poem

Dryden's title itself presents us with a knotty problem. Three earlier works from which Dryden may have derived the name *Religio Laici* are Sir Thomas Browne's *Religio Medici* (London, 1642), Lord Herbert of Cherbury's *De Religione Laici* (London, 1645), and Sir George Mackenzie's *Religio Stoici* (Edinburgh, 1663). Browne's work is at once too well known and too complex to require or allow brief description. Suffice it to say that its similarities to Dryden's poem are few and vague.[10] Herbert's brief treatise belongs to a series of publications for which he has come to be known as the "Father of Deism." His chief work, *De Veritate* (Paris, 1624), one of the first purely metaphysical works by an Englishman, promulgates

---

to doubt that Dryden and his circle were genuinely interested in Simon's work—which was, after all, just the kind of book which would have attracted an *au courant* group of Restoration intellectuals.

10. Though Browne tells us in *Religio Medici* that he judges "points indifferent" according to his "private reason" (i.5) and that he once held the "error" of Origen that "God would not persist in his vengeance for ever" (i.7), he (unlike Dryden) leaves "no gap for Heresies, Schisms, or Errors" (i.6). Like Dryden in *Religio Laici* (ll. 210–11), Browne suggests that there are "many . . . that . . . have their names in Histories and Martyrologies, who in the eyes of God, are not so perfect Martyrs as was that wise Heathen *Socrates*, that suffered on a fundamentall point of Religion, the Unity of God" (i.26); but he closes the Arian gap emphatically in his assertion that there is "no salvation to those that beleeve not in Christ"—not even for "those honest Worthies and Philosophers which died before his Incarnation. . . . Men that live according to the right rule and law of reason," Browne adds, "live but in their owne kinde, as beasts doe in theirs . . . the perfectest actions of earth have no title or claime unto Heaven" (i.54). Browne emphasizes charity and skepticism (ii.1 and 8), but he does not marshal them against the Egyptian bishop, as Dryden does. (Citations are from the text in *Religio Medici and Other Works*, ed. L. C. Martin, Oxford, 1964.)

The one passage in *Religio Medici* which we know Dryden remembered, relates to guardian angels and has something in common with *The Hind and the Panther* but little or nothing with *Religio Laici* (cf. *The Poetical Works of Dryden*, ed. George R. Noyes, Cambridge, Mass., 1950, pp. 365 and 1002).

a theory of knowledge which is substantially the same as that
of the Cambridge Platonists. De *Religione Laici* is a synopsis
of Herbert's essential views. There can be no doubt that
Dryden was familiar with Herbert's work when he wrote
Religio Laici. Harold Hutcheson has pointed out that Dryden's lines,

> The *Deist* thinks he stands on firmer ground;
> Cries ἕυρεκα: the mighty Secret's found,

[ll. 42–43]

as well as the following twenty lines, sound like "an unmistakable echo of Herbert's reference to Archimedes when
recounting his 'discovery' of the essential religious notions inherent in all pagan religions" in *De Religione Gentilium*.[11]
The Preface to *Religio Laici*, Hutcheson notes, refers explicitly to Herbert's *Henry VIII*.[12] Mackenzie's *Religio Stoici*
is an orthodox work of mild rationalistic tendency, not note-
worthy for any special features except that it too shares a
common tradition with the Cambridge Platonists.

The relation of *Religio Laici* to Herbert's work is, at very
best, puzzling. Why should Dryden have taken a title that had
been used for a work whose principles, we assume, he wished
to condemn? A publication by Charles Blount that immediately followed the first appearance of Dryden's poem further
complicates matters. Scott, in *The Life of John Dryden*, was
aware of the work and troubled by it:

> It is remarkable, that his friends do not seem to have
> considered the *"Religio Laici"* as expressive of his de-
> cided sentiments [i.e. Anglicanism]; for Charles Blount, a
> noted free-thinker, in consequence of that very work,
> wrote a deistical treatise in prose, bearing the same title,
> and ascribed it with great testimony of respect to "his

11. Harold R. Hutcheson, *Lord Herbert of Cherbury's "De Religione
Laici"* (New Haven, 1944), pp. 49 and 57.
12. Ibid., p. 57.

much-honoured friend, John Dryden, Esquire." Mr
Blount, living in close habits with Dryden, must have
known perfectly well how to understand his polemical
poem; and, had he supposed it was written under a deep
belief of the truth of the English creed, can it be thought
he would have inscribed to the author a tract against all
revelation? [13]

13. Sir Walter Scott, *The Life of John Dryden,* ed. Bernard Kreissman
(Lincoln, Neb., 1963), p. 268. Cf. the dedication to Blount's *Religio Laici*
(London, 1683). Blount's first published work was a spirited defense of
Dryden against the charge of "Profaneness" in *Tyrannic Love: Mr. Dreyden Vindicated, in a Reply to the Friendly Vindication of Mr. Dreyden*
(London, 1673). Scott's view of Blount's relation to Dryden is diametri-
cally opposed to that of Phillip Harth who believes that Blount's treatise and dedication were maliciously calculated to embarrass Dryden *(Contexts of Dryden's Thought,* pp. 92–94). In spite of the evidence of Blount's
early friendship for Dryden, Harth feels that Blount meant to harm
Dryden in 1683. A decade after the publication of *Religio Laici,* Dryden
joined the project to bring out an edition of Lucian. Blount was one of
the translators. In his prefatory *Life of Lucian* (probably written in
1696) Dryden speaks of the translators and is careful to leave out one of
them—Tom Brown, who had ridiculed him many times. "As for the
translators," he writes, "all of them, that I know, are men of established
reputation, both for wit and learning, at least sufficiently known to be so
among all the finer spirits of the age. . . . The wit of Mr. Blount, and
his other performances, need no recommendation from me; they have
made too much noise in the world to need a herald" *(Works of John
Dryden,* XVIII, 78–79).
    Harth thinks that the tone of Dryden's remarks on Blount is "coldly
ambiguous" *(Contexts of Dryden's Thought,* p. 93). Yet Scott took the
same words to be a genuine expression of Dryden's "kindness and respect"
(Life of John Dryden, p. 152). We might note that six months before
Blount committed suicide (August, 1693) in despair at not being allowed
to marry his deceased wife's sister, he wrote a desperate attempt *"to Jus-
tifie the Marrying of two Sisters, the one after the other"* and weighted
the last lines of his argument with a four-line quotation from *The Hind
and the Panther.* (The essay was included in *The Oracles of Reason,* London, 1693.) I can see no compelling reason to discard Scott's view that the
expressions in Blount's dedication of his *Religio Laici* to Dryden are "such
as to preclude all idea but of profound respect" *(Life of John Dryden,*
p. 268). Charles Gildon, Blount's close associate in *The Oracles of Reason*
and the editor of Blount's *Miscellaneous Works* (London, 1695), was un-

Scott proceeds to the conclusion that Blount secretly knew Dryden did not mean what he said about belief in "Mother Church" and that he wrote "out of compliment to church and state." Yet Blount speaks in the most forthright terms: "I have endeavoured that my Discourse should be onely a Continuance of yours; and that, as you taught Men how to Believe, so I might instruct them how to Live." Blount does not reveal any knowledge of Dryden's familiarity with Herbert's work. On the contrary, he describes his essay to Dryden as "this small Piece, which I Entitle by the Name of *Religio Laici* from a Treatise of the *Lord Herbert of Cherburie*'s so called; whose Notions [i.e. common notions of deism] I have often made use of, and grounded the Chief of my Discourse upon his Five Catholick or Universal Principles." [14] For some reason, Blount never wondered where Dryden got *his* title. So it must seem. Luttrell must have thought that he too knew "perfectly well how to understand" Dryden's *Religio Laici*; on the title page of his copy of the poem he was satisfied to describe it with one word, "Atheisticall." [15]

Dryden's "Learned Friend"

One other circumstance of composition must be examined here. In the Preface, Dryden describes his opinions as follows:

> whatever they are, I submit them with all reverence to my Mother Church, accounting them no further mine, than as they are Authoriz'd, or at least, uncondemn'd by her. And, indeed, to secure my self on this side, I have

doubtedly a genuine friend to Dryden, as his letter to the poet reprinted in *Miscellaneous Letters and Essays* (London, 1694), pp. 1–3, proves beyond a doubt. (The letter was written at the peak of Gildon's deistic identification; in 1697 he was converted to a nonjuring faith.) Cf. also Gildon's defense of Dryden in *The Lives and Characters of the English Dramatick Poets* (London, 1699), p. 40.

14. *Religio Laici* (London, 1683), sigs. [A11r]–[A11v] and [A8v].

15. See Macdonald, p. 33, n. 2.

us'd the necessary Precaution, of showing this Paper
before it was Publish'd to a judicious and learned Friend,
a Man indefatigably zealous in the service of the Church
and State: and whose Writings, have highly deserv'd of
both. He was pleas'd to approve the body of the Discourse, and I hope he is more my Friend, than to do it
out of Complaisance: 'Tis true he had too good a tast
to like it all; and amongst some other faults recommended
to my second view, what I have written, perhaps too
boldly on St. *Athanasius:* which he advised me wholy
to omit. [ll. 24–35]

David Nichol Smith identified Dryden's "judicious and learned
Friend" as "Tillotson, preacher at Lincoln's Inn and Canon
of St Paul's before he was appointed Dean" in 1689.[16] Tillotson's role as adviser raises serious problems for that interpretation of the poem which argues that Dryden's antirationalistic feeling in *Religio Laici* is incipient fideism. Why
should Dryden have asked the leading rationalistic Anglican
of the day for his opinion of a fideistic poem?[17] Bredvold
stated categorically that

> Dryden's disagreement with the central principle of re-
> ligious rationalism is . . . so complete and conclusive
> in *Religio Laici* that it separates him not only from Deism,
> but from the rationalistic tendencies of such Anglican

16. David Nichol Smith, *John Dryden* (Cambridge, 1950), p. 88. John
Mackay substantially agreed with Smith's identification but pointed out
an attendant difficulty; see Kinsley, IV, 1933. This difficulty too has been
explained and the identification stands unchallenged again; see David R.
Brown, "Dryden's 'Religio Laici' and the 'Judicious and Learned Friend',"
MLR, LVI (1961), 66–69. For further confirmation of this point, cf. Bruce
King, "Dryden, Tillotson, and *Tyrannic Love,*" *RES,* XVI (1965), 364–77.

17. This difficulty in Bredvold's interpretation was first noted by Thomas
Fujimura, "Dryden's *Religio Laici:* An Anglican Poem," pp. 207–08.

leaders as Chillingworth, Stillingfleet, Tillotson, and the Cambridge Platonists.[18]

Perhaps Dryden's disagreement not only with Tillotson but with others on this list was not nearly as complete and conclusive as Bredvold supposed.

Problems of Interpretation

It is clear that any acceptable reading of *Religio Laici* must be able to account for the external facts that relate to the poem. Still more important, however, are the crucial problems of interpretation which arise from the body of the poem itself. All these problems, it seems to me, revolve around one major question: how does the poem proceed meaningfully from the hymn of faith in the opening lines to the proselike ratiocination on politic behavior in the conclusion? The first eleven lines of the poem have been recognized as among the most lyrical in all English poetry.[19] They are also a direct contradiction to the epigraph of the poem, *Ornari res ipsa negat, contenta doceri,* and to Dryden's assertion that he has chosen to avoid the "Florid, Elevated and Figurative way" (Preface, l. 350):

> Dim, as the borrow'd beams of Moon and Stars
> To *lonely, weary, wandring* Travellers,
> Is *Reason* to the *Soul:* And as on high,
> Those rowling Fires *discover* but the Sky
> Not light us *here;* So *Reason*'s glimmering Ray
> Was lent, not to *assure* our *doubtfull* way,
> But *guide* us upward to a *better Day.*

18. Bredvold, p. 109.

19. Henry Crabb Robinson tells us that Landor once said to him: "Nothing was ever written in hymn equal to the beginning of Dryden's 'Religio Laici,'—the first eleven lines"; cf. Thomas Sadler, ed., *Diary, Reminiscences, and Correspondence of Henry Crabb Robinson* (London, 1872), II, 229.

> And as those nightly Tapers disappear
> When Day's bright Lord ascends our Hemisphere;
> So pale grows *Reason* at *Religions* sight;
> So *dyes,* and so *dissolves* in *Supernatural Light.*

We have come a long way from this, both in style and content, by the time we reach Dryden's clipped conclusion:

> . . . points obscure are of small use to learn:
> But *Common quiet* is *Mankind's concern.*
>
> [ll. 449–50]

What, we cannot help asking, has become of religion? [20] Why was the lyrical impulse abandoned?

The last six lines of the poem, which are presented as an afterthought on the style and content of the poem, seem oblivious to any such questions:

> Thus have I made my own Opinions clear:
> Yet neither Praise expect, nor Censure fear:
> And this unpolish'd, rugged Verse, I chose;
> As fittest for Discourse, and nearest Prose:
> For, while from *Sacred Truth* I do not swerve,
> *Tom Sternhold's,* or *Tom Shadwell's Rhimes* will serve.
>
> [ll. 451–56]

Dryden seems to offer these lines as clarification, yet they only prompt further, more vexed questioning: what does "Common quiet" have to do with "Sacred Truth"? how does the description "unpolish'd, rugged Verse" apply to the exordium? what do Tom Sternhold and Tom Shadwell have to do with considering the religion of a layman? The use of the word *Discourse* (l. 454), in particular, points up what seems to be a serious contradiction between earlier and later parts of

---

20. A. W. Verrall, *Lectures on Dryden* (Cambridge, 1914), p. 155, asked, "Now in all this, is there any religion at all? *Religio Laici* might well be dismissed as mere politics but for its astounding commencement."

the poem. At line 64 the poet reprimands the deist for his gross presumption:

> Vain, wretched Creature, how art thou misled
> To think thy Wit these God-like Notions bred!
> These Truths are not the product of thy Mind,
> But dropt from Heaven, and of a Nobler kind.
> *Reveal'd Religion* first inform'd thy Sight,
> And *Reason* saw not, till *Faith* sprung the Light.
> Hence all thy *Natural Worship* takes the *Source:*
> 'Tis *Revelation* what thou thinkst *Discourse.*

Here discourse is completely unacceptable. It is the tool of reason and as such it stands opposed to the true method of apprehending religious knowledge—through revelation. Discourse is the deist's delusion. Yet, as the poem ends, Dryden is content and even proud to tell us that *Religio Laici* has been designed as discourse (l. 454). In a similar way Dryden first tells us how "dim" the light of reason is and how "Reason saw not, till Faith sprung the light" (l. 69); yet later he insists that "those who follow'd Reasons Dictates right; / Liv'd up, and lifted high their Natural Light;/With Socrates may see their Maker's Face" (ll. 208–10).

It is clear from the Preface that Dryden was aware of this apparent contradiction. After rehearsing a large part of the poem's argument, he muses,

> I have dwelt longer on this Subject than I intended; and longer than, perhaps, I ought; for having laid down, as my Foundation, that the Scripture is a Rule; that in all things needfull to Salvation, it is clear, sufficient, and ordain'd by God Almighty for that purpose, I have left my self no right to interpret obscure places, such as concern the possibility of eternal happiness to Heathens: because whatsoever is obscure is concluded not necessary to be known. [ll. 139–45]

This quotation is a paragraph complete in itself. Dryden has
no further explanation to give us on the matter. He obviously thought that no good answer was possible, or that it
would all become clear somewhere else.

The "paradox of a reasoned critique of Reason" [21] is more
serious than commentators have seen. Only if we take the
position that already in *Religio Laici* Dryden is a Roman
Catholic apologist employing fideistic strategies can we accept the paradox without further questioning. But not even
Bredvold takes such a position. Dryden's hostility to Roman
Catholic authoritarianism is overt and unmistakable in the
poem. In 1682 the Church of Rome was clearly associated in
Dryden's mind with the worst "medievalism" and oppression
of the human spirit:

> In times o'ergrown with Rust and Ignorance,
> A gainfull Trade their Clergy did advance:
> When want of Learning kept the *Laymen* low,
> And none but *Priests* were *Authoriz'd* to *know:*
> When what small Knowledge was, in them did dwell;
> And he a *God* who cou'd but *Reade* or *Spell;*
> Then *Mother Church* did mightily prevail:
> She parcel'd out the Bible by *retail:*
> But still *expounded* what She *sold* or *gave;*
> To keep it in *her Power* to *Damn* and *Save.*
>
> [ll. 370–79]

Dryden is obviously not tearing down reason in order to build
up Roman Catholicism. Bredvold's account of Dryden's religious development can explain how the paradox or contradiction of a "reasoned critique of Reason" functioned in bringing
about the poet's conversion, but it does not explain the place
of the paradox in an integrated poem in 1682. The implication

21. Arthur W. Hoffman's phrase in *John Dryden's Imagery* (Gaines-
ville, Fla., 1962), p. 63. Hoffman makes the useful suggestion that Dryden
differentiated between the use and abuse of reason.

of Bredvold's view is that *Religio Laici* is unfinished and un-
satisfactory as a poem by itself:[22] it must become "a sort of
prelude or introduction" [23] to *The Hind and the Panther* in
order to be understood. Dryden was no fledgling when he sat
down to write *Religio Laici*; nor was he then going through a
poetic "dry spell." His publications during the previous twelve
months include many of his most impressive poems.[24] Dryden
must have been concerned with the integrated meaning of the
poem. This must be our premise in investigation. Why, then,
we ask, does he attack reason one moment and praise the
High-Critical lucubration of Simon's work the next?

> . . . this weighty Book, in which appears
> The crabbed Toil of many thoughtfull years,
> . . . .
> A Work so full with various Learning fraught,
> So nicely pondred, yet so strongly wrought,
> As Natures height and Arts last hand requir'd:
> As much as Man cou'd compass, uninspir'd.
>
> [ll. 234–47]

It is not immediately clear what it is about Simon's method
of "uninspir'd" reason which somehow makes *it* acceptable.

Dryden's friends were quick to point out that mystery—
Christian or otherwise—is close to the heart of *Religio Laici*.
When the poem first appeared, John Vaughan apostrophized
Dryden as follows:

> So strong thy reasons, and so clear thy sense,
> They bring, like day, their own bright evidence;
> Yet, whilst *mysterious truths* to light you bring,

---

22. Bredvold implies that the conclusion of the poem is "only base
compromise for the sake of an external quiet" (p. 126).

23. Bredvold, p. 121.

24. During these months appeared *Absalom and Achitophel* (Parts One
and Two) and *The Medall*.

And heavenly things in heavenly numbers sing,
The joyful younger choir may clap the wing.[25]

The following year, Roscommon added:

Let free, impartial men from Dryden learn
Mysterious secrets of a high concern.[26]

Dryden himself has told us that *The Hind and the Panther* is
a "mysterious writ" (III, 2). It is true that not all evidence is
equal; yet if we are to elucidate the mysteries embodied in
Dryden's poems, no scrap of information should be declared
inadmissible without a hearing.[27] Though, of course, no
identity can be assumed between earlier and later views in a
man's career, opinions and attitudes are not usually acquired
suddenly and ex nihilo. The theological utterances of young
man Dryden are, therefore, not irrelevant to our investigation.

25. *Works of John Dryden*, x, 36 (italics added).
26. Ibid., x, 34 (italics added). The word *a* (present in the first editions
of the poem) was erroneously omitted by Scott-Saintsbury.
27. Harth, p. vii, disqualifies without examination the theological views
that Dryden assigned to his dramatic heroes, and feels that the religious
views that Dryden records in his essays are not "inherently important."

3

Dryden's Early Theological Opinions

Dryden's writings before 1682 do not reveal consistent religious convictions.[1] Pierre Legouis's catalogue of his early opinions concludes with this apt summation:

> dans cette partie de sa carrière notre auteur, qui n'a jamais à formuler sa doctrine directement ni de façon cohérente, se montre antipuritain et anticlérical (il restera l'un et l'autre); antipapiste, mais sans grande âpreté pour un Anglais du XVIIe siècle; libertin (dans le double sens du mot) avec son public; déiste par la tendance de l'esprit classique; antithéiste parfois, surtout lorsqu'il envisage les rapports de la liberté humaine et de la toute-puissance divine; religieux par accident, mystique jamais, mais scolastique souvent; par tempérament sceptique, c'est-à-dire suspendant son jugement et réservant sa décision jusqu'au jour prévu où les circonstances extérrieures, le sérieux qu'apportaient alors l'approche de la vieillesse (vers la cinquantaine) et la pensée plus présente de la

---

1. We have almost no firsthand information concerning Dryden's early religious training. Derrick passed on the tradition that Dryden was "bred" in the German Anabaptist theology, and Langbaine asserted that Dryden was an adherent of something like Anabaptism as late as 1659: see *The Critical and Miscellaneous Prose Works of John Dryden*, ed. Edmond Malone (London, 1800), I, 37 n. Whatever Dryden's early faith was, it surely was not Anabaptism itself. James M. Osborn has shown that Dryden was, in fact, baptized on 14 August 1631: *John Dryden: Some Biographical Facts and Problems* (New York, 1940), p. 270.

mort à laquelle il fallait se préparer, l'amèneront à choisir.[2]

The pattern or tendency of these various positions is clear: they reflect the unsettled mind of a humanist in a Christian age.

"Grounded on Human Reason"

Dryden's retrospective remarks on religion in the *Life of Plutarch* (1683) confirm this view and furnish a valuable starting point for a more precise discussion of Dryden's early views of the relation of reason and religion:

> I have ever thought, that the wise men in all ages have not much differed in their opinions of religion; I mean, as it is grounded on human reason: for reason, as far as it is right, must be the same in all men; and truth being but one, they must consequently think in the same train. Thus it is not to be doubted but the religion of Socrates, Plato, and Plutarch was not different in the main; who doubtless believed the identity of one Supreme Intellectual Being, which we call God.[3]

This emphasis on "human reason . . . as far as it is right" is the hallmark of humanistic Christian thought.[4] Even the autobiographical passage in *The Hind and the Panther* tends to indicate that, prior to his conversion to Roman Catholicism, Dryden put substantial trust in his own reason once he began to consider religious questions at all. An account of his early

2. Pierre Legouis, "La religion dans l'œuvre de Dryden avant 1682," *Revue Anglo-Américaine,* IX (1931–32), 536.

3. *Works of John Dryden,* XVII, 33.

4. Cf. Herschel Baker, *The Wars of Truth: Studies in the Decay of Christian Humanism in the Earlier Seventeenth Century* (Cambridge, Mass., 1952), pp. 91 ff. I have resisted the phrase "Christian humanism" because in certain contexts (and in this one in particular) it implies a body of thought and belief with clear demarcations. Such a precise implication cannot apply to Dryden in this period.

thinking which denies rationalistic tendencies cannot fail to
have difficulty with these lines:

> My thoughtless youth was wing'd with vain desires,
> My manhood, long misled by wandring fires,
> Follow'd false lights; and when their glimps was gone,
> My pride struck out new sparkles of her own.
>
> [I, 72–75]

We cannot know precisely what "fires," "false lights," and
"sparkles" mean, but it seems clear that they represent various
kinds and degrees of reliance on reason. The passage in which
these lines appear begins:

> What weight of antient witness can prevail
> If private reason hold the publick scale?
>
> [I, 62–63]

A. W. Verrall logically interpreted the sparkles of Dryden's
own pride as an admission that "he has held no recognised
creed"—"presumably some sort of Deism." [5] Scott took the
sparkles to mean "those sentiments which he imbibed after the
Restoration, and which immediately preceded his adoption
of the Catholic faith." This he defines as being "sceptical concerning revealed religion" and hovering "between natural religion and the faith of Rome." [6] This suggestion of Dryden's
early Roman Catholic tendencies is the mild ancestor of the
modern radical interpretation that until recently dominated
Dryden studies in this area. Scott's feeling that some kind of
inclination towards Roman Catholicism is detectable as early
as *Religio Laici* and that Dryden was eventually converted
from "a state of infidelity, or rather of Pyrrhonism" [7] provided
Bredvold with the foundation for his study. Bredvold's plan,
however, to enforce a strict technical definition of Pyrrhonism

5. Verrall, *Lectures on Dryden,* p. 150.
6. *Life of John Dryden,* pp. 262–68.
7. Ibid., p. 269.

required that he explain away all traces of rationalism or "natural religion"—especially deism—in Dryden's early thought. Bredvold's explanations led to what seemed the only hope for redeeming the integrity of the poet's thought (i.e. its Pyrrhonist tendencies) but in reality they involved us in distortions which have had to be rectified. Although there is a large element of significant truth in Bredvold's understanding of Dryden's thought, the meaning of *Religio Laici* depends on a body of thought very different from the one he emphasized. We must be able to see that Dryden's connection with this thought—to be described in the next chapter—flows directly from a continuous development of his early opinions.

"Cautious Rationalism"

Even Bredvold was willing to concede a "religious rationalism . . . of very limited application" in Dryden's early thinking.[8] The cause of his concession is the passage in the *Defence of an Essay of Dramatic Poesy* (1668) in which Dryden remarks that men can prove the existence of a deity and deduce that He should be worshiped but they "differ afterwards in the manner of the worship." [9] George Williamson pointed out that examples of limited applications of reason of this type are more plausibly interpreted as "a cautious form of rationalism" than as "anti-rationalism." [10] The view that Dryden was rationalistic and even, in some sense, deistic in the earlier part of his career, is corroborated by suggestive evidence in the plays.[11] Here we find sentiments which parallel Dryden's remark in 1683 about the religious opinions of "the wise men in all ages." In the *Indian Emperour* (first performed, 1665),

---

8. *The Intellectual Milieu of John Dryden*, pp. 116–17.

9. *Of Dramatic Poesy*, ed. Watson, I, 122.

10. *MLN*, LI (1936), 195–96.

11. Such evidence, it must be emphasized, cannot be considered conclusive by itself. Verrall's interesting view, for example, that *The State of Innocence* (1677) "is really Deistic and not Christian in tone" (p. 150) is highly subjective.

act v, scene ii, Montezuma (one of Dryden's noblest protago-
nists) is being stretched on the rack, together with his High
Priest, by a Christian priest who wants to convert them and
who also wants their gold.

> *Chr. Pr. (to Mont.).* Fond man, by heathen ignorance mis-
> led,
> Thy soul destroying when thy body's dead:
> Change yet thy faith, and buy eternal rest.

> *High Pr. (to Mont.).* Die in your own, for our belief is
> best.

> *Mont.* In seeking happiness you both agree;
> But in the search, the paths so different be,
> That all religions with each other fight,
> While only one can lead us in the right.
> But till that one hath some more certain mark,
> Poor human-kind must wander in the dark;
> And suffer pain eternally below,
> For that, which here we cannot come to know.

> *Chr. Pr.* That, which we worship, and which you believe,
> From nature's common hand we both receive:
> All, under various names, adore and love
> One Power immense, which ever rules above.
> Vice to abhor, and virtue to pursue,
> Is both believed and taught by us and you:
> But here our worship takes another way—

> *Mont.* Where both agree, 'tis there most safe to stay:
> For what's more vain than public light to shun,
> And set up tapers, while we see the sun?

> *Chr. Pr.* Though nature teaches whom we should adore,
> By heavenly beams we still discover more.

> *Mont.* Or this must be enough, or to mankind
> One equal way to bliss is not designed;

> For though some more may know, and some know less,
> Yet all must know enough for happiness.

Chr. Pr. If in this middle way you still pretend
  To stay, your journey never will have end.

Mont. Howe'er, 'tis better in the midst to stay,
  Than wander farther in uncertain way.

Chr. Pr. But we by martyrdom our faith avow.

Mont. You do no more than I for ours do now.
  To prove religion true—
  If either wit or sufferings would suffice,
  All faiths afford the constant and the wise:
  And yet even they, by education swayed,
  In age defend what infancy obeyed.

Chr. Pr. Since age by erring childhood is misled,
  Refer yourself to our unerring head.

Mont. Man, and not err! What reason can you give?

Chr. Pr. Renounce that carnal reason, and believe.

Mont. The light of nature should I thus betray,
  'Twere to wink hard, that I might see the day.[12]

Legouis is undoubtedly correct in noting, "ce n'est plus l'empereur aztèque, c'est un déiste anglais du xviie siècle." [13]

Another scene which deserves a second look in this context appears in *Tyrannic Love* (1670), act II. Here the content is not deistic but—what is equally important for our discussion—is markedly rationalistic in its approach to religious questions.

12. Quotations from Dryden's plays are taken from the Scott-Saintsbury edition.

13. Legouis, p. 529. Bredvold, p. 112, essentially agrees with this assessment but objects that "it would be unwarranted to affirm on the strength of this debate that Dryden, like Montezuma, rejected Christian revelation." This is true but irrelevant to the main question of Dryden's *tendency* toward a rationalistic position.

Saint Catherine argues the superiority of Christianity without once mentioning grace or even God, and this is enough to bring her success in converting a heathen philosopher, Apollonius, to the Christian faith. She never once appeals to formal religious authority, a church, to win her point. Her "Enlightened" mind, her human reason endowed by heaven, seems to be sufficient:

> *S. Cath.* Nor pride, nor frenzy, but a settled mind,
>   Enlightened from above, my way does mark.

> *Max.* Though heaven be clear, the way to it is dark.

> *S. Cath.* But where our reason with our faith does go,
>   We're both above enlightened, and below.
>   But reason with your fond religion fights,
>   For many gods are many infinites:
>   This to the first philosophers was known,
>   Who, under various names, adored but one;
>   Though your vain poets, after, did mistake,
>   Who every attribute a god did make;
>   And so obscene their ceremonies be,
>   As good men loathe, and Cato blushed to see.

> *Max.* War is my province!—Priest, why stand you mute?
>   You gain by heaven, and, therefore, should dispute.

> *Apol.* In all religions, as in ours, there are
>   Some solid truths, and some things popular.
>   The popular in pleasing fables lie;
>   The truths, in precepts of morality.
>   And these to human life are of that use,
>   That no religion can such rules produce.

> *S. Cath.* Then let the whole dispute concluded be
>   Betwixt these rules, and Christianity.

> *Apol.* And what more noble can your doctrine preach,
>   Than virtue, which philosophy does teach?

To keep the passions in severest awe,
To live to reason, nature's greatest law;
To follow virtue, as its own reward;
And good and ill, as things without regard.

S. Cath. Yet few could follow those strict rules they gave;
For human life will human frailties have;
And love of virtue is but barren praise,
Airy as fame; nor strong enough to raise
The actions of the soul above the sense.
Virtue grows cold without a recompence.
We virtuous acts as duty do regard;
Yet are permitted to expect reward.

Apol. By how much more your faith reward assures,
So much more frank our virtue is than yours.

S. Cath. Blind men! you seek e'en those rewards you
blame:
But ours are solid; yours an empty name.
Either to open praise your acts you guide,
Or else reward yourselves with secret pride.

Apol. Yet still our moral virtues you obey;
Ours are the precepts, though applied your way.

S. Cath. 'Tis true, your virtues are the same we teach;
But in our practice they much higher reach.
You but forbid to take another's due,
But we forbid even to desire it too:
Revenge of injuries you virtue call;
But we forgiveness of our wrongs extol:
Immodest deeds you hinder to be wrought,
But we proscribe the least immodest thought.
So much your virtues are in ours refined,
That yours but reach the actions, ours the mind.

Max. (*to Apol.*). Answer, in short, to what you heard her
speak.

> *Apol.* Where truth prevails, all arguments are weak.
>   To that convincing power I must give place;
>   And with that truth that faith I will embrace.

Rarely has a saint been thus canonized with a rationalistic halo.[14]

Lord Herbert

The animadversions upon deism in *Religio Laici* do not, it seems to me, constitute a complete rejection of Cherbury's thinking. The first of Cherbury's five "common notions," that human reason can discover the existence of a deity, is stated and confirmed immediately after the exordium without reference to "the Deist":

> Some few, whose Lamp shone brighter, have been led
> From Cause to Cause, to *Natures* secret head;
> And found that *one first principle* must be.
>
> [ll. 12–14]

14. Dryden tells us in the preface to *Tyrannic Love* that he has been "charged by some ignorant or malicious persons with no less crimes than profaneness and irreligion." He asserts that his "outward conversation . . . shall never be justly taxed with the note of atheism or profaneness." Of this Verrall remarked, "But this disclaimer proves nothing as to his positive belief; Deism is not profane" (p. 150).

Bredvold argued, p. 109, that the "most obvious and most serious objection" to the theory that "Dryden was really a Deist from 1660 to 1686" is that "in *Religio Laici*, both in the preface and in the poem, [he] rejects Deism and contrasts its presumption with his own skeptical habits of thought." But the observations on deism in *Religio Laici* have no explicit retrospective force. Where Dryden does not say "I have ever thought" (as he does about his more deistic views of 1683 in the *Life of Plutarch*) about an opinion in 1682, we have no "obvious" reasons for extending that opinion to 1660–81. Dryden wrote no poetry of exclusive religious concern before *Religio Laici*. The main reason for considering his religious opinions up to 1681 is to gain some notion of his *probable* opinions in 1682. Where a later statement in the poem itself has no retrospective force, we defeat our own purposes by seeing it as the "most obvious and most serious objection" to an alternative interpretation of earlier material.

The poet denies that human reason can also discover "what, or who, that UNIVERSAL HE" (l. 15) but this does not even contradict the other four elements of Cherburian deism. These are: "that He is to be worshiped, that virtue and piety are the chief part of worship, that we should repent of our sins, and that there is reward or punishment after this life." [15] Dryden's version of these principles (ll. 42–61) indicates that he is attacking the abuses of the Restoration deist who rejected available revelation rather than deism itself:

> The *Deist* thinks he stands on firmer ground;[16]
> Cries ἔυρεκα : the mighty Secret's found:
> *God* is that *Spring* of *Good; Supreme,* and *Best;*
> *We,* made to *serve,* and in that Service *blest;*
> If so, some *Rules* of Worship must be given,
> Distributed alike to all by Heaven:
> Else *God* were *partial,* and to *some* deny'd
> The Means his Justice shou'd for *all* provide.
> This *general Worship* is to *PRAISE,* and *PRAY:*
> One part to *borrow* Blessings, one to *pay:*
> And when frail Nature slides into *Offence,*
> The *Sacrifice* for *Crimes* is *Penitence.*
> Yet, since th' Effects of Providence, we find
> Are variously dispens'd to Humane kind;
> That *Vice Triumphs,* and *Vertue suffers* here,
> (A Brand that Sovereign Justice cannot bear;)
> Our Reason prompts us to a *future* State:
> The *last Appeal* from *Fortune,* and from *Fate:*
> Where God's all-righteous ways will be declar'd;
> The *Bad* meet *Punishment,* the *Good, Reward.*

Dryden attacks the deist because he has reduced religion to a calculated transaction; words such as *distributed, provide,*

15. Hutcheson, *Cherbury's "De Religione Laici,"* p. 30.
16. That is, firmer than the ground that "vanishes" from beneath the ancients (l. 28).

borrow, pay, dispens'd, appeal, and *reward* are the vocabulary
of commercialism rather than of theology. But, however much
Dryden used Herbert's work for information concerning
deism, it is clear that "the Deist" is not Herbert himself. The
point which Dryden attacks most vigorously is not one of the
Cherburian "common notions" at all: "This general Worship
is to *PRAISE* and *PRAY:* / One part to borrow Blessings,
one to pay." This forms the basis of the pervasive commercial
imagery in the poem which, as Arthur Hoffman notes, "presents the mean departures from and venal corruptions of the
relationship rendered initially in the borrowing of light lent
from above." [17] But this is also a mean departure from the
principles of Lord Herbert, for whom "virtue and piety are
the chief part of worship": *"Virtutem cum pietate conjunctam
(quæ proba Facultatum conformatione hoc in Opere descri-
bitur) præcipuam partem Cultus Divini habitam esse et semper
fuisse."* [18] Dryden himself assents to this view when he tells us
that

> those who follow'd *Reasons* Dictates right;
> Liv'd up, and lifted high their *Natural Light;*
> With *Socrates* may see their Maker's Face.
>
> [ll. 208–10]

In *De Religione Laici,* moreover, Herbert explicitly deplores
the commercialistic aspects of any kind of worship: "Nor . . .
let priests promise that sins will be remitted by a transaction
of little moment, or one thrust away too far among other
affairs (much less by a mercenary arrangement)." [19]

Deism and Informed Rationalism

It is misleading and erroneous to suggest that there was a
recognized, clear-cut body of thought called deism which

17. *John Dryden's Imagery,* p. 69.
18. Quoted by Hutcheson, p. 40.
19. Ibid., p. 111.

Dryden dismissed. In fact, the first recorded use of the word *deism* appears in Dryden's Preface to *Religio Laici*.[20] As Hutcheson points out, the seventeenth-century deists "had no party, no formulated common creed, no patron saint. If Lord Herbert was 'the father of English deism,' his children did not recognize his paternity. Only the first, Charles Blount, professed to be his disciple; the rest ignored him. And, for the most part, they ignored each other. The deists were individual religious malcontents."[21] The ideological identity of "the Deist" in *Religio Laici* is not a simple matter and it cannot be assumed that Dryden's attack on him implies a rejection of all deistic principles. We have already seen substantial evidence—in the poem and outside it—that Dryden was sympathetic to some of these principles.

In order to understand Dryden's attack on "the Deist" in 1682, it is essential that we know the broad outlines of the history of deism in the seventeenth century. As Hutcheson tells us, there were two distinct periods of deistic thought in the century, "the earlier and far more interesting having received only the most incidental attention from scholars, and the later, better known, covering in England approximately the last quarter of the seventeenth century and the first half of the eighteenth. The history of the first period is part of the history of the efforts to achieve religious toleration after the Reformation had divided Christendom into armed sects; the second period was one of guerrilla warfare on orthodoxy once toleration had been substantially won."[22]

Modern deism first sprouted from the skepticism of the Italian academies in the second quarter of the sixteenth century. It grew up as a movement whose purpose was to defend

20. The first recorded occurrence of the word *deist* in English is in Burton's first edition of the *Anatomy of Melancholy* (1621), and the next citation for even this word is for the year 1670; see Hutcheson, p. 56, and the *OED*.

21. Hutcheson, p. 55.

22. Ibid., pp. 59–60.

the heterodox rather than to attack the orthodox. Its main
foci were a denial of the doctrine of exclusive salvation and
an attempt to pacify religious dispute. As Hutcheson says,
"alone among the unorthodox of their day, they were fighting
only incidentally for a new faith. The greater objective of
their fight, waged passionately yet with rigidly disciplined
logic, was a new charity. Or, perhaps more exactly, charity
was their new faith." [23] This is the tradition and the spirit
in which Herbert wrote. Here we find little of the belligerency
of the late seventeenth-century deist toward revealed religion.
Fujimura has remarked that, "after a conventional attack on
the Deists, [Dryden] reverses his position in a curious manner.
He argues that God's boundless mercy may extend salvation
even to pagans who never heard of Christ, and who conse-
quently followed only the light of natural reason." [24]

Once we recognize that Dryden was writing at a turning
point in the history of deism, we realize that there is nothing
"curious" and no reversal involved in Dryden's various opinions. He deplores the presumption and the hostility to revealed
religion of the new deism ("the Deist") even while the main
skeptical, tolerant, irenic character of his poem has strong
affinities with the old deism or natural religion. The foundation of Dryden's campaign for the salvation of heathens is, as
he twice tells us, "Charity" (ll. 212 and 224). He was satisfied
to conclude his argument with the single statement that "Common quiet is Mankind's concern" (l. 450). There are, as we
shall see, more immediate and more illuminating sources
for the opinions of the poem. It is important, however, to
recognize here that Dryden's attack on "the Deist" is not
a rejection of all the principles of deism.

Yet a major part of Dryden's opposition to the deist does,
at first, seem to be explicitly antirationalistic. After he has
finished his exposition of the deist's principles, he continues,

23. Ibid., pp. 60–67.
24. Fujimura, "Dryden's *Religio Laici*," pp. 208–09.

Thus Man by his own strength to Heaven wou'd soar:
And wou'd not be Oblig'd to God for more.
Vain, wretched Creature, how art thou misled
To think thy Wit these God-like Notions bred!
These Truths are not the product of thy Mind,
But dropt from Heaven, and of a Nobler kind.
Reveal'd Religion first inform'd thy Sight,
And *Reason* saw not, till *Faith* sprung the Light.
Hence all thy *Natural Worship* takes the *Source:*
'Tis *Revelation* what thou thinkst *Discourse.*

[ll. 62–71]

Later in the poem, however, we recall that Dryden contends

those who follow'd *Reasons* Dictates right;
Liv'd up, and lifted high their *Natural Light;*
With *Socrates* may see their Maker's Face.

The Preface makes clear that these two passages are not con-
tradictory. Following "Reason's Dictates right" and lifting
"high their Natural Light" are obviously not simple activities
for Dryden:

Deism, or the Principles of Natural Worship, are onely
the faint remnants or dying flames of reveal'd Religion
in the Posterity of *Noah* . . . and unatainable by our
Discourse, *I mean as simply considerd,* and without the
benefit of Divine illumination. So that we have not lifted
up our selves to God, by the weak Pinions of our Reason,
but he has been pleasd to descend to us: and what
Socrates said of him, what *Plato* writ, and the rest of
the Heathen Philosophers of several Nations, is all no
more than the Twilight of Revelation, after the Sun of it
was set in the Race of *Noah.* That there is some thing
above us, some Principle of *motion,* our Reason can

apprehend, though it cannot discover what it is, *by its own Vertue.* [ll. 67–84][25]

Reason and discourse "as simply considerd," acting only by their "own Vertue," can discover little of divine truth. But Dryden clearly holds that even the reason of "righteous" pagans partakes of "Divine Illumination" without the aid of any Christian church. This can hardly be called antirationalism. In fact, it is the most exalted kind of informed rationalism, and it constitutes the backbone of *Religio Laici.* It will be closely considered in chapters 4, 5, and 6.

"Modest Inquisitions"

A passage which has often been quoted as evidence of Dryden's philosophical skepticism occurs in *A Defence of an Essay of Dramatic Poesy* (1668) where Dryden defends himself against the charge of "being magisterial":

> in vindication of myself, I must crave leave to say that my whole discourse was sceptical, according to that way of reasoning which was used by Socrates, Plato, and all the Academics of old, which Tully and the best of the Ancients followed, and which is imitated by the modest inquisitions of the Royal Society.[26]

What Dryden understood by the phrase "modest inquisitions of the Royal Society" is problematical and remains to be discussed below. What he meant by "the Academics of old" is spelled out for us, I think, in *The Life of Plutarch* (1683) where he tells us that his author was "at least an Academic, that is, half Platonist half Sceptic": "Plutarch endeavours to teach others, but refuses not to be taught himself, for

25. Italics are mine in the phrases "I mean as simply considerd" and "by its own Vertue."
26. *Of Dramatic Poesy*, I, 123.

he is always doubtful and inquisitive." [27] This is hardly philosophical skepticism. Yet Bredvold ignored such considerations
and took at face value the sentences which immediately
follow the above passage from the *Defence*:

> That it is so, not only the name will shew, which is *An
> Essay*, but the frame and composition of the work. You
> see it is a dialogue sustained by persons of several opin-
> ions, all of them left doubtful, to be determined by the
> readers in general; and more particularly deferred to the
> accurate judgment of my Lord Buckhurst, to whom I
> made a dedication of my book.

Dryden's deference to his patron is obvious in these lines.
The "frame and composition" of the *Essay*, we have already
seen, are not really impartial to the opinions expressed; nor
are all of the opinions "left doubtful." [28] Neither in intention
nor in achievement is the *Essay* evidence of Pyrrhonistic
skepticism.

Another passage which has been quoted to reinforce the
Pyrrhonistic interpretation is really striking evidence of Dryden's continuous rationalistic inclination. In the preface to
Sylvae (published in 1685, only two years before *The Hind
and the Panther*) Dryden tells us:

> If I am not mistaken, the distinguishing character of
> Lucretius (I mean of his soul and genius) is a certain
> kind of noble pride, and positive assertion of his opinions.
> He is everywhere confident of his own reason, and as-
> suming an absolute command, not only over his vulgar
> reader, but even his patron Memmius. . . . These are the
> considerations which I had of that author, before I at-
> tempted to translate some parts of him. And accordingly
> I laid by my natural diffidence and scepticism for a while,
> to take up that dogmatical way of his, which, as I said,

27. Ibid., II, 12.
28. As Bredvold (p. 13) thought was really the case.

is so much his character as to make him that individual poet.

This is as much of the passage as Bredvold reproduces. Two sentences later, however, Dryden says, "I think a future state demonstrable even by natural arguments." [29] Thus, even two years before the publication of *The Hind and the Panther,* Dryden evidently did not think that his kind of skepticism was incompatible with accepting a rationalistic argument for the immortality of the soul.

In the Preface to *Religio Laici* too Dryden seems to declare himself a disciple of Sextus:

Being naturally inclin'd to Scepticism in Philosophy, I have no reason to impose my Opinions, in a Subject which is above it: But whatever they are, I submit them with all reverence to my Mother Church, accounting them no further mine, than as they are Authoriz'd, or at least, uncondemn'd by her. And, indeed, to secure my self on this side, I have us'd the necessary Precaution, of showing this Paper before it was Publish'd to a judicious and learned Friend, a Man indefatigably zealous in the service of the Church and State: and whose Writings, have highly deserv'd of both. [ll. 22–30]

But, if the "judicious and learned Friend" was the rationalist divine John Tillotson, it is difficult to understand why Dryden, in the very same passage, should appeal to him and to "philosophical skepticism." [30] The answer to this contradiction does not lie in a rejection of the Tillotson identification, but in an understanding of Dryden's complex attitude toward "Scepticism."

Dryden's views on skepticism are bound up with the *scepsis scientifica* of the Restoration. In 1672 he wrote, "we live in an age so sceptical, that as it determines little, so it takes

29. *Of Dramatic Poesy,* II, 25–26.
30. See Fujimura, pp. 207–08.

nothing from antiquity on trust." [31] This was an opinion
which stayed with him until the last years of his life. All
"knowing ages," he declared in 1696, are "naturally sceptic,
and not at all bigotted; which, if I am not much deceived,
is the proper character of our own." [32] Nowhere does he differentiate between his own skepticism and that of his age;
and that skepticism, we have by now realized, was generally
in the service of rationalism rather than, as Bredvold believed, Pyrrhonism.[33] In religion and science, said Sprat,
"we cannot make War against *Reason*, without undermining
our own strength, seing it is the constant weapon we ought
to imploy." [34] "I do not," Boyle wrote, "with the true Scep-
ticks propose doubts to persuade men, that all things are
doubtful and will ever remain so (at least) to human understanding; but I propose doubts not only with design, but
with hope, of being at length freed from them by the at-
tainment of undoubted truth." [35]

Once we have freed ourselves from the notion that Dryden's
early thought was simplistically antirationalistic or hostile
to all deistic principles, at least some of the puzzling circumstances attending the poem become clearer. We can understand why Dryden, with his rationalistic *scepsis scientifica*,
would have appealed to the rationalist divine, John Tillotson,
to pass on his opinions.[36] At the same time we can see that
Blount extended his warm welcome to a continuance of Dryden's sympathy for at least some of the deistic principles.

In addition, we are now in a better position to understand why *An Essay by the Celebrated Poet, John Dryden,*

31. *Of Dramatic Poesy*, I, 169.
32. *Works of John Dryden*, XVIII, 70.
33. Cf. chap. 1, n. 22.
34. Sprat, *History of the Royal Society*, p. 362.
35. Quoted by Prior, *MP*, XXXII (1935), 327–28.
36. The extent of contemporary suspicion of Tillotson's liberal tendencies can be seen in Charles Leslie's *The Charge of Socinianism against
Dr. Tillotson Considered* (Edinburgh, 1695).

Esq; to prove that Natural Religion is alone necessary to Salvation (London, 1745) was attributed to Dryden forty-five years after the poet's death.[37] Close examination of this essay in terms of our corrected perspective on Dryden's early thought reveals that if the attribution is not accurate it is at least logical (see Appendix A). This fascinating "Deistical" work contradicts the central principle of most deists in that it posits God's immanence or continued activity in the universe:[38] "there is one infinite eternal God, Creator of all Things," we read, and "he governs the World by Providence." [39] That this essay should have been thought to be by Dryden is perhaps one more indication of the view of Dryden's thought taken by men closer to him than ourselves.

Toward the end of the essay, the author tells us, "It has been demanded of me, Whether I should be convinc'd of my Opinion, and admit of supernatural Religion, in case the Gospel (i.e.) a supernatural Religion had been promulgated to all the World? I answer'd, I should; and was contented that the whole stress of the Dispute should be terminated in that one Point. It was reply'd, That then if it could be proved that this universal Revelation was unnecessary, I ought to acquiesce; I granted that also." [40] The Dryden who wrote *Religio Laici* in 1682 was obviously convinced of both these points: namely, that the universal availability of saving gospel truths should be, and *is,* one of the characteristics of the true "supernatural Religion"; and that God's mysterious ways have made formal "universal Revelation" of those truths "unnecessary" for every individual. In fact, it is these

37. See Hutcheson, p. 58, n. 8. It was first printed in 1693 without any mention of Dryden. Internal evidence (see Appendix A) indicates that it was written after 1672.

38. See Hutcheson, p. 55.

39. *Oracles of Reason,* p. 195. John Leland, *A View of the Principal Deistical Writers That Have Appeared In England In The Last And Present Century* (London, 1798), I, 45–46, noted this peculiarity.

40. *Oracles of Reason,* p. 208.

ideas which dominate the poem and which, as we shall see, combine to produce the strange sequence of theological argument which concludes without any mention of religion. Both points are deeply rooted in the liberal theology of the period—in both its conventional and abstruse aspects.

"Things We Must Believe"

There were powerful forces of intellectual change abroad during the months preceding the publication of *Religio Laici*. Dryden did not wish to escape them. It is true that his feeling —that the function of reason in relation to the Scriptures is "to apprehend them to be the word of God" (Preface, ll. 99– 100) and that then the "things we must believe" in Scripture "are few, and plain" (l. 432)—lies securely within the tradition of rationalistic or humanistic Anglicanism exemplified by Hooker.[41] But an event of some moment separated Dryden from all Anglicans writing before 1682: Father Simon's *Critical History* had now made impossible the rational proof of "the infallibility of Scripture." In the not too distant future other Anglican writers would absorb Simon's blow to their structure of belief—with no great trembling.[42] But for the moment, the potency of Simon's findings seemed considerable: Dryden, as we have seen, identifies them as the occasion of his poem.

It is possible to contend that Simon's work had no substantial effect on Dryden's thinking and that *Religio Laici* is essentially a reiteration of the views of Hooker or Taylor.[43]

41. Cf. Fujimura, p. 209.

42. See Thomas Baker, *Reflections upon Learning* (London, 1700), pointed out in this connection by Williamson, *MLN*, LI (1936), 196.

43. "Essentially," says Fujimura (p. 217), "Dryden asserts the *via media* of the Church of England of his time. Such a position was perhaps lacking in religious fervor and depth, but it was a reasonable and moderate faith, tolerant of minor doctrinal differences, and hence most efficacious in assuring peace and stability in England." This is the view repeated by Harth, *Contexts of Dryden's Thought*, pp. 215 ff.

But the elaborate Anglican exposition of "necessary" or "plain" truths is lacking in the poem. Commentators of the generation before Dryden were fond of pointing out that Anglicans could rest safe and assured in the "perfection" of Scripture. In addition to Dryden's own arguments for the authority of Scripture (ll. 126–67) they could assert that "there is nothing lame, nothing idle, nothing impertinent in them, they were not written by chance, and at all adventure; there's not a syllable, not a tittle, but hath a masse of treasure comprehended and contrived in them." [44] Now that this simple answer could no longer be given, the only way to safety led through danger and darkness.

44. Hamon L'Estrange, *Considerations, upon Dr Bayly's Parenthetical Interlocution* (London, 1651), p. 91. This was one of the treatises which a man named Dryden bought at auction on 15 May 1682. Cf. chap. 1, n. 1, and Appendix B, n. 3.

4

Innatism and the "Candle of the Lord"

A major obstacle in the way of apprehending the intellectual content of *Religio Laici* and *The Hind and the Panther* is the close identification of Dryden with the Enlightenment. It is undoubtedly true, as Marjorie Nicolson has noted, that "Dryden, Pope and Johnson no longer lived in the old animate world of the Elizabethans." But the conclusion that theirs "was a world and a universe made by Descartes and Newton and Locke" [1] must seem, in relation to Dryden at least, largely unwarranted. The evidence of Cartesian influence in Dryden's work is small; and the works of Newton and Locke did not even begin to appear until the last years of the decade in which Dryden wrote his religious poems. It is true, of course, that most great works in the history of ideas have harbingers, and that a pioneering atmosphere usually precedes great discoveries; but it is also true that poets rarely stand close to the frontiers of intellectual innovation. Certainly Dryden did not in his own time. His generally conservative mind was most productive during a period in history when there was a hiatus in the progress towards enlightenment so far as the nonscientist was concerned. [2]

1. Marjorie Hope Nicolson, *The Breaking of the Circle: Studies in the Effect of the "New Science" upon Seventeenth Century Poetry* (Evanston, Ill., 1950), p. 181.

2. Sir George Clark, *The Later Stuarts, 1660–1714* (Oxford, 1961), p. 30, has pointed out that "Most of the scientists of the time were men who ranged widely over the still little-developed branches of scientific study, but there was something of an interruption in the co-ordination of their results into a general synthesis or philosophy. Thomas Hobbes, who had undertaken this in the previous generation, was now an old man—he

If Dryden was not an Elizabethan, he was also not a son of the yet unborn Enlightenment. In fact, of all the elements in *Religio Laici,* the one I think most charged with intellectual energy has been disregarded by critics who have looked too soon to the horizon of the coming century. This neglected element is the complex doctrine of man's innate capacity for saving truths. It is alluded to at many points in *Religio Laici* and receives its traditional formulation in lines 136–37:

> Heav'ns early Care prescrib'd for every Age;
> First, in the *Soul,* and after, in the *Page.*

With the reader's permission, I will now take leave of Dryden, for the space of a chapter, in order to explain the history and the characteristics of this doctrine.[3]

"These Men of Innate Principles"

When Locke published *An Essay Concerning Humane Understanding* in 1690, he found it necessary to devote his first Book to an attack on the un-Enlightened notion of innate ideas. Some of his contemporaries wondered who could still hold such outlandish opinions and questioned whether he had "got the story right." [4] Locke's reference was simply to "these men of innate principles," whom, unfortunately, he

---

had been born in the year of the Spanish Armada—and, although his sceptical and materialistic spirit did much to clear the way for the scientists, he was himself no scientist and little of a mathematician, and his scornful unorthodoxy was distasteful to the England of the restoration. The next Englishman to make a philosophy . . . was Locke, whose publications of this kind came a generation later."

3. Although there are many available accounts of "innate ideas," no one has offered an adequate description of the development of the non-literalistic innatism of the Cambridge Platonists or of the problems of aesthetics (especially metaphor) which they encountered. The studies by Lamprecht, Yolton, and Lichtenstein (noted below) have been the most helpful in this respect.

4. See John W. Yolton, *John Locke and the Way of Ideas* (London, 1956), p. 2

never bothered to identify. That such believers still existed in the last decades of the seventeenth century has also been doubted by some modern commentators. Ernst Cassirer believed them to be straw men constructed by Locke only for purposes of attack.[5] This, however, is a minority opinion. Closer examination of the question by other scholars has left no doubt about the very real existence of Locke's opponents, although he did exaggerate or distort their opinions to suit his argument. There is still no agreement as to their exact identity, but a precise determination is not necessary for our considerations here. The idea of innatism itself and its current language are more relevant to the present study. The content, purpose, and even the nebulousness of the idea must be examined if we are to understand in what forms it was available for Dryden's use.

Although the notion of innatism is a commonplace of western thought, it did not become important in formal English thinking until after the Reformation, when the sharp decrease in church authority shifted greater responsibility for religious knowledge to the individual.[6] On the continent, the idea commanded a central, shadowy place in mystical theology (especially in the German tradition from Eckhart to Boehme); and in the writings of Descartes it became prominent as the keystone of a theory of natural knowledge in which nature and grace were separated. On English soil, however, formal mysticism did not strike deep roots and, in spite of such writers as Bacon, the alternative entree for innatism in the vacuum created by the separation of grace and nature was not a real possibility until the end of the seventeenth century.[7] Yet the Cambridge Platonists were moving in this direction

5. *Das Erkenntnisproblem in der Philosophie und Wissenschaft der neueren Zeit* (Berlin, 1922), II, 230–31.

6. Cf. *Philosophical Writings of Henry More*, ed. Flora Isabel MacKinnon (New York, 1925), p. 276.

7. Cf. Sterling P. Lamprecht, "Innate Ideas in the Cambridge Platonists," *PhR*, XXXV (1926), 572–73.

as they attempted to avoid Bacon's separation of science and religion by adapting the new mechanical philosophy to bolster Christianity and by sustaining Lord Herbert's emphases on an innate capacity for learning religious truths.[8] They stressed the potential value of a common body of generally acceptable doctrine in freeing mankind from theological disputes and in saving righteous heathens.

In seventeenth-century England there was great diversity in the definition and "proof" of ideas supposed to be innately derived.[9] Comenius complained to the Royal Society

8. Cf. Richard Foster Jones, *Ancients and Moderns: A Study of the Rise of the Scientific Movement in Seventeenth-Century England* (St. Louis, Mo., 1961), p. 185.

9. Universal or common consent was not the only, nor even the chief, support of the doctrine. Men of the stature and scientific reputation of Walter Charleton, Dryden's "Honour'd Friend," did indeed hold this as an adequate basis for the doctrine in spite of obvious contradictions reported from other lands and other religions. In *The Immortality of the Human Soul* (London, 1657) he argued that it does *not* follow from these contradictions "that the perswasion" of the soul's "Immortality ought not to be reputed General" inasmuch as "the dissent of a few persons doth not make a General Consent not to be Natural."

> For, as, though some men are born only with one foot, and some lay violent hands upon themselves; it is not lawful for us thence to argue, that it is not natural to men to have two feet, or that the desire of life is not natural to all men. [Quoted by Yolton, p. 38.]

But this was by far a minority view. Most upholders of innatism subscribed to various arguments from "self-evidence" (see Lamprecht, p. 571).

Whichcote, the "father" of the Cambridge group, held that "Things of Natural Knowledge, or of first Inscription in the Heart of Man by God . . . are known to be true as soon as ever they are proposed": quoted by E. T. Campagnac, *The Cambridge Platonists, Being Selections from the Writings of Benjamin Whichcote, John Smith, and Nathanael Culverwel* (Oxford, 1901), p. 5. Though Descartes defined self-evident truths as those which cannot be denied without self-contradiction (see MacKinnon, *Writings of Henry More*, p. 277) and was led by this concern with self-contradiction to declare a fundamental dualism in human knowledge, Platonists such as More, who fell out with Descartes on the question of dualism (see Rosalie L. Colie, *Light and Enlightenment: A Study of the Cambridge Platonists and the Dutch Arminians*, Cambridge, 1957, pp.

in 1668 that, though philosophers have spoken a great deal
about "innate" and "common" notions "not one of them has
ever brought these into order and arrangement." [10] The situation was not much improved by 1682. Yet Comenius's criticism and the criticism of modern-day writers on the "vagueness
and confusion" [11] of the theory are irrelevant to its importance
for the age. The notion of innatism was neither secular nor
religious; it was one of the last holdouts on the misty marches
between the natural and the supernatural in respectable
English thought: it was one of the last English myths. Myths,
we know, are not often rigorously defined. In fact, part of
their power derives from their adaptability and availability
for many uses. It is not surprising, therefore, that the theory
of innatism in the second half of the seventeenth century
manifests itself as a wide, shifting spectrum of thought rather
than as a single, clear-cut proposition.

The doubts which have been raised concerning the existence,
at any time in the century, of a literal—so-called naïve—
formulation of innate ideas are not completely without basis.
This formulation, as Locke represented it, contended that
men are born with a specific number of full-blown ideas
which are independent of experience or God's grace. Dryden
rejects this view of "Philosophising Divines" in the Preface
to *Religio Laici* (ll. 69–77); and even in the early years of

----

49–65), avoided contradiction as a test of truth and kept to intuitive apprehension and immediate certainty (cf. MacKinnon, p. 277). For More,
innatist truths are as self-evident as the propositions that *"The whole is
bigger then the part: . . . Every number is either Even or Odde;* which
are true to the soul at the very first proposal; as anyone that is in his
wits does plainly perceive": *An Antidote against Atheisme, or An Appeal
to the Natural Faculties of the Minde of Man, whether there be not a
God* (London, 1653), p. 17. He does not find it necessary to examine his
evidence more closely than this.

   10. John Amos Comenius, *The Way of Light*, trans. E. T. Campagnac
(London, 1938), p. 7.

   11. James Gibson, *Locke's Theory of Knowledge and its Historical Relations* (Cambridge, 1917), p. viii and pp. 29 ff.

the century most writers who employed the theory were careful to avoid this version.[12]

It may be that part of Locke's campaign against innatism in its naïve form was due to misunderstanding, on his part, of the language employed by advocates of a more moderate formulation. Lord Herbert of Cherbury, for example, spoke constantly of certain *Veritates Catholicae* which were "divinely inscribed in the understanding itself" [13]—just as Dryden speaks, more subtly, of "pre-scribed" truths (ll. 136–37). The consequence for Herbert was that later writers classified him as a proponent of the naïve form of the doctrine. Yet Harold Hutcheson has pointed out that what Herbert "thought innate was not ideas, but modes of thought. Man's faculties are innate." [14] It is significant that Hutcheson's correction, to-

12. William Sclater's reference is typical: "The law of nature, is that rule of pietie, and honestie, that the Lord hath written in the hearts of all men: whereby they know *confusedly, and in generall,* what is good; what is euill; what to be done; what to be forborn." It is "vouchsafed vnto all by a generall influence of Gods grace, which is indeed as common as nature: and therefore called the law of nature." *A Key to the Key of Scriptvre* (London, 1611), p. 170 (italics added); cf. Yolton, p. 33. There can be no question, however, that Locke was not merely battling the phantoms of his own imagination. Richard Carpenter, for example, advocated an unquestionably naïve form of the doctrine in his *The Conscionable Christian* (1623), where he tells us, that "the whole and intire work of conscience . . . consists, as I conceive it, in a practicall syllogisme: the major proposition whereof ariseth from the *Synteresis* or treasury of morall principles, and of sacred rules wherewith the practicall understanding is furnished for the saving direction of us in all actions": quoted by Yolton, p. 31. The conception of a moral *synteresis* was quite common in the seventeenth century; cf. John F. Huntley, *"Proairesis, Synteresis,* and the Ethical Orientation of Milton's *Of Education,*" *PQ,* XLIII (1964), 40–46.

The advocates of the naïve form of the doctrine were themselves often aware of its vulnerability, and for the majority of advocates of innatism some qualification of the extreme was the only way to preserve the conception at all.

13. Hutcheson, *Lord Herbert of Cherbury's "De Religione Laici,"* p. 89.

14. Ibid., p. 37.

gether with observations on the need for it, were anticipated
three hundred years before. In 1651 Culverwel made the following comment on Herbert's opinions: "at the first dash
you would think him in a Platonical strain; but if you attend
more to what he says, you will soon perceive that he prosecutes
a far different notion. . . . For he doth not make these
instincts any connate ideas, and representations of things,
but tells us that they are powers and faculties of the soul,
the first-born faculties and beginning of the soul's strength,
that are presently espoused to their virgin-objects, closing and
complying with them long before discourse can reach them." [15]

Metaphors of Innatism

Culverwel foresaw what Hutcheson's historical investigations have revealed as fact: the metaphors of innatism or
"inscription" used by Herbert carried the liability of being
easily exaggerated by unsympathetic, though honest, readers.
The extent of this liability can only be appreciated when
we realize that the history of innatism in the seventeenth
century is more a history of metaphors than of concepts. The
traditional metaphor of "inscription" allowed of little shading
or elaboration to represent more complex views of innateness.
William Sclater's speculations on what "the Lord hath written
in the hearts of all men: whereby they know confusedly, and
in generall, what is good" is a graphic example of the resulting imprecision.[16] The early Cambridge Platonists suffered
extensively from misconstruction on this count. Whichcote
spoke of "Things of Natural Knowledge, or of first Inscription
in the Heart of Man by God." John Smith spoke of "truths
of natural inscription." Naturally such positions were attacked

15. Nathanael Culverwel, *Of the Light of Nature*, p. 128.
16. Cf. n. 12. It is an example which could be multiplied many times
—in the habitual references of such men as William Chillingworth to
"common notions written by God in the hearts of all men": quoted by
John Tulloch, *Rational Theology and Christian Philosophy in England
in the Seventeenth Century* (Edinburgh, 1874), I, 331.

as formulations of the naïve theory, although there is little clear evidence to support the charge.[17] In fact, the Cambridge group, both early and late, usually tried—though not always with complete success—to avoid the misleading implications of the inscription metaphor and, to do this, adapted to their own ends the immemorial metaphor of interior light.

It was through the writings of Whichcote that the "new" metaphor, the "Candle of the Lord," first came into English innatist thought. The metaphor was borrowed from Proverbs 20:27: "The spirit of man is the candle of the Lord, searching all the inward parts of the belly." Though we do not have an accurate record of the development of the metaphor's implications in Whichcote's teaching at Cambridge, or of its dissemination, his writings give us a fair outline of the progress of his ideas and imagery. His "two lights" are fundamental to his thinking:

> God hath set up *Two Lights;* to enlighten us in our Way: the Light of *Reason,* which is the Light of his Creation; and the Light of *Scripture,* which is After-Revelation from him. Let us make use of these two Lights; and suffer neither to be put out. . . . The *Spirit of a Man is the Candle of the Lord;* Lighted *by* God, and Lighting us *to* God. *Res Illuminata, illuminans.*[18]

It remained only to complete the connection between the innate capacity and light and then to transfer the burden carried by the inscription metaphor to the candle:

> . . . I cannot distinguish Truth in itself; but in way of descent to us:) *Truth* either *of first Inscription,* or *of After-revelation* from God.
> The Truth of first Inscription is connatural to Man,

17. See Yolton, p. 40; cf. n. 9.
18. Benjamin Whichcote, *Moral and Religious Aphorisms* (London, 1753), nos. 109 and 916.

it is the Light of God's Creation, and it flows from the
Principles of which Man doth consist, in his very first
Make: This is the Soul's Complexion. . . . Things that
are of an immutable and indispensible Nature, we have
Knowledge of them by the Light of first Impression. The
voluntary Results of the Divine Will, we have by Revelation from God.

Man's Observance of God in all Instances of Morality;
these are Truths of *first Inscription;* and these have a
deeper Foundation, greater Ground for them, than that
God gave the Law on Mount *Sinai;* or that he did after
ingrave it on Tables of Stone; or that we find the Ten
Commandments in the Bible. For God made Man to
them, and did write them upon the Heart of Man, before
he did declare them upon Mount *Sinai,* before he ingraved them upon the Tables of Stone, or before they
were writ in our Bibles; God made Man to them, and
wrought his Law upon Mens Hearts; and, as it were,
interwove it into the Principles of our Reason.

The "Light of first Impression" is first described as written
and then as "wrought" in the hearts of men. In the end the
vocabulary of light becomes independent of inscription:

This is the Sum. All Divine Truth is of one of these
two Emanations:—Either it flows from God, in the first
Instant and Moment of God's Creation; and then it is
the Light of that Candle which God set up in Man, to
light him; and that which by this Light he may discover,
are all the Instances of Morality; of good Affection, and
Submission towards God; the Instances of Justice and
Righteousness to Men, and Temperance to himself:—
Or else, it is of an after Revelation and Discovery.[19]

As Cassirer has noted, Whichcote's use of the "Candle of

19. *The Cambridge Platonists,* ed. Campagnac, pp. 4–10.

the Lord" metaphor became the center around which Cambridge Platonism revolved.[20]

Dispositional Innatism

Distinguishing between metaphors of innatism may seem to the modern reader a matter of less than compelling philosophical or theological importance. Yet it is clear from the literature of innatism that the step from metaphor to epistemology was not great. Seventeenth-century writers were themselves aware of this. In *A Demonstration of the Divine Authority of the Law of Nature* (London, 1681) Parker accounted for the development of the naïve form of the theory in terms of its faulty language of inscription—especially its material metaphors—which we saw him reject earlier as "the meer Products of Imagination." [21]

> As to the Sufficiency of the Publication of the Law of Nature, the plain Account of it has been obscured by nothing more, then that it has alwaies been described and discoursed of in metaphorical and allusive Expressions, such as *Engravings,* and *Inscriptions,* and the *Tables of the Heart,* etc. As if the Law of Nature consisted of a certain number of Propositions that were imprinted upon the Minds of Men, and concreated with their Understandings, by attending to and reflecting upon which they were instructed or bound to govern their moral Actions. [p. 5]

This was not an attack on innatism per se. Parker himself maintained that "the Laws of Nature" are "drawn forth into use and bound upon the Conscience . . . by vertue of the workings of our own Minds" and he even argued, after making

20. Ernst Cassirer, *The Platonic Renaissance in England,* trans. James P. Pettegrove (Austin, Tex., 1953), p. 26.
21. *Free and Impartial Censure,* p. 79.

short shrift of exceptions, that universal consent is "a great
proof and confirmation of the Laws of Nature" (pp. 7–12);
"The natural Activity of the Mind," according to Parker,
gives man "Knowledge" of "the Laws of Nature" (p. 42). The
candle metaphor of the Cambridge Platonists could avoid the
naïve implications which Parker objected to by leaving the
form of innatism unspecified. They advocated a *dispositional*
theory of innate ideas which was emphatically dependent on
experience or the immediate influence of God.[22] Culverwel
commented that "the Platonists in this were commendable,
that they looked upon the spirit of a man as 'the candle of the
Lord,' though they were deceived in the time when it was
lighted." [23] More also was generally anxious to qualify his
position on "actual" innate knowledge and to distinguish it
from the material idealism suggested by an inscription representation:

> when I say *actuall Knowledge,* I doe not mean that there
> is a certain number of *Ideas* flaring and shining to the
> *Animadversive faculty* like so many *Torches* or *Starres*
> in the *Firmament* to our outward sight, or that there
> are any *figures* that take their distinct place & are legibly
> writ there like *Red Letters* or *Astronomicall Characters*
> in an *Almanack;* but I understand thereby an active
> sagacity in the Soul, or quick recollection as it were,
> whereby some small businesse being hinted unto her, she
> runs out presently into a more clear & larger conception.[24]

We have some *Ideas* that we are not beholding to our
Senses for, but are the mere exertions of the Mind occa-
sionally awakened by the Appulses of the outward Objects;
which the outward Senses do no more teach us, then he

22. Cf. Yolton, pp. 39–40.
23. *Of the Light of Nature,* p. 132.
24. Quoted by Yolton, p. 40.

that awakened the *Musician* to sing taught him his skill.[25]

Cudworth wrote that the teaching of experience is "the kindling" of the soul "from within; or helping it so as to excite and awaken, compare and compound, its own notions, as whereby to arrive at the knowledge of that which it was before ignorant of." [26] This dispositional form of the theory was the major contribution of the Cambridge Platonists to the history of innatism. It gave the doctrine a new lease on life in the second half of the seventeenth century. Through the dispositional formulation and the candle metaphor which represented it, the doctrine of innatism was not only freed from scholastic literalness but also given an independent organic quality which it had formerly lacked. The layman could lift the candle of his own spiritual power to light up essential questions whenever the sun of revelation was missing or eclipsed or clouded over by sectarian dispute.

The Cambridge Platonists did not do their work in a vacuum. The materials for their achievement were present in the mainstream of English theology, though they floated and bobbed there like driftwood, unpiloted and, for the most part, unwanted. The candle metaphor and the dispositional formulation of innatism were implicit in earlier Anglican views of "natural light" and were perhaps reinforced in

25. Quoted by Lamprecht, p. 569. The Platonists' "Candle" may mark a transition point between the "mirror" and the "lamp" which M. H. Abrams has described for us. It is not a mirror, a mere "reflector of external objects" and, though it is a lamplike "radiant projector," it does not, like the lamp, make a truly independent "contribution to the objects it perceives," in that its light is more expressly derivative than that of the lamp: man sees only what God has given him to see. Thus the main difference between the candle and the lamp lies in the strong sense of an active, gracious God which the former metaphor carries. See M. H. Abrams, *The Mirror and the Lamp: Romantic Theory and the Critical Tradition* (New York, 1958), pp. vi and 59–60.

26. Quoted by Lamprecht, p. 570.

England by the popularization of German mystical thought during the years Dryden spent at Cambridge.[27] The Cambridge men were exploiting a well-known image when they compressed the glow of natural light into a single flame and located it in the soul of every man. But with their help the light of the candle, "excited" and awakened by God and by external experience, tended to become a class of knowledge unto itself. This is the higher kind of "Reason" which the Cambridge group constantly wrote about.

Innatism, Reason, or Discourse

S. L. Bethell has pointed out that English theologians of the late sixteenth and early seventeenth centuries commonly subscribed to "natural reason and natural theology; it was

27. Many of the elements of the innatist tradition, for example, are apparent in this passage from Hooker's *Laws*, I, viii, 3 (citations from Hooker are to *The Works of that Learned and Judicious Divine Mr. Richard Hooker,* ed. John Keble, rev. R. W. Church and F. Paget, Oxford, 1888):

> The general and perpetual voice of men is as the sentence of God himself. For that which all men have at all times learned, Nature herself must needs have taught; and God being the author of Nature, her voice is but his instrument. By her from Him we receive whatsoever in such sort we learn. Infinite duties there are, the goodness whereof is by this rule sufficiently manifested, although we had no other warrant besides to approve them. The Apostle St. Paul having speech concerning the heathen saith of them, "They are a law unto themselves." His meaning is, that by force of the light of Reason, wherewith God illuminateth every one which cometh into the world, men being enabled to know truth from falsehood, and good from evil, do thereby learn in many things what the will of God is; which will himself not revealing by any extraordinary means unto them, but they by natural discourse attaining the knowledge thereof, seem the makers of those Laws which indeed are his, and they but only the finders of them out.

Cf. Jakob Boehme, *Concerning the Election of Grace* (London, 1655), p. 12: "Look upon a kindled candle, and thou seest a similitude both of the *Divine* and of the *Natural* Being Essence or Substance"; Boehme adds that in the soul "the Word of God formeth and Imageth it self into a Natural and creaturely ground" (p. 66).

an inheritance from the scholastic middle ages and was shared
by the generality of educated men." [28] But the rejection of
scholastic thinking and the incipient separation of grace and
nature opened a painful fissure between faith and reason.
"Sacred theology," wrote Bacon, "must be drawn from the
word and oracles of God, not from the light of nature, or
the dictates of reason." [29] This is the same antirational tendency which persisted throughout the century and which was
opposed by every writer in the Cambridge camp. It was also in
evidence before Bacon wrote. Hooker shows us that what we
have identified as a central concern of the Cambridge group
derived much of its direction from traditional Anglican
thought:

> But so it is, the name of the light of nature is made
> hateful with men; the "star of reason and learning,"
> and all other such like helps, beginneth no otherwise to
> be thought of than if it were an unlucky comet; or as if
> God has so accursed it, that it should never shine or give
> light in things concerning our duty any way towards
> him, but be esteemed as that star in the Revelation, called
> *Wormwood,* which being fallen from heaven, maketh
> rivers and waters in which it falleth so bitter, that men
> tasting them die thereof. A number there are, who think
> they cannot admire as they ought the power and author-
> ity of the word of God, if in things divine they should
> attribute any force to man's reason. For which cause
> they never use reason so willingly as to disgrace reason.[30]

The spirit of this protest persists in the exaltation and re-
definition of reason at Cambridge. Culverwel's famous "luta-
nist" passage expresses Hooker's protest in the language of
dispositional innatism:

28. S. L. Bethell, *The Cultural Revolution of the Seventeenth Century* (London, 1951), p. 34.
29. Quoted by Willey, *The Seventeenth Century Background,* p. 36.
30. Hooker, *Laws,* III, viii, 4.

> Is it not better to enjoy the faint and languishing light
> of this 'candle of the Lord,' rather than to be in palpable
> and disconsolate darkness? . . . Would you persuade the
> lutanist to cut all his strings in sunder because they are
> out of tune? . . . Because men have not so much of
> reason as they should, will they therefore resolve to
> have none at all? . . . Reason, when awakened, . . .
> hears her own jarrings, sees the dimness of her own
> sight.[31]

Culverwel, moreover, is among the more moderate of the
Cambridge writers in his approach to reason. He was, it is
true, willing to say that "the vigour and triumph of reason
is principally to be seen in those first-born beams, those pure
and unspotted irradiations, that shine from it; I mean those
first bubblings up of common principles that are owned and
acknowledged by all." [32] But then he would add that "the rise
of these first principles is very cryptical and mysterious," [33]
and he demurred from going further.[34]

The Cambridge Platonists' attitude toward reason is best
represented in the writings of More. In his effort to define
the higher kind of reason, he sought a concomitant principle
which could identify the light of the Candle:

> I should commend to them that would successfully philos-
> ophize, the belief and endeavor after a certain Principle
> more noble and inward than Reason it self, and without
> which Reason will faulter, or at least reach but to mean
> and frivolous things. I have a sense of something in me
> while I thus speak, which I must confess is of so retruse
> a nature that I want a name for it, unless I should adven-
> ture to term it Divine Sagacity, which is the first Rise of

31. Culverwel, *Of the Light of Nature,* pp. 19–20.
32. Ibid., p. 24.
33. Ibid., p. 130.
34. Cf. ibid., pp. 7, 75, 81, and 165.

successful Reason, especially in matters of great comprehension and moment.[35]

Man, according to More, is endowed with a particle of the
divine which gives him the use of independent spiritual power
in his apprehension of reality.

It should not be supposed, however, that the concept of
a higher reason was limited to the small group of Cambridge
Platonists. The Cambridge men were the center of a large
and diverse group of thinkers who were known by a term as
broad in its application as in its meaning: latitudinarians.
Most of the liberal men of the century belonged in one way
or another to the ranks of the "men of latitude." In time,
this nominal association of intellectuals, like that of progres-
sives or liberals in our own century, acquired a connotation
of opprobrium in some quarters. In 1662 an observer ("S.P.")
identified the term most closely with the Cambridge Platonists
themselves but noted that the "name of Latitude-men" is
"daily exagitated amongst us both in Taverns and Pulpits, and
very tragical representations made of them. . . . A Latitude-
man therefore (according to the best definition that I can
collect) is an image of clouts that men set up to encounter
with for want of a real enemy; it is a convenient name to re-
proach a man that you owe a spight to, ('tis what you will,
and you may affix it upon whom you will) 'tis something will
serve to talke of when all other discourse fails." [36]

35. Quoted by Lamprecht, p. 563. See page 155 of the excellent study
by Aharon Lichtenstein, *Henry More: The Rational Theology of a Cambridge Platonist* (Cambridge, Mass., 1962).

36. *A Brief Account of the new Sect of Latitude-Men* (Cambridge,
1662), pp. 4–5, by "S. P." Douglas Bush, *English Literature in the
Earlier Seventeenth Century, 1600–1660* (Oxford, 1962), p. 364, notes that
after the appearance of More's "much-discussed book, *The Grand Mystery
of Godliness* (1660), the term 'latitude-men' began to be used by some
'Cholerick gentlemen' as equivalent to 'heretics.'" It was a name which
many a coffee-drinker, possibly a poet among them, would have wished

If the latitudinarians did have any one distinguishing characteristic, it was their attitude towards reason. They were not
extreme rationalists. They distinguished sharply between common reasoning and the reason which is associated with innatism. Joseph Glanvill voiced the typical latitudinarian
devaluation of reason and exaltation of Reason: "Reason
of the far greatest part of mankind, is but an aggregate of
mistaken phantasms." He noted that even the "highest and
most improved parts of Rationality, are frequently caught in
the entanglements of a tenacious Imagination." [37] In his Λογου
θρησκεια: Or, *A Seasonable Recommendation, and Defence of
Reason, In the Affairs of Religion* (London, 1670) Glanvill
distinguishes explicitly between the two kinds of reason and
shows us how much the distinction depends on the tradition
of innatism:

> *Reason* is sometimes taken for *Reason* in the *Faculty,*
> which is the *Understanding;* and at other times, for *Rea-
> son* in the *object,* which consists in those *Principles,* and
> *Conclusions* by which the *Understanding* is *informed.*
> *This latter* is meant in the *dispute* concerning the *agree-
> ment,* or *disagreement* of *Reason,* and *Religion.* And
> *Reason* in *this* sense, is the same with *natural truth.* . . .
> By the *Principles* of *Reason* we are not to understand the
> *Grounds* of any mans *Philosophy;* nor the *Critical Rules*
> of *Syllogism;* but those *imbred fundamental notices,* that
> God hath implanted in our Souls; such as arise not from
> *external objects,* nor *particular* humors, or *imaginations;*
> but are *immediately* lodged in our minds; *independent*
> upon other *principles* or *deductions;* commanding *a sud-
> den assent;* and *acknowledged* by *all* sober mankind. [pp.
> 6–7]

to avoid. (The pamphlet by "S. P." is generally attributed to Simon
Patrick, although this ascription has sometimes been disputed; see Lichtenstein, p. 26, n. 40.)

37. Quoted by Willey, p. 184.

Jackson Cope well observes that "roughly similar epistemologies left Lord Herbert of Cherbury a deistic irenicist and Glanvill an Anglican apologist." [38]

The same position is evident in men of latitude who were substantially distant from Glanvill's Platonism. [39] When the Jesuit fideist, Edward Knott, complained that if the infallibility of the Church is denied, "every man is given over to his own wit and discourse," William Chillingworth had a ready answer: "if you mean by *discourse,* right reason grounded on Divine revelation, and common notions written by God in the hearts of all men, and deducing, according to the neverfailing rules of logic, consequent deductions from them; if this be it which you mean by *discourse,* it is very meet and reasonable and necessary, that men, as in all their actions, so especially in that of greatest importance, the choice of their way to happiness, should be left unto it; and he that follows this in all his opinions and actions, and does not only seem to do so, follows always God; whereas he that followeth a company of men, may oft-times follow a company of beasts." [40] Chillingworth's distinction between the two kinds of "discourse," or reason, is less refined than Glanvill's but it is still unmistakable and effective in identifying one kind of discourse as an instrument which is divinely endowed. [41]

38. Jackson Cope, *Joseph Glanvill: Anglican Apologist* (St. Louis, Mo., 1956), p. 72.

39. See Cope, pp. 127–43.

40. *The Works of William Chillingworth, M.A.* (Oxford, 1838), I, 14–15. The passage is quoted by Tulloch, *Rational Theology,* I, 131, and by Bredvold, *Intellectual Milieu of Dryden,* p. 81.

41. It should be noted that the same ideas were expressed in less systematic forms by a wide range of thinkers, including Sir Walter Ralegh, Lancelot Andrewes, Donne, Jeremy Taylor, Milton, and John Tillotson (see Baker, *The Wars of Truth,* pp. 97, 131–32; Lamprecht, p. 566; and Charles Coffin, *John Donne and the New Philosophy,* New York, 1937, p. 290). Even the extreme anti-Puritan William Laud held that one of the "three main grounds" of Christian faith was "the light of Nature." (*The Works of the Most Reverend Father in God William Laud,* Oxford, 1849, II, 130.)

The relationship between Descartes's assertion of "clear and distinct

Charity, Synergism, and Heresy

The writings of the latitude men did not, in the end, bolster orthodox Anglicanism. The efforts of these men, especially of the Cambridge Platonists, preserved and even resuscitated, for a few decades, the spiritual unity of the cosmos in the minds of many men. But this work was done at great cost. The history of latitudinarian thought in the seventeenth century is attended and defined by a series of propositions and tendencies which were philosophically or theologically contingent upon innatism. As long as these satellite conceptions were held together by the binding energy of a belief in an innate capacity for saving truth, they constituted an orderly system of religious comprehension and theological balance. Once, however, this belief began to fail, the same conceptions became runaway forces in a process of rapid disintegration.

The position of the Cambridge Platonists in the history of British theology is therefore an ironic and even tragic one. Their sturdy intellects were capable of sustaining a devout religious life built on a single profound abstraction with many subordinate principles held in firm check. Unfortunately, they were incapable of communicating the essentials of their faith. Only the husk of their religious outlook passed to posterity, and it was this husk which was substituted, by many, for orthodox religion.

The idealism of the Cambridge school was, like traditional Platonism, an effort to get closer to the true reality. In spite

---

ideas" and the English tradition of innatism was not causal, but it reinforced the English tradition and helped to make it respectable among those who were loitering in the basilica of Enlightenment (see Lamprecht, p. 571).

If it was objected that innatist views were difficult to distinguish from aspects of Socinianism or deism, the ready answer was, "because Socinus has burnt his wings at this *Candle of the Lord,* must none therefore make use of it?" (Culverwel, p. 23).

of certain notorious aberrant preoccupations in the writings of More, the main concern of the Cambridge Platonists and of More himself was decidedly not mystical. "God forbid," says More in the person of his Philotheus, "that the sweet of Contemplation should ever put your Mouth out of tast with the savoury Usefulness of Secular Negotiations. . . . The exercise of Love and Goodness, of Humanity and Brotherly-kindness, of Prudence and Discretion, of Faithfulness and Neighbourliness, of unfeigned Devotion and Religion, in the plain and undoubted Duties thereof, is to the truly regenerate Soul a far greater pleasure than all the fine Speculations imaginable." [42] "Give me religion that is grounded in reason . . . and that doth attain real effects," said Whichcote.[43] Ultimately this interest in the "real effects" of religion was to contribute to the weakening of orthodox Anglicanism.[44]

All the Cambridge Platonists were pious members of the Anglican Church. How they came to be the heralds of dis-solution in that Church is hinted at by S. P. when he notes that there is not "any Article of Doctrine held forth by the Church, which they can justly be accused to depart from, unlesse absolute reprobation be one, which they do not think themselves bound to believe." [45] S. P.'s "unlesse" describes a major focus of the entire philosophy of the Cambridge school and the source of their injurious effect on orthodox Anglican belief. The doctrine of innatism itself, the cardinal intel-lectual tool of the whole group, was employed by them to deny absolute reprobation. In this lies the chief difference between

42. Quoted by Lichtenstein, p. 104.

43. Quoted by Frederick J. Powicke, *The Cambridge Platonists: A Study* (London, 1926), p. 80.

44. Lichtenstein has remarked that "the overmastering concern with moral conduct—often to the neglect and detriment of the specific con-tent of religion proper—is the most characteristic feature of Restoration and eighteenth-century theology. In large measure, this concern derives from the fountainhead of Cambridge Platonism" (p. 160).

45. "S.P.", *A Brief Account*, p. 9.

the continental and English uses of innatist ideas. Descartes, as Sterling Lamprecht has pointed out, used innatism "as part of his equipment for insisting on the clarity and demonstrability of the new view of external nature," while the Cambridge Platonists appealed to innatism as "an escape from the fatalism of Protestant confessional statements." [46]

The candle of the Platonists gave light wherever it was needed: no one, they held, was born in darkness; mere circumstance sent no man to hell. This universalism was not a desirable extra but the heart of their matter. "Universal charity is *a thing final* in religion," wrote Whichcote.[47] The assertion of "universal charity" as a terminal value left no room for half-committed statements on the possibility of salvation for men of other beliefs.[48] The Cambridge men, as a group, turned Erasmus's prayer, *"Sancte Socrates ora pro nobis"* into a creed: "If men contend for the effects of real goodness and deny wickedness, they do truly and properly preach Christ . . . for this is the effect of Christ and this is Christ's business." [49] "Nothing," Whichcote concluded, "is desperate in the condition of good men; they will not live and die in any dangerous error." [50]

The Cambridge men posited a kind of charitable synergism which was the very opposite of Calvinistic or Hobbesian views of human nature. Whichcote asserted that "in all Moral Perfections, God is imitable by us; We may resemble God: God is communicable to us; We may partake of Him." [51] At the same time, he avoided Augustine's frantic concern with grace. One of Whichcote's favorite texts was, "The Grace of God

46. See Lamprecht, pp. 562 and 572–73.

47. Quoted by Powicke, p. 17; italics added.

48. Culverwel's dissent from this view is one of the major points which distinguish him from the Cambridge Platonists; see Culverwel, pp. 265–69.

49. Quoted by Powicke, p. 63.

50. Quoted by Tulloch, II, 103.

51. *Moral and Religious Aphorisms,* no. 50.

that bringeth salvation hath appeared to all men, teaching us that, denying ungodliness and worldly lusts, we should live soberly, righteously, and godly in this present world." [52] The Cambridge men, as S. C. Carpenter has remarked, "trod seldom in the deep, dark ravines, where sin is fought and redemption is found a vital need." [53] Christ is taken by them as an exemplum of "what human nature may attain to, and how it may by humility, self-denial, Divine love, and a Christ-like life, rise above all visible heavens into a state of immortal glory and bliss." [54] It is no wonder, therefore, that Anthony Tuckney could find in Whichcote's work "a kind of moral divinity minted, only with a little tincture of Christ added," something very close, as Tuckney saw it, to the Arminian and Socinian heresies.[55] "Truth is Truth," Whichcote answered, "whosoever speaks it, and I will readily agree with Papist, Socinian, or any, so far as he asserts it; because it is not his but God's." [56] One symptomatic and unfortunate result (from the point of view of maintaining orthodox Anglicanism) of this charity and objectivity was to be that a pupil of Whichcote's, Archbishop Tillotson, would soon be offering pragmatic definitions of religion which did not even mention God: religion, Tillotson tells us, is "the thwarting and crossing of our vicious inclinations, the curing of our evil and corrupt affections, the due care and government of our unruly appetites and passions, the sincere endeavour and constant practice of all holiness and virtue in our lives." [57]

Through the influence of the Cambridge Platonists a greater homocentric emphasis became acceptable in English religious thought. Lichtenstein's important remark concerning More,

52. Quoted by Powicke, p. 33.
53. S. C. Carpenter, *The Church in England, 597–1688* (London, 1954), p. 383.
54. Quoted by Powicke, p. 72.
55. Ibid., p. 57.
56. Ibid., p. 56.
57. Quoted by Lichtenstein, p. 187.

in this connection, applies equally to the general position of
the Cambridge men: "the unicity of God and the resultant
uniqueness of man's relation to Him—totally dissimilar from
any mere political or social relation—are definitely mini-
mized, if not, indeed, overlooked." [58] This attitude becomes
of great practical significance in relation to the authority of
the Bible. Whichcote tells us that "the Scripture is to be read
as a man would read a letter from a friend, in which he doth
only look after what was his friend's mind and meaning." [59]
Such a statement assumes *prior knowledge* of the "friend's
mind and meaning." "The written word of God," Whichcote
says elsewhere, "is not the first or only discovery of the duty
of man. It doth gather and repeat and reinforce and charge
upon us the scattered principles of God's creation." [60] This
convenient application to the Candle of the Lord freed the
Cambridge men from self-torment about obscure places in the
revealed text. "Suppose there be a place of Scripture," Whichcote argued, "about some notion that doth transcend the reach
of human reason, and which is knowable only by divine revelation; and divine revelation is comprehended in a form of
words that I cannot fully comprehend; in this case I refer
myself to God, and believe that that is true which God intended in those words. This I call an implicit faith." [61] We
might call it a healthy ability to dismiss imponderables; de-
fenders of a church-oriented orthodoxy, like Tuckney, regarded it as incipient atheism.

"Common Quiet" and "Rationalistic Anti-Intellectualism"

The relaxed attitude of the Cambridge men towards "unessential" matters of scriptural interpretation was for them only
a means to an end. Their goal in all such questions was to

58. Ibid., p. 168.
59. Quoted by Powicke, p. 78.
60. Ibid., p. 31.
61. Ibid., pp. 40–41.

pacify religious dispute in order to attain peace and tranquility. Their technique, as Willey notes, was "not to confront the cloud of credal warfare, but 'to put it by'; to dwell always upon the real, the saving truths, and by simply not using the weapons of controversy to let them silently rust away."[62] It is clear that they pursued this end quite consciously. "What we have openly driven at all this while," Smith tells us, "is, To learn not to devote or give up our selves to any private Opinions or Dictates of men in matters of Religion, nor too zealously to propugne the Dogmata of any Sect. . . . They are not alwaies the Best men that blot most paper."[63] For this work, the light of their candle was eminently useful. As Lamprecht remarks, "all the sectarian spirit of the century, all the dogmatism of partisan groups were challenged by the theory" of innatism.[64] According to the dynamic, dispositional formulation of the Cambridge men no one group could claim the absolute necessity of its creed for salvation because the Candle of the Lord always provided a sufficiency of light to save any good man: it always burned more brightly wherever the sun of revelation was unknown or obscured. This reliance on a formula for the insurance of a necessary minimum was in accord with a widespread tendency in Anglicanism towards submerging "doctrinal differences in the few essential truths necessary for salvation."[65] The mobility, however, with which the Cambridge men endowed this concept was soon to move it out of the pale of the Church. The "few essential truths" could easily be reduced to secular morality. To the third earl of Shaftesbury and his generation, Whichcote was merely a "Preacher of Good-Nature."[66]

The "naturalism" to which Cambridge Platonism so easily

62. Willey, p. 140.
63. *The Cambridge Platonists,* ed. Campagnac, pp. 88–89.
64. Lamprecht, p. 564.
65. Baker, p. 117.
66. Noted by W. C. de Pauley, *The Candle of the Lord: Studies in the Cambridge Platonists* (London, 1937), p. 3.

lent itself is nowhere to be found, however, in its propounders. Nature for them is still the habitation of a living, acting God. The reason which they find in every man is, in Smith's words, "a living principle of Holiness within." [67] Nor is there anything of mere syllogistic "rationalism" in this concept of reason. The uninspired *process* of reasoning is to them almost useless in religious matters. In fact, one discovers among the Cambridge school a distinctly anti-intellectual bias. "To the Hypocrite and disobedient that read them for to peep into knowledge, or to furnish themselves with learned and relligious partes," even the Scriptures, More tells us, "are a snare to the understanding, and fill them with a very misshapen conceit and imagination, that neither true Divinity nor Nature will allow of." [68] The path to the "internal Kingdom of God" is through "the Mysteries of the Heart, . . . not of the Head, which in comparison, is but an outward Shop of Phancies and fine Pictures." [69] This anti-intellectual tendency was produced or reinforced by other currents in the age. Here the Cambridge school found itself in agreement with Bacon's dislike of "excessive rationalism" [70] and with the general reaction of the new science to heavy reliance upon ratiocination.[71] It was a tendency which also coincided with the development of what Lovejoy has called "an intellectual equalitarianism" and a paradoxical "rationalistic anti-intellectualism" in related areas of British thought.[72] The tradition of innatism accommodated itself readily to such attitudes.[73]

67. *The Cambridge Platonists,* ed. Campagnac, p. 81; cf. Lamprecht, 562–63, on this point.

68. Quoted by Lichtenstein, p. 98.

69. Ibid., p. 99.

70. Willey, p. 43.

71. See Alfred North Whitehead, *Science and the Modern World* (New York, 1954), pp. 83–108.

72. A. O. Lovejoy, "The Parallel of Deism and Classicism," in *Essays in the History of Ideas* (Baltimore, 1948), pp. 84–85.

73. Matthew Hale, for example, in *The Primitive Origination of Mankind* (London, 1677), wrote that there "are some truths so plain and

Ultimately it was the belief of the Cambridge Platonists in the innate Candle of the Lord which kept their program from being in their own time what it was to become a generation later. Their opposition to absolute reprobation, their decreased emphasis on the fall of man, their lessened concern with grace and God's unicity, their small dependence on scriptural authority, their tolerant attitude towards heresiarchs, their efforts to pacify religious dispute, their emphasis on practical morality and communal tranquility—all these were bound together by the energy of innatism.

Uncommunicated Light

At least part of the reason for the demise of these ideas can be traced to a problem of communication. The Cambridge men developed a literary position which confronted—or reacted to—many of the problems of prose and poetry in the later seventeenth century. Because they proceeded on the assumption that concepts alone are real and that these concepts, as they are intuitively apprehended, should not be toyed with, they too, as we saw in the first chapter, were reluctant to use concrete images or metaphors. Their beloved candle and other kinds of light seemed to them to be concepts of truth in themselves; their epistemology, like Culverwel's *Discourse,* was to be "weaved of sunbeams." [74] And they showed no less regard for style than for imagery. For them the religious life, like the works that taught it, had to be an achievement in regenerate tone: the "first thing in religion," said Whichcote, "is to refine a man's temper." [75]

Yet, in the final analysis, a large part of their failure must

---

evident, and open, that need not any process of ratiocination to evidence or evince them; they seem to be objected to [i.e. made objects of] the Intellective Nature when it is grown perfect and fit for intellectual operation" (quoted by Yolton, p. 33).

74. Culverwel, p. 5.
75. Quoted by Tulloch, II, 106.

be attributed to shortcomings in their means of expression.
The representation of an inner vision of religion was their
life's work, but they defined that vision as essentially incapable of representation. Religion, Whichcote insisted, must not
be "Mystical, Symbolical, Ænigmatical, Emblematical; but
uncloathed, unbodied, intellectual, rational, spiritual." [76]
Though they had in their possession a magnificent tool for
the creation of a "true" poetry—a Candle of the Lord, an
image which was "real" in itself—they refrained from using
it to the fullest.[77] Michael Roberts has pointed out that "by
abandoning the poetic use of language, which alone is competent to deal with . . . internal knowledge, they themselves
had made certain the defeat of their own cause." [78] Their
light, however, did not die in the dust. Dryden found a way
to mend their lamp.

76. *Moral and Religious Aphorisms,* no. 889.

77. "Divinity," said Smith, is "rather to be understood by a *Spiritual
sensation,* then by any *Verbal description*" (*Select Discourses,* London,
1660, p. 2).

78. Michael Roberts, *The Modern Mind* (London, 1937), p. 115. Roberts's
discussion of the Cambridge Platonists is interesting but it does not take
into account the innatist tradition or the significance of the "Candle of the
Lord" metaphor.

5

Religio Laici: I

The content and the form of *Religio Laici* depend, in my view, on an adaptation of the Cambridge Platonist thought which we examined in the last chapter. In chapters 9 and 10 I hope to show that the work of the Cambridge men also provided, in a quite different way, the germinal inspiration for *The Hind and the Panther*. In *Religio Laici,* the strongest argument for their influence is the presence of certain ideas in the body of the poem that, when given their proper weight, may be seen to contribute to a poetic totality of great interest. The description of this totality is the main business of the next chapter. At this point it is worth recalling the secondary and external indications of Dryden's relation to the Cambridge group.

"Wandring Fires"

When, in *The Hind and the Panther* (1687), Dryden tells us that his "manhood, long misled by wandring fires, / Follow'd false lights" (I, 73–74) we cannot be sure that this is a reference to the particular kind of Anglicanism espoused by the Platonists; but it surely refers, as Verrall and Scott realized, to something like it. The suggestion that Dryden did have the Cambridge latitudinarians in mind is reinforced later in that poem when the Hind tells the Panther:

> Your sons of Latitude that court your grace,
> Though most resembling you in form and face,
> Are far the worst of your pretended race.
>
> [III, 160–62]

It seems plausible that where Dryden now saw danger he had
once found strength.

Even as late as 1693 he maintained that the Platonists had
opened up a fertile field of subjects for poetry. He recommends to "Christian poets" (who "have not hitherto been
acquainted with their own strength") the "perusing of one
chapter in the prophecy of Daniel, and accommodating what
there they find with the principles of Platonic philosophy
as it is now Christianised." [1] This is probably a direct reference to the introduction and the text of More's *Exposition of
the Prophecies of Daniel*,[2] published in 1681. In the same
place, Dryden describes the qualifications of the epic poet and
remarks, "If any of so happy a genius be now living, or any
future age can produce a man . . . conversant in the philosophy of Plato, as it is now accommodated to Christian use
. . . he may build a nobler, a more beautiful, and more perfect poem than any yet extant since the Ancients." [3] We need
not wonder where or when Dryden was exposed to the Cambridge Platonists. Saintsbury remarked that Dryden had "a
strong dash of the . . . latitudinarianism of his university" [4]
which was, especially during Dryden's college years, the Platonism of Whichcote and More and Cudworth.[5] Even after he
left Cambridge, there was still opportunity for direct contact
with at least one of the Cambridge group. Whichcote moved
to London in 1668 and became Rector of St. Lawrence Jewry.
We know that he preached there twice a week—alternating

1. Dryden, *Of Dramatic Poesy*, ed. Watson, II, 88.

2. See Watson's note, ibid., II, 88, n. 2.

3. Ibid., II, 90.

4. *Works of John Dryden*, XVIII, 321.

5. Charles E. Ward, *The Life of John Dryden* (Chapel Hill, N.C.,
1961), p. 15, has noted similarly that "the liberal climate of thought" at
Cambridge, inspired in large measure by "Henry More, Cudworth, Culverwel, and Whichcote," must have "exercised its influence upon Dryden as
an undergraduate."

with Tillotson much of the time—to a small but "very considerable and judicious auditory" until his death in 1681.[6]

The opportunities for indirect exposure to the ideas of the Platonists were legion and inescapable. Not only were their most important books appearing throughout the two decades preceding 1682, but their sphere of influence extended into many areas beyond their immediate reach. Their systematic application of innatist doctrine to support a belief in universal salvation profoundly influenced the work of at least two of Dryden's friends. His "Honour'd Friend," Walter Charleton, was an articulate spokesman for innatism.[7] The epistle to Charleton (1663) contains evidence suggesting that the poet was acquainted especially with those of Charleton's writings which were most strongly influenced by the Cambridge men. In recounting the great achievements of English thinkers, he offers Charleton this compliment:

> Nor are *You,* Learned Friend, the least renown'd;
> Whose Fame, not circumscrib'd with *English* ground,
> Flies like the nimble journeys of the Light;
> And is, like that, unspent too in its flight.
>
> [ll. 33–36]

This is probably an allusion to Charleton's *The Darknes of Atheism Dispelled by the Light of Nature. A Physico-Theologicall Treatise* (London, 1652). In *A Discourse concerning . . . Satire* Dryden also refers to a conversation which he had around the year 1673 with "that noble wit of Scotland, Sir George Mackenzie."[8] The part of the conversation which

6. Quoted by Powicke, *The Cambridge Platonists,* p. 53. Dryden was supposed to have been an ardent admirer of Tillotson, at least. According to the "character" of the poet which Congreve included in his edition of Dryden's *Dramatick Works* (London, 1735), I, sig. [A8v], Dryden frequently said, "that if he had any Talent for *English* Prose, it was owing to his having often read the Writings of the great Archbishop *Tillotson.*"
7. Cf. chap. 4, n. 9.
8. *Of Dramatic Poesy,* II, 150.

Dryden records does not concern religion, but since Mackenzie's chief claim to fame at that time was his philosophical-
religious treatise (mentioned earlier), *Religio Stoici* (1663), it
is difficult to believe the two men did not also discuss religion.[9]
Dryden's poem does not resemble Mackenzie's opinions at
many points, but *Religio Stoici* does defend *recta ratio* in
much the same way as did the Platonists. One of Mackenzie's
best passages gives us some idea of what he might have said
to Dryden on the subject of religion:

> I am alwayes ashamed, when I hear reason call'd the
> step-mother of faith, and proclaimed rebel against God
> Almighty, and such declared traitors, as dare harbour it,
> or appear in it's [*sic*] defence. These are such fools as they
> who break their Prospects, because they bring not home
> to their sight the remotest objects; and are as unjust as
> *Jacob* had been, if he had divorc'd from *Leah,* because
> she was tender-eyed: whereas, we should not put out the
> eyes of our understanding, but should beg from God the
> eye-salve of His Spirit for their illumination. Nor should
> we dash the Prospect of our reason, against the rockie
> walls of dispair; but should rather wash it's glasses with
> the tears of unfeigned repentance.[10]

Dryden's Montezuma, as we have seen, expresses a similar
sentiment about reason soon after the appearance of Mackenzie's treatise:

> . . . what's more vain than public light to shun,
> And set up tapers, while we see the sun? [11]

The truths which reason makes available to us should not be

9. Smith, *John Dryden,* p. 62, suggested that Dryden may have taken
the idea for his title from Mackenzie's treatise.

10. Sir George Mackenzie, *Religio Stoici* (Edinburgh, 1663), pp. 122–23.
The passage is an unmistakable paraphrase of Culverwel, *Of the Light of
Nature,* p. 128.

11. *The Indian Emperour* (1665), v, ii.

wasted—even if, Mackenzie adds, they do not tell us everything we wish to know.

These indications of influence constitute only a presumption; they do not, of themselves, make a certainty. Such a certainty, however, is not necessary for our study. *Religio Laici*
itself is the best possible evidence of the influence on Dryden
of the spectrum of thought which radiates from the Cambridge
men and their followers. That the "Law" was in some sense
inscribed or *pre-scribed,* "first, in the Soul, and after, in the
Page" (l. 137) is made explicit in *Religio Laici* as well as in
the writings of the Platonists.[12] Without much searching we
can (and will, at a later point) find other reflections of Cambridge Platonist views. But such indications of debt, I must
stress, are only superficial. They were shared by the multitude
of writers and thinkers who are known to us as latitudinarians.
The larger debt of *Religio Laici* to the Cambridge Platonists
is fundamental to its entire fabric and determines the order
of its unity. This must now be described in some detail.

The Necessary Minimum

It will be useful for the conduct of our discussion to offer
a preliminary outline of *Religio Laici* in terms of the problems

12. John Vaughan was convinced that innatism had a key role in
Religio Laici. In his commendatory poem, he wrote to Dryden:

> 'Tis time at last to fix the trembling soul,
> And by thy compass to point out the pole;
> All men agree in what is to be done,
> And each man's heart his table is of stone,
> Where he, the god-writ character may view;
> Were it as needful, faith had been so too.
> [*Works of John Dryden,* x, 36]

Dryden's word *prescrib'd* and the lines which follow it are surely meant
to avoid the naïve literalness into which the Cambridge men sometimes
strayed. It may be that his catchall criticism of naïve "Philosophising
Divines" in the Preface (l. 70) was intended to include their aberrations
of this kind, even though he was profoundly indebted to them for their
more hardheaded moments.

we have seen in previous chapters and the solutions that will
be presented in this one. The poem treats two different though
related topics. First is the way of life which the layman must
follow if he is to win the *summum bonum* or salvation. The
poet compares reason and religion in their ability to provide
guidance on this question. The second topic is the authority
of the revealed way of life, the Scriptures, and the ability of
reason to help faith establish such authority. The views of
the poem on this subject are clear. Reason must employ its
best powers to establish the plausibility of belief in Scripture;
faith must do the rest.

We noted, however, that one major difficulty arises for
Dryden in this connection. For earlier writers in the Anglican
tradition the infallibility of Scripture was, to a lesser or greater
extent, an inseparable part of belief in the authority of Scripture. Once one believed that God had given the Bible, few
serious problems were raised concerning the accurate transmission of the text. As a result one could feel certain that, although the meaning of individual passages might be disputed,
the necessary minimum for salvation always remained available to the layman. But with the publication of Simon's
Histoire critique du Vieux Testament, modern biblical criticism was born.[13] Now the transmitters of the Scriptures
were believed to have "Let in gross Errours to corrupt the
Text: / Omitted paragraphs, embroyl'd the Sense" (ll. 265–66).
The reliability of the text was gone together with the simple
assurance that a necessary minimum for salvation was available outside the arena of theological dispute or, indeed, within
it. A text with complex problems of authorship and accuracy
could no longer yield God's plain truths by any direct
method.[14] In *Religio Laici,* Dryden's great concern with the

13. For a discussion of recent studies of Simon's work, see Harth,
Contexts of Dryden's Thought, pp. 174–78. Harth's remarks on previous
views of the influence of Simon's work on the poems of Dryden seem un-
necessarily dismissive.

14. Cf. Appendix B.

question of a necessary minimum is evidenced in no fewer than five separate passages which assert the availability of this mysterious quantity without telling us where it is to be found.

The manner of these assertions is itself interesting. They are all, in themselves, incomplete. Their function is to deny extreme positions and to clear the way for an unspecified middle course. Dryden denies the fideistic account of the modern Christian's situation that men like François Veron employed.[15]

> Or *Christian Faith* can have no *certain* ground,
> Or *Truth* in *Church Tradition* must be found.
>
> [ll. 280–81]

It is, Dryden tells us, "More Safe, and much more modest" to say that

> *God wou'd not leave Mankind without a way:*
> And that the *Scriptures,* though not *every where*
> Free from Corruption, or intire, or clear,
> Are uncorrupt, sufficient, clear, intire,
> In *all* things which our needfull *Faith* require.
>
> [ll. 295–300]

The reversal of negatives (*corrupt, not entire, not clear*) in line 299 derives its effectiveness from the unobtrusive addition of "sufficient" which begs the crucial question and leads to its complement, the requirements of "needfull Faith." Later, when the divinity of Christ is debated, "From the same Scripture" (l. 313), the poet interrupts and affirms that

> many have been sav'd, and many may,
> Who never heard this Question brought in play.
> Th' *unletter'd* Christian, who believes in *gross,*
> Plods on to *Heaven;* and ne'er is at a loss.
>
> [ll. 320–23]

15. See Bredvold, *The Intellectual Milieu of John Dryden,* pp. 78–80.

The reason for this assurance is that

> the *Streight-gate* wou'd be made *streighter* yet,
> Were *none* admitted there but men of *Wit*.
>
> [ll. 324–25]

No appeal to a specific untainted part of Scripture or to a creed is attempted. We are never told what the layman must believe "in gross," and the use of "unletter'd" in this context tends to deny dependence on any specific passages in Scripture. Somehow the essential message of the Bible does reach the layman:

> It *speaks* it *Self,* and what it does contain,
> In all things *needfull* to be *known,* is *plain*.
>
> [ll. 368–69]

As the poem nears its close, the assertions of an available minimum continue, though no new basis for them is made apparent. The poet condemns the enthusiasts who wrangle over endless interpretations of Scripture:

> Plain *Truths* enough for needfull *use* they found;
> But men wou'd still be itching to *expound*.
>
> [ll. 409–10]

The peroration (ll. 427–50) repeats the availability of the necessary minimum for the fourth and final time, though again nothing is specified: "men," unfortunately, "will [i.e. want to and will] believe more than they need," though the "things we must believe, are few, and plain" (ll. 432–33).

Nor should we delude ourselves into thinking that the end of the poem really offers a definition of "what is necessary." The poet does say that

> Even *Arius* and *Pelagius* durst provoke [i.e. appeal]
> To what the *Centuries preceding* spoke.
>
> [ll. 346–47]

The poet recalls this difficulty in the peroration when he considers the possibility that "after all" the Fathers themselves may "stand suspected still" when "we see / The Scripture, and the Fathers disagree" (ll. 439–41). In the end, he does not designate any external authority as absolute in matters of salvation. His final admonition to the layman only considers the effects of theological discord on civil order:

> . . . after hearing what our Church can say,
> If still our Reason runs another way,
> That private Reason 'tis more Just to curb,
> Than by Disputes the publick Peace disturb.
> For points obscure are of small use to learn:
> But *Common quiet* is *Mankind's concern.*
>
> [ll. 445–50]

The reliance on the Church which the poet advocates is clearly secondary and external. His main concern in these lines is the layman's obligation to public peace. He tells him to "curb" his public expression, not to change his private beliefs. The layman should not become too much involved in the process of debating "points obscure." The poet speaks to him in terms of what is just to mankind, not of what God requires for salvation. The latter question can only be settled in the secluded space of one's own breast, and the layman—like the poet, who is himself a layman (Preface, l. 5 and l. 317 of the poem)—can be sure that he will find there "all things which our needfull Faith require" (l. 300).

> If *others* in the *same Glass better* see
> 'Tis for *Themselves* they look, but not for *me:*
> For *MY* Salvation must its Doom receive
> Not from what *OTHERS,* but what *I* believe.

The specification of which scriptural truths are "needful" for salvation must come from some other quarter. At this point in the overall plan of the poem its two topics come together.

The layman, whose faith the poet is considering, is not only the Christian confirmed in traditional views; he is also the Athenian bred in darkness and the "Indian" soul born into savagery. If, indeed, "God wou'd not leave Mankind without a way" (l. 296), a necessary minimum for salvation must be available to them without knowledge of a formal revelation. At the same time, however, Scripture must somehow be *necessary* for those who have been exposed to revelation. The poet's entire conception of mankind in its spiritual aspect is involved here. That he himself suspected that his views would not be easily understood is evident from his painstaking explication of this topic in the Preface, where he rehearses what amounts to a spiritual history of mankind. Scott's incomplete understanding of this history and of the poet's conception of man's spiritual knowledge led him to exclaim in wonderment that Dryden "somewhat fantastically, argues as if it were some remnant of the original faith revealed to Noah, and preserved by the posterity of Shem." [16]

Man's Spiritual History

The starting point of Dryden's prefatory history is his disagreement with Athanasius. But he soon forgets about the Egyptian Bishop and by the time his account is concluded he is discussing deism. This range of relevance is significant, I think, for indicating the centrality of spiritual history to the topics of the poem. Yet it is the specific historical conclusion which is now of most interest to us and which must first be understood. Dryden writes,

> It has always been my *thought,* that Heathens, who never did, nor without Miracle cou'd hear of the name of Christ were yet in a possibility of Salvation. Neither will it enter easily into my belief, that before the coming of our Saviour, the whole World, excepting only the Jewish Nation, shou'd lye under the inevitable necessity of everlasting

16. *Works of John Dryden,* x, 3.

Punishment, for want of that Revelation, which was con-
fin'd to so small a spot of ground as that of *Palæstine.*
Among the Sons of *Noah* we read of one onely who was
accurs'd; and if a blessing in the ripeness of time was reserv'd for *Japhet,* (of whose Progeny we are,) it seems un-
accountable to me, why so many Generations of the same
Offspring, as preceeded our Saviour in the Flesh, shou'd
be all involv'd in one common condemnation, and yet
that their Posterity shou'd be Intitled to the hopes of
Salvation: As if a Bill of Exclusion had passed only on
the Fathers, which debar'd not the Sons from their Succession. Or that so many Ages had been *deliver'd over* to
Hell, and so many *reserv'd* for Heaven, and that the Devil
had the first choice, and God the next. Truly I am apt to
think, that the revealed Religion which was taught by
Noah to all his Sons, might continue for some Ages in the
whole Posterity. That afterwards it was included wholly
in the Family of *Sem* is manifest: but when the Progenies
of *Cham* and *Japhet* swarm'd into Colonies,[17] and those
Colonies were subdivided into many others; in process of
time their Descendants lost by little and little the Primitive and Purer Rites of Divine Worship, retaining onely
the notion of one Deity; to which succeeding Generations
added others: (for Men took their Degrees in those Ages
from Conquerors to Gods.) [ll. 38–62]

At this point Dryden asserts the intercession of providence in
the scheme of salvation:

Revelation being thus Eclipsed to almost all Mankind,
the light of Nature as the next in Dignity was substituted;
and that is it which St. *Paul* concludes to be the Rule of
the Heathens; and by which they are hereafter to be
judg'd. [ll. 62–66]

17. One of the contemporary works which described the founding of
these colonies was Dickinson's *Delphi Phœnicizantes.* Cf. chap. 2, n. 4.

He then returns to his history and the importance of it for his poem:

> If my supposition be true, then the consequence which I have assum'd in my Poem may be also true; namely, that Deism, or the Principles of Natural Worship, are onely the faint remnants or dying flames of reveal'd Religion in the Posterity of *Noah:* And that our Modern Philosophers, nay and some of our Philosophising Divines have too much exalted the faculties of our Souls, when they have maintain'd that by their force, mankind has been able to find out that there is one Supream Agent or Intellectual Being which we call God: that Praise and Prayer are his due Worship; and the rest of those deducements, which I am confident are the remote effects of Revelation, and unatainable by our Discourse, I mean as simply considerd, and without the benefit of Divine Illumination. So that we have not lifted up our selves to God, by the weak Pinions of our Reason, but he has been pleasd to descend to us: and what *Socrates* said of him, what *Plato* writ, and the rest of the Heathen Philosophers of several Nations, is all no more than the Twilight of Revelation, after the Sun of it was set in the Race of *Noah.* That there is some thing above us, some Principle of *motion,* our Reason can apprehend, though it cannot discover what it is, by its own Vertue. [ll. 66–84]

Reason, "by its own Vertue" as a ratiocinative instrument, can only proceed by the methods of "Discourse, . . . simply considerd," by the methods of ratiocination, to secular truths. But reason that has added to its own virtue, during the course of history and by divine intercession, the benefits of divine illumination and the saving "light of Nature" can—not "simply considerd"—attain to certain divine truths. This is the same quantity which Hooker distinguishes as "true, sound, divine reason; . . . reason proper to that science whereby the things of God are known." [18] Dryden denies that any man's reason can reach divine truths unaided; but he affirms that every man's reason is, in fact, aided by divine agency. He does not wish man to seek a lower position in the order of creation, but he hopes that men will stand more humbly before the God who placed them there. To interpret such an account of man's reason, as man now has it, as antirationalism, is a mistake. It is Dryden's complex notion of the endowments of reason which enables him to find a solution to the major theological problems of the poem. With it he can justify his trust that the Christian will always find a necessary minimum of truth for salvation in the Scriptures, no matter what their textual state; and with it he can be sure that another necessary minimum, "the light of Nature as the next in Dignity," will always be available to supplement the "dying flames of reveal'd Religion in the Posterity of Noah." Reason is thus Dryden's adjustable recourse to saving knowledge.

Richard Burthogge and the *Traditio Lampadis*

Although Dryden gives an appearance of novelty to his historical exposition by using such a phrase as "if my supposition be true," he really presents nothing new. A whole literature concerning Noah's travels and his "colonies" existed in the Renaissance and the Restoration.[19] The use of the expanded Noah legend to authenticate conceptions of reason was less common, but it too is of an early date in the century. Culverwel declaimed vehemently against such applications because those that he encountered were designed to assert the authority of tradition and, therefore, to deny absolutely the mysterious substitution of "the light of Nature as the next in Dignity." In *Of the Light of Nature* he writes, "This is to tell you that men have no 'candle of the Lord' within them, but only

18. *The Works of Richard Hooker,* ed. Keble, III, 594.
19. See Don Cameron Allen, *The Legend of Noah: Renaissance Rationalism in Art, Science, and Letters* (Urbana, Ill., 1949), pp. 83 ff.

there must be a *Traditio lampadis,* a general and public light, that must go from one hand to another." [20] It would seem, therefore, that the coupling or supplementation of the *Traditio lampadis* with the light of nature was an innovation of comparatively late date. Here again, however, Dryden cannot make any claims to having been first. The particular combination of ideas and images which constitute his adjustable source of reason and saving knowledge had been elaborated by Richard Burthogge[21] in 1675. Burthogge's interesting position in the intellectual history of the Restoration, together with the fascinating parallel between his work and crucial sections of Dryden's Preface and poem, gives his work special value as an introduction to the complex unity of *Religio Laici* as an artistic whole.[22]

Burthogge's reputation rests primarily on his later philosophical works, which include an important critique of Locke and a theory of knowledge which is "a remarkable anticipation of Kant." [23] The work which concerns us is an early theological treatise, *Causa Dei,* today little known.[24] Burthogge's apolo-

---

20. Culverwel, p. 102.

21. In his *Causa Dei, Or An Apology For God* (London, 1675). Burthogge "was born at Plymouth about 1638. He was educated at Exeter grammar school, became a servitor or chorister of All Soul's College, Oxford, in 1654, proceeded B.A. in 1658, migrated to Lincoln College, and completed his degree 'by determination'. He afterwards went to Leyden University to study medicine. . . . On returning to his native country he settled at Bowden, near Totnes, where he acquired a large medical practice" (*DNB*). He died about 1694.

22. For a possible direct connection between Dryden and Burthogge's writing of *Causa Dei* see Appendix A.

23. See *The Philosophical Writings of Richard Burthogge,* ed. Margaret W. Landes (Chicago, 1921), p. xvi.

24. For a brief discussion of Burthogge's theological views see Yolton, pp. 46–48. My discussion of Burthogge's *Causa Dei* and its relation to Dryden's *Religio Laici* first appeared in my dissertation on *Religio Laici,* Yale, 1966. I recorded the importance of Burthogge for Dryden in *DA* 27 : 4216A. Much of the same material has since appeared in Harth, *Contexts of Dryden's Thought,* pp. 117, 121, 129 n., 164. Harth's view of Burthogge and his importance to Dryden is substantially different from the one presented here.

getical works offer a striking example of the Restoration intellectual with one foot on either side of the threshold of Enlightenment. "The influence of the Cambridge Platonists," his editor tells us, "is obtrusively evident" throughout his religious writings. Like them, he "teaches that apart from all sensuous experience we know the form of truth, which enables us to distinguish truth from error just as immediately as we distinguish sense-qualities." Burthogge, however, "holds an empirical theory of truth which contradicts this view." [25] It seems to me that it was the joining of these two views in an exposition of theological history that produced the two-part system which is also found in Dryden's work. Given the historical fact of revelation, Burthogge, in the person of an empiricist, requires some form of sense experience—some *Traditio lampadis*—to explain the presence of even faint glimmers of revealed ideas:

> *as* all men came from *Adam* in the *first* World, so . . . in the *second* all did Descend from *Noah,* who had the knowledge of the true Religion, and instructed all his children in it, which children cannot be imagined but also to instruct and teach theirs, and so onward. . . .
>
> Now, those *General Articles,* Heads, or Points of Religion, wherein all men all the World over commonly agree, and which are therefore called ᴄᴏᴍᴍᴏɴ ꜱᴇɴᴛɪᴍᴇɴᴛꜱ *though* they be *not* (what by some they be imagined) *Innate Idea's,* or Notions ingrafted and imprinted on the Minds of Men by Nature, but (as I have evinced them) *main* and *substantial Points of the first Tradition,* and consequently, *Retained* in all the following, with more or less Disguise; *yet* be they as *Infallibly and Indubitably true, as if they were.*[26]

25. Landes, pp. xiii–xv. Harth disregards Burthogge's affinities with the innatist theology of the Cambridge Platonists (see *Contexts of Dryden's Thought,* p. 132 n.).

26. *Causa Dei,* pp. 335–41.

Burthogge thus rejects, as did most of the Cambridge men, a naïve formulation of innate ideas; but, like them, he develops a dispositional form of the same doctrine when he comes to consider the minimum necessary for salvation:

> there is no Nation under Heaven so Inhumane, Barbarous and Savage, but that though it may not have as much as many others, yet it hath sufficient light concerning God, and concerning common Offices and Duties of men. . . . This is the true Light that enlightens every man that comes into the world. By [this] Light within,[27] I understand nothing but . . . Practique Reason, that Ray of Jesus Christ [the Sun of Righteousness] [sic] who is Original, First and Primitive Reason; by which a man enabled to discern Good and Evil, Vertue and Vice, Rectitude and Turpitude, is agreeably inclined to Pursue one, and to Refuse the other.[28]

This is Burthogge in the person of a Cambridge Platonist, exalting and sanctifying reason by a direct connection with the source of the divine. It is the same "light of Nature as the next in Dignity" which Dryden learned to graft on to his history of revelation. Like Dryden, too, he accounts for knowledge of vital religious principles in two ways: first, as we have seen,

27. On page 408, Burthogge also considers the part of the Light of Nature which he calls the "light without." He tells us that it, too, is given to every man and that it "is a manifestation and Discovery in the things that are made, and in the Providential Dispensation, Government and Conduct of them, That God is, and that he is Almighty, Infinite, Eternal, Immense, All-wise, All-knowing, Bountiful and Benign, which is principally shewed in the former: And that he is Supream Rector and Governour of all, that he loveth Righteousness and doth Right, that he is Gracious and Merciful, and that his Mercy is to All, and over All his works, and that is principally shewn in his Providence." Burthogge's account of the "Light of Nature" in his philosophical treatise, Organum Vetus et Novum (London, 1678), is more brief and more mechanistically fitted to a scientific account of man and the universe. See especially pp. xiii, 19–20, and 187–88 of the Landes edition.

28. Causa Dei, pp. 394–95.

he derives "those General Articles, Heads, or Points of Religion" from the light of a *Traditio lampadis;* second, he notes that man also has knowledge of these articles because God "has been pleasd to descend to us" in the "Practique Reason, that Ray of Jesus Christ":

> The *System* of *Prime, Common Plain Self-evident Dictates of the Practique Understanding* or Reason (whose Number can no better be Determin'd than that of Fundamentals in Religion) is generally *called* the 𝕷𝖆𝖜 𝖔𝖋 𝕹𝖆𝖙𝖚𝖗𝖊: not only because it is described as it were in *Nature,* and in the very *habitudes* and Respects of things themselves, but also because (as our Apostle happily expresseth it) it is a *Law* whereby a man *is so* unto himself; [29] that is, his very *faculties* themselves, which are his Nature, do as it were prescribe him Laws, which in Opposition unto *Positive* and *written* Laws, are called 𝕳𝖚𝖓𝖜𝖗𝖎𝖙𝖙𝖊𝖓, and under that Notion were acknowledged by the Wisest *Heathen,* by *Plato,* by *Aristotle,* by *Cicero* to be the *Catholique* or common *Law* of all mankind.[30]

Yet Burthogge, like Dryden, is careful to frame this acknowledgment of man's own spiritual knowledge in a context of subordinacy. The precise manner of Burthogge's subordinating frame is, in fact, the most striking point of similarity between *Causa Dei* and *Religio Laici.* Dryden's opening lines are as follows:

> Dim, as the borrow'd beams of Moon and Stars
> To *lonely, weary, wandring* Travellers,[31]

29. Thus Burthogge extends the application of St. Paul's dictum from heathens to all men.

30. *Causa Dei,* p. 400.

31. For some reason it has not been previously noted that "weary, wandring Travellers" is a descendant, if not a direct echo, of Spenser, *Faerie Queene,* VII. VI. 9. 9. The stanza in which this phrase appears, describes the goddess of the moon, Cynthia, who has been "by highest *Ioue* assign'd . . . to beare / Nights burning lamp" (VII. VI. 12. 2–3),

> Is *Reason* to the *Soul:* And as on high,
> Those rowling Fires *discover* but the Sky
> Not light us *here;* So *Reason*'s glimmering Ray
> Was lent, not to *assure* our *doubtfull* way,
> But *guide* us upward to a *better Day.*
> And as those nightly Tapers disappear
> When Day's bright Lord ascends our Hemisphere;
> So pale grows *Reason* at *Religions* sight;
> So *dyes,* and so *dissolves* in *Supernatural Light.*

Burthogge describes the larger context of the "Practique Reason, that Ray of Jesus Christ [the Sun of Righteousness]" in the following manner:

> verily it is a great Truth, that as *he* would not have the Jewish *Law,* so much less would he have the Gentile Wisdom to supplant the Gospel. All the *Light* before Christ, whether that among the Jews, or that among the Gentiles, was but *Moon,* or *Star-Light,* designed only for the *night* preceding; but it is the *Sun* must Rule by *Day.* Now the Gospel *dispensation* is the *Day,* and *Christ* the Sun that makes it; by whose Alone Light we must walk. For as in Nature, the *Light* afforded by the Moon and Stars,

---

> sitting on an Iuory throne . . . ,
> Drawne of two steeds, th' one black, the other white,
> Environd with tenne thousand starres around,
> That duly her attended day and night;
> And by her side, there ran her Page, that hight
> *Vesper,* whom we the Euening-starre intend:
> That with his Torche, still twinkling like twylight,
> Her lightened all the way where she should wend,
> And ioy to weary wandring trauailers did lend.

Dryden's interest in Spenser dates essentially from the appearance of the 1679 edition of Spenser's poetry (see Osborn, *John Dryden: Facts and Problems,* pp. 227–29.) Dryden's copy of this edition contains notes in his own hand which indicate that he read the *Cantos of Mutabilitie,* at least, with a professional eye: between stanzas twelve and thirteen of VII.ii, Dryden wrote, "Groundwork for a Song on St Cecilias Day." This copy is now in the library of Trinity College, Cambridge. (In the end, Dryden did not use this groundwork for any of his poems.)

which is of great Advantage, and very much administers to our Direction, and Comfort in a Journey by night, yet in the day is *none;* The Moon and Stars that shine by night, and then make other things Visible, they are Invisible themselves, and Dark by day; So in the *Moral* world, not only the *Law* of *Moses* to the Jews, but that *Philosophy* and Wisdom among the Gentiles, that before the coming of the Lord Christ, while it was yet extream Dark, was of extraordinary Use and Benefit, *It* is no longer *now* of any to them, nor to be insisted on, since He is come. For now 'tis *broad Day*. One would be glad of Moon-light, or Star-light, that is to travel by night; but he delires, and is out of his Wits, that would preferr it before the Sun by Day.

By this time, you see how my *Opinion of the Old Philosophy,* that it was a kind of *Starlight* derived from the Sun of Righteousness, and pointing to him, is so far from being in *Derogation* to the Gospel **Grace,** that *it* rather highly Illustrates and Establishes it; the Philosophers themselves, as well as the Prophets, being (as it were) as so many *Stars* that shined in a Dark Place, and with a borrowed lustre, until (in *Peters* own expression) the *Day-Star* arose from on high.[32]

The similarities between Burthogge's and Dryden's passages are striking: [33] both use the appearance of "borrow'd beams"

---

32. *Causa Dei,* pp. 194–96. Another variation of this traditional metaphor which bears a resemblance to Dryden's opening lines was pointed out by Douglas Bush, *Science and English Poetry: A Historical Sketch, 1590–1950* (New York, 1950), p. 49, in Donne's *Biathanatos* (London, 1646?), pp. 153–54. Donne's passage lacks, among other things which are present in Dryden's lines, the mention of a traveler or a journey. For interesting observations on the possible relation of Donne to *Religio Laici,* see Jerome McGann, "The Argument of Dryden's *Religio Laici,*" *Thoth,* III (1962), 78–89.

33. For evidence suggesting that Burthogge derived these passages from the Cambridge Platonist, Henry More, see chap. 6.

or "borrowed lustre" of moon and stars to travelers on a night-time journey as a metaphor for the power of reason to bring the soul to salvation; in both, the main function of reason or starlight is to "guide us upward to a better Day," to point to "the Sun of Righteousness"; in both, "Day's bright Lord ascends" or "the Day-Star" arises "from on high" to signify the coming of Christ and the Gospel.[34]

Yet the main significance of these similarities is not that they indicate an analogue or possible source for a part of Dryden's poem. What is most important is the particular combination of history, metaphysics, metaphor, and concern that runs parallel in Burthogge's and Dryden's work and helps place *Religio Laici* and its conception of reason as an adjustable source for saving knowledge in the context of the same liberal theology upon which Burthogge was relying. For the purposes of our outline and in the process of sketching the nature of Dryden's intellectual debt, we have discussed only isolated parts of the poem; yet all of its parts and its meaning as a whole are also significantly related to the framework we delineated in chapter 4. To show this, I must now begin at the beginning and present an analysis in essentially linear form.

34. In relation to line 11 of the poem, it is interesting to note that on page 289 Burthogge quotes an English translation of the famous sibylline acrostic on doomsday which reads, in part, *"Great Heaven shall be dissolv'd, the Moon depriv'd / Of all her Light."* See also Dryden's *Britannia Rediviva,* ll. 311–12.

6

Religio Laici: II

In *Religio Laici,* the process of finding the necessary minimum of gospel truth for laymen of all persuasions consists of two simultaneous and complementary operations. One is a dialectic of ideas conducted through two patterns of metaphor which oppose and modify each other until a final equilibrium is achieved. The other is a gradual shift in concern which eventually brings the poem to consider the essential questions of man's spiritual existence. Both are directly related to the theology exemplified by Cambridge Platonism and both rise in the dawn of the poem, the exordium, where they must be discovered now.

The "Great Automaton"

The great beauty of the opening lines of *Religio Laici* has often been recognized, but their complexity and their function in the poem have rarely been inspected closely. It has never been pointed out, for example, that the first seven lines contain a subtle paradox:

> Dim, as the borrow'd beams of Moon and Stars
> To *lonely, weary, wandring* Travellers,
> Is *Reason* to the *Soul*: And as on high,
> Those rowling Fires *discover* but the Sky
> Not light us *here;* So *Reason*'s glimmering Ray
> Was lent, not to *assure* our *doubtfull* way,
> But *guide* us upward to a *better Day.*

The light of the moon and stars is first described as "borrow'd" or reflected, but then the imagery of "Fires (l. 4) and
"Tapers" (l. 8) suggests that this light is generated by those
bodies themselves. This idea is reinforced by the shift in noun
from *beam* to *ray*, which may suggest radiated rather than
reflected light. Even radiated light is, in the larger picture of
Creation, *lent* to the light-giving bodies of the universe, but
in their present situation they have at least *some* independent
power. In this way the power of reason as man's God-given
taper or "Candle of the Lord" is first insinuated, and the
"time when 'twas lighted" [1] is emphasized to remind the
reader of its ultimately derivative nature.

In my view, Dryden's exploitation of the generative power
of "Moon and Stars" is in a sense typical of his particular
position in the history of English poetry. He lived at a time
when the old metaphysics and the new science tended to over-
lap in striking ways. It was a situation which begged for treat-
ment by a poet. Marjorie Nicolson informs us that "the
most persistent of themes, throughout two centuries," had
been "that of the 'borrow'd light' of the moon." In 1640, "a
dispute still raged as to whether she [the moon] received *most*
or *all* of her light, the majority, following Cardan, holding
that there was some slight lunar illumination in addition to
the solar reflection." Miss Nicolson notes that the "paradoxical Margaret of Newcastle" was one of the few writers who, as
late as 1666, defended "the idea that the moon is an illuminating body, here, as elsewhere, refusing to accept the evidence of experimental science." [2] That the dissemination of
experimental knowledge was slow even among less froward
members of the modern community is evident from the writings of Comenius who, in 1668, addressed his *Way of Light*
"To the Torch Bearers of this Enlightened Age, Members of

1. Cf. chap. 4 for a discussion of this point in Culverwel.
2. Marjorie Hope Nicolson, "A World in the Moon," *Smith College
Studies in Modern Languages*, XVII (1936), 11–14.

the Royal Society of London" and told them that, a "light-giving thing is one which scatters rays from itself. Such are the sun, the moon, the stars, candles and so on." [3]

At this rate of diffusion, it is not surprising that the partial use of the older conception should still appeal to a poet writing in 1682, especially when he wished to indicate by it a form of spiritual energy which had been available to men of the dim past. The exordium, however, is completely in the present tense (unlike Burthogge's similar imagery), so that even while the lines serve as an historical account of how heathens, who "follow'd Reasons Dictates right" (l. 208), were saved before the coming of the Gospel, they are also a formula for contemporary use during the eclipse of revelation occasioned by the loss of a reliable text for Scripture. It is the innate power or disposition of man's divinely endowed reason that assures him a necessary minimum of guidance in all contingencies. Reason's power adjusts to man's needs: reason and religion are complementary; they vary inversely so that a constant minimum quantity of spiritual knowledge is always offered to the soul.

A sense of jointure and adjustability is stressed in the structure of the exordium, which we gradually come to realize is designed as a dazzling imitation of what "S.P." called (in describing the mechanical cosmology of the Cambridge Platonists) "Divine Art in the great automaton of the world." [4] It is divided into three parts by two "and as" clauses, at lines three and eight, which mark readjustment points in the light situation. This function in the second "and as" clause is obvious:

And as those nightly Tapers disappear

3. *The Way of Light,* trans. E. T. Campagnac, p. 66. On the same page he also explicitly distinguishes between a "light-giving thing" and "anything which is filled with light or has been lit up."

4. *A Brief Account,* p. 19. Here *automaton* means something like "a piece of mechanism having its motive power so concealed that it appears to move spontaneously" (*OED*).

When Day's bright Lord ascends our Hemisphere;
So pale grows *Reason* at *Religions* sight;
So *dyes,* and so *dissolves* in *Supernatural Light.*

In the first use of *and as* the same function is less apparent.
Although it has been remarked by one critic of the poem that
the light of moon and stars is usually considered adequate for
a night journey,[5] lines 1–3 have never been differentiated from
lines 4–7, in which reason cannot "light us here" by itself.
The lines, however, must be differentiated because they describe two different stages of the light situation. "And as on
high, / Those rowling Fires discover but the Sky" describes a
change in the illumination of those "rowling Fires" because
the Day is coming which will itself "assure our doubtfull
way." In the middle states, the function of reason's light is to
make us turn our eyes to the dawn: at this point, when revelation becomes available, "to apprehend [the Scriptures] to be
the word of God, is all our Reason has to do" (Preface, ll. 99–
100). In the third state (ll. 8–11), when the gospel revelation
is completely discovered to the soul, reason's guiding light is
no longer required at all and it "dissolves" in a sea of "Supernatural Light."

For the layman of 1682 this sea is no longer at the full. His
sunrise of revelation has been clouded over not by doubts
but by the *certainty* of textual corruption. His inner light of
reason must supplement the partially eclipsed supernatural
light and lead him to the "needfull" truths which are "uncor-
rupt, sufficient, clear, intire" (l. 299). This, as I see it, is the
middle stage delineated in the exordium. But for the heathen
the sea of revelation was never at the full. There was no
Scripture that his reason could help him "apprehend . . . to
be the word of God." His situation is that of the first stage
where the dim light of reason enables him to achieve the

5. Fujimura, "Dryden's *Religio Laici,*" p. 207. We should also recall
(cf. chap. 5) that Spenser's and Burthogge's uses of the same metaphor
leave no doubt as to the adequacy of this light.

necessary minimum of truth for his journey in the night. After the closing lines of the exordium, in which a standard of spiritual perfection is depicted that may be reached again in a Second Coming, we descend to the reality. We begin again with the heathen's situation and then move on to the present situation of the Christian. The poem is thus planned as a necessarily incomplete fulfillment of the blueprint in the exordium and as an exemplar of the formula that Dryden believed must be reversible. In both stages or situations that the poem can include it is man's reason, the taper of the Lord, that is developed into an assurance of man's ability to gain sufficient knowledge for salvation.

Light and the Ground of Reason

The exordium, I think, is a blueprint for the poem in another sense. It outlines a solution to the problems of poetics that we saw in chapter 1. It is what made it possible for Dryden to adopt the motto *Ornari res ipsa negat* and still continue to write poetry. Imagination and its product, imagery, as we have seen, had become suspect in poetry, especially in religious poetry. The falsifications or misrepresentations of "material Phantasmes" would not be tolerated.[6] If Dryden was to write a religious poem, he had to find some way to do it without imagery, or at least without obvious reliance on imagery. Here Dryden took a lesson from the Cambridge Platonists and improved on them.

The Cambridge men, as we saw, were constantly substituting abstractions for images. For them, light was the only "Ornament" which was "True and Real" in itself. The fundamentals of their system were expressed in images of light but, on the whole, they abandoned the poetic use of language. Dryden, in the close of the Preface, abjures the "Florid, Elevated and Figurative way" (l. 350) and then, in the opening of the poem develops a magnificent lyrical image of light be-

6. Glanvill, *Vanity of Dogmatizing*, pp. 95–97, cf. chap. 1.

cause light, he believed in 1682, is "True and Real" in itself and cannot be construed as the cheating way of the passions. Light could be used, in the last words of the Preface, to reason a man "into Truth" (ll. 354–55). But the imagery of light essentially ends at line eleven. After this there is not only far less imagery of any kind than in the exordium; there is even less than is usual in Dryden's other poems.[7] If Dryden, like the Cambridge men, had truly abandoned the use of imagery we may suspect that his attempt at poetic communication of religious ideas would have met with no more success than theirs.

We have already seen that the *borrow'd ray* of reason in the exordium is a mixed quantity which, when circumstances require, may have considerable and *increasing* independent power. In order to see that the imagery of the poem is progressive as well as recessive (to use Hoffman's term),[8] we must note another important fact in the exordium. Even in the final stage of light adjustment, when revelation bursts forth in seemingly unrestrained glory, a small, almost inaudible, dissonant note is heard:

> And as those nightly Tapers disappear
> When Day's bright Lord ascends our Hemisphere;
> So pale grows *Reason* at *Religions* sight;
> So *dyes,* and so *dissolves* in *Supernatural Light.*

Day's bright Lord, we observe, ascends *our* hemisphere only. Much of the world, at the moment of revelation,[9] was or still is, left with only its fires and tapers of reason. This implication is developed explicitly in the poem when the poet repeats

---

7. See Smith, *John Dryden,* p. 61 and Hoffman, *John Dryden's Imagery,* pp. 69–70 on this point.

8. Hoffman, p. 70.

9. We do not, I think, run the risk of reading Dryden's metaphors too carefully. Even the implication that "Day's bright Lord" must once have been, in some sense, in the other "Hemisphere" to which it will also return is, as we shall see later, diligently developed in the poem.

and admits the staggering force (l. 185) of the deist's objection that

> a *general* Law is that alone
> Which must to *all,* and every *where* be known:
> A Style so large as not *this* Book can claim
> Nor ought that bears *reveal'd* Religions *Name.*
> 'Tis said the sound of a *Messiah's Birth*
> Is gone through all the habitable Earth:
> But still that Text must be confin'd alone
> To what was *Then* inhabited, and known:
> And what Provision could from *thence* accrue
> To *Indian* Souls, and Worlds discover'd *New?*
> In other parts it helps, that Ages past,
> The Scriptures there were *known,* and were *imbrac'd,*
> Till Sin spread once again the Shades of Night:
> What's that to these who never *saw* the Light?

> [ll. 170–83]

Men living in the other hemisphere have never seen the light on high. For them, there must be at least a minimum of light provided in the part of God's creation which is available to them below. This use of *hemisphere* together with the description of man's earthbound journey forges an unobtrusive opposition between the light above, which comes immediately from beyond man's world, and the dimly illuminated ground below, which always offers man the light of reason promising a necessary minimum of spiritual knowledge.

In acknowledging the problematical use of metaphor in religious poetry as well as the crisis in the "rule of faith" described by Simon's work, Dryden moves away from the image of supernatural light (l. 11) and closer to the complete abstraction of reason; yet at the same time, it seems to me, he does not lose the possibility of writing poetry because he is progressively incorporating light, as an *entelechy,* into the "ground" of reason. The inconspicuous, almost anamnestic, metaphor of "ground" [10]—and the network of metaphors associated with it—is made part of the tissue of abstract argument concerning reason's proper sphere of activity and its synergistic capacity for providing saving truth. Because the exordium contains assurance that the light which disappears in one form must appear in another, reason and its invisible ground metaphor can function as a quasi-abstract counterpart to visual light.

It is obvious that English writing—before, during, and after the Restoration—abounds with commonplace uses of the word *ground* to denote base, basis, foundation, cause, reasoning, logic, etc. But Dryden's use of a ground metaphor in *Religio Laici* to suggest a body of divine truths which God's grace makes available to ordinary human reason may carry ancillary resonances of a more specialized usage—or tradition of usage. "Venerable Hooker" (as Dryden refers to him in the Preface to *Religio Laici*) tells us, for example, that

> The main principles of Reason are in themselves apparent. . . . In every kind of knowledge some . . . grounds there are, as that being proposed the mind doth presently embrace them as free from all possibility of error, clear and manifest without proof. . . . This . . . is the ground whereupon the wisdom of the Apostle buildeth a law. . . . Upon the same ground our Saviour proveth the law most reasonable. . . . whatsoever such principle there is, it was at the first found out by discourse, and drawn from out of the very bowels of heaven and earth. . . . Touching the several grand mandates, which being imposed by the understanding faculty of

10. Conventional uses of this word abound in Dryden's other writings. Even in the Preface to *Religio Laici* the word appears (e.g. l. 309) with little sense of an attached set of specific ideas. *Religio Laici* and (for different though related reasons, as we shall see) *The Hind and the Panther* are his only works which systematically develop this special aspect of the word.

the mind must be obeyed by the Will of Man, they are by the same method found out, whether they import our duty towards God or towards man.[11]

Using the conventional illumination metaphor, Hooker emphasizes that the vital center of man's reason is enlightened by God's grace:

The light of natural understanding, wit, and reason, is from God; he it is which thereby doth illuminate every man entering into the world.[12]

Although, like Dryden, Hooker rejects a naïve account of innate ideas, he does not discard all forms of innatism:

the laws which the very heathens did gather to direct their actions by, so far forth as they proceeded from the light of nature, God himself doth acknowledge to have proceeded even from himself, and that he was the writer of them in the tables of their hearts.[13]

Hooker is careful to point out that such views do not represent capitulation to graceless natural religion:

there is no kind of faculty or power in man or any other creature, which can rightly perform the functions allotted to it, without perpetual aid and concurrence of that Supreme Cause of all things.

In all which . . . hath been spoken touching the force and use of man's reason in things divine, I must crave that I be not so understood or construed, as if any such thing by virtue thereof could be done without the aid and assistance of God's blessed Spirit.[14]

We may feel that Hooker's notion of reason aided by grace

11. *Laws,* I, viii, 5–7.
12. Ibid., III, ix, 3.
13. Ibid.
14. Ibid., I, viii, 11, and III, viii, 18.

—of "divine reason" [15]—represents, in the words of a recent commentator, "an astonishing turn to a kind of irrationalism" that is "no solution at all of the problem of the relationship between faith and reason." [16] But it is a notion which Dryden probably realized was lodged securely in Anglican thought. From Hooker's point of view it is a ground which avoids the pitfalls of Puritan "illumination":

> albeit the Spirit lead us into all truth and direct us in all goodness, yet because these workings of the Spirit in us are so privy and secret, we therefore stand on a plainer ground, when we gather by reason from the quality of things believed or done, that the Spirit of God hath directed us in both, than if we settle ourselves to believe or to do any certain particular thing, as being moved thereto by the Spirit.[17]

The Cambridge Platonists were especially active in adopting such language. We hear echoes of Hooker's words in John Smith's description of the capacity of "Reason . . . *Lumen de Lumine* . . . to enable Man to work out of himself all those Notions of God which are the true Ground-work of Love and Obedience to God, and conformity to him." [18] To the same effect, Rust speaks of "our common Notions and Principles of natural instinct, whereupon we ground all our reasonings and discourse," [19] and Whichcote tells us that the "Truths of

15. *The Works of Richard Hooker,* III, 594.

16. Gunnar Hillerdal, *Reason and Revelation in Richard Hooker* (Lund, Sweden, 1962), p. 135. Yet conceptions of this kind warn us against simplistic schematization of the background of Dryden's poem, such as that presented in *Contexts of Dryden's Thought,* p. 133, where Harth tells us that Dryden's "whole conception of the two distinct orders of reason and faith stems from the tradition of Thomas Aquinas, Hooker, and many of his contemporaries."

17. *Laws,* III, viii, 15.

18. Quoted in *The Cambridge Platonists,* ed. Campagnac, p. 181.

19. George Rust and Joseph Glanvill, *Two Choice and Useful Treatises* (London, 1682), p. 179.

first Inscription" have a "greater Ground . . . than that God gave the Law on Mount Sinai." [20]

This use of the ground metaphor in seventeenth-century English theology was nurtured by the writings of Jakob Boehme who taught that "the Most inward Ground in Man is CHRISTUS . . . the other or second ground of Nature is the Soul. . . . And the third ground is the created Man out of the Limus of the Earth." "What is Grace?," Boehme asks; "It is the inward Ground viz. CHRISTUS." [21] Boehmistic language of this kind was probably familiar to Dryden as an undergraduate. In 1650, the year of his matriculation at Cambridge, More's former tutor, Charles Hotham, addressed his *Introduction to the Tevtonick Philosophie* to the University Vice-Chancellor, and More himself later devoted a treatise to Boehme's cosmology.[22] In any case, Boehme's mystical ground of knowledge would not have seemed very bizarre to a seventeenth-century Anglican. The synergism which it involved is clearly present in Hooker, as we have seen, as well as in the traditional notion of a *synteresis* or "a ground of the soul" [23] which is expounded at length by Aquinas[24] and which Robert Burton describes as "an innate habit, . . . a conversation of the knowledge of the law of God and Nature, to know good or evil." [25]

Uncondensed Imagery

Dryden's characteristic use of a system of metaphors in an opposition of ideas has been outlined by Martin Price in his

20. *The Cambridge Platonists,* ed. Campagnac, pp. 4–5.

21. Jakob Boehme, *Concerning the Election of Grace,* pp. 76–77. For general information concerning Boehme's influence on Restoration writing, cf. Wilhelm Struck, *Der Einfluss Jakob Boehmes auf die englische Literatur des 17. Jahrhunderts* (Berlin, 1936).

22. Henry More, *Philosophiæ Teutonicæ Censura* (London, 1679).

23. See William Ralph Inge, *Christian Mysticism* (London, 1918), p. 360 and chap. 4, n. 12.

24. See *Summa Theologica,* I, Q. 79, Art. 12.

25. *Anatomy of Melancholy* (London, 1923), I, 1, 2, X.

excellent analysis of "the dialectical nature of Dryden's verse."
Price notes that Dryden sets up an initial opposition and then
carries it further so that the logic of the opposition "governs" the lines: "We shift, as we might in Donne, from figure
to figure within the logical opposition. The shift of figures is
neither so bold nor so ostentatious as in Donne; no image is
pursued so far as to build up an extended figure." Dryden's
style "plays upon a tissue of metaphors without condensing
them into firm images." His best poetry, Price finds, "achieves
its end with less violence of paradox than the Metaphysicals
and less fullness of image than the Romantics." [26]

Dryden's use of paradox also differs from that of the Metaphysicals in that they were more interested, as Basil Willey
has noted, in "the actual process of fusing disparates than . . .
any 'truth' that may emerge from the process," [27] while Dryden's opposition and dialectic are constructed to yield "Sacred
Truth." The opposing forces in *Religio Laici* combine to produce the ground of reason which has elements of both initial
dialectical extremes: the light above and the darkness below.
In writing *The Hind and the Panther,* Dryden would learn to
use the same reactants to yield a strikingly different synthesis.
A description of his dialectic in *Religio Laici* constitutes an account of a significant part of the inner workings of the poem
and of the process of defining the necessary minimum for salvation of all men.

A cardinal point which makes possible the dialectical argument of the poem is the assumption that the minimum of
spiritual knowledge necessary for salvation is obscure only because of man's abuses of the very reason which could otherwise provide that knowledge without difficulty. This view

26. Martin Price, *To the Palace of Wisdom: Studies in Order and
Energy from Dryden to Blake* (New York, 1964), pp. 29–30. See also
Maynard Mack, " 'Wit and Poetry and Pope': Some Observations on his
Imagery," reprinted in *Eighteenth-Century English Literature: Modern
Essays in Criticism,* ed. James L. Clifford (New York, 1959), pp. 21–41.
27. Willey, *The Seventeenth Century Background,* p. 51.

has little to do with skepticism. It is part of the rationalistic anti-intellectualism which, as we have seen in chapter 4, ran through much of the liberal theology of the time. The second section of the poem (ll. 12–41, immediately following the exordium), which describes the spiritual situation of the ancients, parallels the first stage of reason in the exordium. The heathens, in their earthbound travels, have no supernatural light of revelation, but they have been endowed with an inner light of nature—their reason—which should be an adequate guide to their souls in the quest for salvation. Their reason was sufficient to give them full knowledge of the earth they inhabited. Their "Lamp" led them "from Cause to Cause, to Natures secret head" (l. 13). This knowledge of nature carried with it the important recognition of a deity of some kind. Merely by the exercise of their reason, merely by searching their own ground, they were able to find "that one first principle must be" (l. 14). But their reason was led astray when they tried to extend it, by ratiocination, onto planes where they could not reach:

> But *what,* or *who,* that *UNIVERSAL HE;*
> Whether some *Soul* incompassing this Ball
> *Unmade, unmov'd;* yet *making, moving All;*
> Or various *Atoms* interfering Dance
> Leapt into *Form,* (the Noble work of *Chance;*)
> Or this great *All* was from *Eternity;*
> Not ev'n the *Stagirite* himself could see;
> And *Epicurus Guess'd* as well as He.
>
> [ll. 15–22]

Human reason cannot achieve specific knowledge beyond its own sphere, beyond "this Ball." Universal knowledge is beyond man, because outside of his sphere the modes of his reason cannot be employed. Human reason reveals truths about man's present, local situation, not about the "great All" or

about a "future State" determined by "Providence and Fate"
(ll. 23–24). The poet's survey of the "Opinions of the several
Sects of Philosophers concerning the Summum Bonum" [28] further reveals that when men try to systematize the obvious, it
vanishes "from 'em, like Enchanted ground" (l. 28). They dig
busily for systems of virtue, but they miss the patent truths:

> The *wiser Madmen* did for *Vertue* toyl:
> A Thorny, or at best a barren Soil.
>
> [ll. 31–32]

These men are "wiser" than the other abusers of their own
reason, the other "Madmen," because they stick closer to the
ground of reason. Others decide that pleasure is the only good
and in this way go beyond the capacity of their reason to understand man's place in the cosmic order: they find "their Line
too short, the Well too deep" (l. 34). When men leave the
ground of reason, they lose their orientation:

> . . . *anxious Thoughts* in *endless Circles* roul,
> Without a *Centre* where to fix the *Soul:*
> In this wilde Maze their vain Endeavours end.
>
> [ll. 36–38]

The concluding part of the poet's discussion of the ancients'
plight makes it still clearer that it is within reason's proper
sphere of activity and through its innate capacity for divine
truth that the necessary minimum for salvation has been provided. The discussion is resumed once again in accordance
with the blueprint of the exordium. In his answer to the deist
(which we have yet to discuss) the poet affirms the final power
of revelation. The deist then elaborates the "hemisphere" objection that the poet has embedded in the exordium's third
part. This elaboration, as we have already noted, distinguishes

---

28. The marginal notes appeared in the early editions of the poem
and seem to have been written by Dryden himself, though there is no
other evidence of his authorship.

between what was "then" (l. 177), at the time of revelation, "inhabited, and known" and "Worlds discover'd New." The other hemisphere contains "Indian Souls . . . who never saw the Light" of revelation (ll. 177–83).[29] The poet preserves the proselike, conversational manner of the poem by avoiding the appearance of closely knit, prepared metaphors and arguments. He speaks as if the deist's objection suddenly presents an unforeseen threat to his own position. The objection is introduced, after a long assurance of revelation's power (ll. 126–67), with the interjection "But stay" (l. 168), and the poet tells us that "Of all Objections this indeed is chief / To startle Reason, stagger frail Belief" (ll. 184–85). Some seemingly new resource must be tapped to meet this challenge.

Yet the *answer*—that which the poet is willing to "grant" (l. 186) the deist—is really a direct extension of the earlier description of the ancients' spiritual state. The foundation for the concession has already been carefully laid in the exordium and in that earlier description. The "lonely, weary, wandring Travellers" who have only the light of reason during their sojourn in the other hemisphere must use their "Lamp" (l. 12); they must investigate the ground which they inhabit. This investigation will yield them not only secular truth but the recognition of a first principle. They must not, however, try to extend their reason, through ratiocination, onto other planes. Their own reason, the poet intimates in the converse of his criticism, would yield them sufficient spiritual truth, if only they did not abuse it. This intimation is now made explicit:

> We grant, 'tis true, that Heav'n from humane Sense
> Has hid the secret paths of *Providence:*
> But *boundless Wisedom, boundless Mercy,* may
> Find ev'n for those *be-wildred* Souls, a *way:*

29. It is clear from the poet's answer to this objection that the other hemisphere also includes pagan souls born into this world, before the common era, in "our Hemisphere." The "Gentiles" of St. Paul and the reference to Socrates are evidence of this.

> If from his *Nature Foes* may Pity claim,
> Much more may *Strangers* who ne'er heard his *Name.*
> And though *no Name* be for *Salvation* known,
> But that of his *Eternal Sons* alone;
> Who knows how far transcending Goodness can
> Extend the *Merits* of *that Son* to *Man?*
> Who knows what *Reasons* may his *Mercy* lead;
> Or *Ignorance invincible* may plead?
> Not onely *Charity* bids hope the *best,*
> But *more* the great Apostle has exprest:
> *That, if the* Gentiles, (whom no Law inspir'd,)
> *By Nature did what* was by *Law requir'd;*
> *They, who the written Rule had never known,*
> *Were to themselves both Rule and Law alone:*
> *To Natures plain indictment they shall plead;*
> *And, by their Conscience, be condemn'd or freed.*
> Most righteous Doom! because a *Rule reveal'd*
> Is *none* to *Those,* from whom it was *conceal'd.*
>
> [ll. 186–207]

The poet's use of the older, hyphenated spelling "be-wildred" reproduces its original meaning, "lost in pathless places," and suggests the identity of these souls and the "lonely, weary, wandring Travellers" of the exordium. Though they cannot come to the higher ground—the secret paths of Providence—without the light of revelation, God has provided them with a candle to show them the paths of their own realm. Thus they too can find a *way* to salvation. As in the case of Hooker and the Cambridge Platonists, this is not "God-forsaken natural-ism." Though the poet finds an illumination outside the light of formal revelation that is also adequate for salvation, he also emphasizes the ultimately derivative character of this light. The use of the word *nature* confirms the divine element which has been incorporated into the heathen's reason. If God's foes can claim pity from his nature, surely righteous heathens

who live by the nature which God created can claim pity from
"Natures plain indictment." The logic of God's mercy proceeds
along providential paths which man cannot distinguish with
his own reason: "Who knows," we are told, "what Reasons
may his Mercy lead?" But there is no doubt that the possibility that God may extend salvation to heathens—expressed
only in terms of *may* (l. 188) and *can* (l. 194)—when analyzed
merely by human reason has been confirmed into a certainty
by the revelation of the great Apostle. It becomes an accomplished fact, a "Most righteous Doom," which the poet "then"
(l. 208) applies freely to the righteous of all times who followed in the paths of their divinely endowed reason:

> Then those who follow'd *Reasons* Dictates right;
> Liv'd up, and lifted high their *Natural Light;*
> With *Socrates* may see their Maker's Face,
> While Thousand *Rubrick-Martyrs* want a place.
>
> [ll. 208–11]

Here is one part of the final resolution of the opposition between the light on high and the darkness below. Through
God's mercy, man has been given a natural light which can be
lifted *above* its merely natural situation to a state comparable
in efficacy to *super*natural light. Thus even though man in-
habits only his own ground of reason, he can travel to the
highest place before his "Maker's Face."

The poet emphasizes, however, that there is no natural continuity between Man's reason and the light of heaven. It is
only through God's mercy that the two can be bridged.[30] Only
through the continued action of Providence in the flickering

30. The mysterious "A.W." put the point very well when he wrote, "I
wholly deny any Natural Light can lead me to a Supernatural; there is
no proportion betwixt those two extreams: There is a Gulph betwixt,
. . . And 'tis not so easy a passage as from *Coventgarden* to *Whitehall;*
'tis rather from *Covent-Garden* to some place beyond the *Cælum
Empyræum,* and wholly out of the boundaries of Nature": *Oracles of
Reason,* p. 202. Cf. Appendix A.

of man's candle can the heathen walk in upward paths. The absolute distinction between the ground of human reason and the divine ground of heaven's ways is first made explicit in the closing lines of the first discussion of the ancients. I have postponed an analysis of these lines to the present place because the distinction forms the basis of the poet's transition to the consideration of the deist.

In concluding that first discussion, in which the ancients are chastised for trying to reach beyond or to penetrate deeper than their own ground of reason, the poet asks:

> How can the *less* the *Greater* comprehend?
> Or *finite Reason* reach *Infinity?*
> For what cou'd *Fathom GOD* were *more* than *He.*
>
> [ll. 39–41]

Dryden, here, as well as in the later discussion of the ancients, makes "Infinity" the inaccessible divine ground of the universe.[31] It is only because God shows "boundless Mercy" (l. 188) that man is ever enabled to move beyond the confines of his own restricted reason. Salvation for men was brought, the poet tells us, in the name of Christ and his revelation. But even before the divine, infinite ground of heaven was made accessible to man in this manner, God's "transcending Goodness" devised a way to "Extend the Merits of that Son to Man" by endowing him with the natural light of "Reasons Dictates." Yet man is not one who "knows what Reasons" motivate God's "transcending Goodness." The distinction between man's reason and God's remains absolute.

31. Willey notes, in another context, that "infinite extension or space became with More . . . the divine ground of the universe" (pp. 168–69). More's achievement on this point was a matter of emphasis. For further comment, see John Tull Baker, *An Historical and Critical Examination of English Space and Time Theories* (Bronxville, N.Y., 1930), p. 12; cf. Appendix C.

The Deist's Delusion

The "Systeme of Deisme" is a more serious abuse of reason than the systems of the ancients because the deist has been a beneficiary of revelation.[32] He lives during the second phase of man's spiritual history when the function of human reason is not to discover the truths which are a necessary minimum for the ancient or the Indian, but "to apprehend" the Scriptures "to be the word of God" (Preface, 1. 100)—to "discover but the Sky" (l. 4). He thinks his reason has penetrated to the plane of the divine which eluded the reasoning of the ancients —which "vanish'd from 'em, like Enchanted ground" (l. 28). In reality, however, the deist does not use his reason at all, though he thinks he stands on "firmer ground" (l. 42). He cries "εὑρεκα [I have found it]" (l. 43),[33] when in fact he is merely repeating part of the revelation of the infinite divine which has

32. Harth's effort to determine the precise identity of the "Deist" is fascinating but inconclusive and finally, I think, distorted. He is right to depend heavily on the deistical essay "Of Natural Religion," which there is good reason to believe Dryden knew firsthand, especially because it refers explicitly to Wolseley's *Reasonablenes of Scripture-Belief* (London, 1672) (cf. Appendix A and my dissertation on *Religio Laici,* Yale, 1966 [misdated 1967]). But Harth's conception of deism is confusing because it is alternately expanded—as in his tenuous lexical extrapolations of deistical terminology (pp. 77 ff.)—and constricted (cf. pp. 85 ff.); we are forced to wonder whether Dryden himself could have had a specific adversary in mind. That he did, seems especially unlikely when we recall that "Of Natural Religion" was amicably addressed to Charles Blount who was (contrary to Harth's new view) Dryden's friend: that Dryden in part used "Of Natural Religion" in *Religio Laici* is more plausibly explained by his *sympathy* for the remarkably moderate tone and argumentation of that essay. Indeed, it may even be true that, according to the eighteenth-century ascription of that essay, Dryden *was* its author and that *Religio Laici* represents an explicit revision of earlier views—in much the same relation as *The Hind and the Panther* bears to *Religio Laici* (cf. chap. 7 and Appendix A).

33. For Dryden's possible borrowing from Herbert of Cherbury in these lines, see Hutcheson, *Cherbury's "De Religione Laici,"* pp. 57–58.

been given to man in the Scriptures. The ancients reached only to "Natures secret head" (l. 13). They could not reach the "God-head" (l. 78). The deist thinks he has reached it by his own rational powers: "God is that Spring of Good" (l. 44), he declares, stumbling unawares onto a proposition about God and an image of source or supply that affiliates equally with flow of bounty (well-spring) and that flow of light (day-spring) in which reason's spiritual constructs will, at the end of days, *dissolve* (l. 11). The conclusions asserted by the deist are not false in themselves. God, he proclaims, is "Supreme, and Best":

> *We,* made to *serve,* and in that Service *blest;*
> If so, some *Rules* of Worship must be given,
> Distributed alike to all by Heaven:
> Else *God* were *partial,* and to *some* deny'd
> The Means his Justice shou'd for *all* provide.
> This *general Worship* is to *PRAISE* and *PRAY:*
> One part to *borrow* Blessings, one to *pay:*
> And when frail Nature slides into *Offence,*
> The *Sacrifice* for *Crimes* is *Penitence.*
> Yet, since th' Effects of Providence, we find
> Are variously dispens'd to Humane kind;
> That *Vice Triumphs,* and *Vertue suffers* here,
> (A Brand that Sovereign Justice cannot bear;)
> Our Reason prompts us to a *future* State:
> The *last Appeal* from *Fortune,* and from *Fate:*
> Where God's all-righteous ways will be declar'd;
> The *Bad* meet *Punishment,* the *Good, Reward.*
>
> [ll. 44–61]

His deductions are, in fact, no more than plagiarisms from revelation, as the poet tells him:

> These Truths are not the product of thy Mind,
> But dropt from Heaven, and of a Nobler kind.
>
> [ll. 66–67]

He imagines that he can walk, by his own power, on the divine ground where God's ways (l. 60) are clear to him.

The poet takes the deist to task for mistaking the plane on which his reason should operate:

> Thus Man by his own strength to Heaven wou'd soar;
> And wou'd not be Oblig'd to God for more.
>
> [ll. 62–63]

The higher truths which the deist has found here below were "dropt from Heaven." The tendency of the deist's thought leads him to forget his dependent state:

> Vain, wretched Creature, how art thou misled
> To think thy Wit these God-like Notions bred!
>
> [ll. 64–65]

The reinforcing use of the word *creature* helps emphasize the fact that man owes his existence to the Creator and not the reverse: man cannot create anything godlike by himself. The spring (l. 44) or source (l. 70) of supernatural light which the deist claims to have discovered is known to man only through revelation:

> *Reveal'd Religion* first inform'd thy Sight,
> And *Reason* saw not, till *Faith* sprung the Light.[34]
> Hence all thy *Natural Worship* takes the *Source:*
> 'Tis *Revelation* what thou thinkst *Discourse.*
>
> [ll. 68–71]

Man's discourse is restricted to finite, earthly reason. As proof of this point the poet reverts briefly to his discussion of the

34. Cf. Henry More, *Discourses on Several Texts of Scripture* (London, 1692), p. 66: "Nor yet is either this Natural or Spiritual Eye to be said to be altogether devoid of light: But as *Plato* conceiv'd, there was an *innate light* in the Eye, and that by the conjunction of this with the external light . . . Vision was performed: . . . in vertue of the happy meeting together of which inwardly pure disposition of the Soul with . . . outward suggestions, she is assured of the reality of the Divine and Spiritual Objects of the Understanding, what is to be believed and what to be done."

ancients. Their brightest lamps, shining at a time before revelation dimmed out the necessity for the light of nature, only
achieved the most obscure (l. 73) and rudimentary notion of
the divine. The poet asks the deist:

> how com'st *Thou* to see these truths so clear,
> Which so obscure to *Heathens* did appear?
> Not *Plato* these, nor *Aristotle* found:
> Nor He whose Wisedom *Oracles* renown'd.
> Hast thou a Wit so deep, or so sublime,
> Or canst thou lower dive, or higher climb?
> Canst *Thou,* by *Reason,* more of *God-head* know
> Than *Plutarch, Seneca,* or *Cicero?*
> Those Gyant Wits, in happyer Ages born,
> (When *Arms,* and *Arts* did *Greece* and *Rome* adorn)
> Knew no such *Systeme:* no such Piles cou'd raise
> Of *Natural Worship,* built on *Pray'r* and *Praise,*
> *To One sole GOD.*
>
> [ll. 72–84]

For the ancients, even this obscure knowledge was sufficient
to win salvation. They could, with Socrates "whose Wisedom
Oracles renown'd," see "their Maker's Face" (l. 210) merely by
the light of nature. They came much closer to being Wits who
bred God-like Notions (l. 65): they were born "Gyant Wits."
Yet even they were not able to leave the restricted plane of
human reason: even their line was too short; they could not
reach infinity or the divine without revelation. The deist, however, with a wit less "deep" and less "sublime" [35] tries to dive
lower and climb higher to planes that human reason cannot
reach even when it is at the height of its powers; even then,
reason cannot raise itself by building rationalistic *systems* or
Babel-like "Piles."

The deist possesses an instrument of reason which stands

35. For another example of Dryden's emphasis on visual height in the
word *sublime,* see his translation of Virgil's *Georgics,* I, 330–33.

much lower than the ancients' in the scale of the finite. He is chained—half-conscious, as the poet intimates—to the ground of human reason, yet he has made much bolder claims to knowledge of the divine by dint of reason.

> Dar'st thou, poor Worm, offend *Infinity?*
> And must the Terms of Peace be given by *Thee?*
> Then *Thou* art *Justice* in the *last Appeal;*
> *Thy easie God* instructs Thee to *rebell:*
> And, like a King remote, and weak, must take
> What Satisfaction *Thou* art pleas'd to make.
>
> [ll. 93–98]

The poor worm's delusion that he can crawl to heaven on his own power stems from his blindness to the possible existence of a justice or a last appeal different in kind from what he can see and comprehend around him. The deist's idea of infinity as an attribute of God extends no further than to make God remote and therefore weak in the affairs of men, who must promulgate the laws of easy salvation—"Satisfaction"—for themselves.

"Relief from Humane Wit"

Man, the poet affirms, can only be saved from impartial justice if God will take man's punishment on Himself:

> But if there be a *Pow'r* too *Just,* and *strong*
> To wink at *Crimes,* and bear unpunish'd *Wrong;*
> Look humbly upward, see his Will disclose:
> The *Forfeit* first, and then the *Fine* impose:
> A *Mulct thy* Poverty cou'd never pay
> Had not *Eternal Wisedom* found the way:
> And with Cœlestial Wealth supply'd thy Store:
> *His Justice* makes the *Fine,* his *Mercy* quits the *Score.*
> See God descending in thy Humane Frame;
> Th' *offended,* suff'ring in th' *Offenders* Name:
> All thy Misdeeds to him imputed see,

And all his Righteousness devolv'd on thee.

[ll. 99–110]

The function of human reason after the Incarnation and the revelation of the Gospel is only to cause us to "Look humbly upward" (l. 101) where we will "see his Will disclose" how the score will be set right by his infinite mercy. It is only because God has "rolled down" or "devolv'd" his righteousness to man below that man has a chance for salvation; reason must make us understand this:

> For granting we have Sin'd, and that th' offence
> Of *Man,* is made against *Omnipotence,*
> Some Price, that bears *proportion,* must be paid;
> And *Infinite* with *Infinite* be weigh'd.
> See then the *Deist lost: Remorse* for *Vice,*
> *Not* paid, or *paid, inadequate* in price:
> What farther means can *Reason* now direct,
> Or what Relief from *humane Wit* expect?
> *That* shews us *sick;* and sadly are we sure
> *Still* to be *Sick,* till *Heav'n* reveal the *Cure:*
> If then *Heaven's Will* must needs be understood,
> (Which must, if we want *Cure,* and *Heaven,* be *Good*)
> Let all Records of *Will reveal'd* be shown;
> With *Scripture,* all in equal ballance thrown,
> And *our one Sacred Book* will be *That one.*

[ll. 111–25]

The question, "What farther means can Reason now direct"? is not left unanswered. Some relief can be given by "humane Wit." "Consider," said Culverwel, in a similar way, "that the very apprehending the weaknesse of *Reason,* even this in some measure comes from *Reason. Reason,* when awaken'd, it feels her own wounds, . . . sees the dimnesse of her own sight." [36]

36. In this instance I have used the first edition of *An Elegant And Learned Discourse Of the Light of Nature* (London, 1652), p. 4, in order to reproduce the original (Culverwel's or his age's) emphasis in italics and capitalization.

Reason serves an important function when it "shews us sick" and reveals that "Heaven's Will" must "reveal the Cure." In this manner the poet gives us an exemplum of his argument by guiding us "upward" (l. 7) to the "one Sacred Book."

The next forty-one lines illustrate the process of apprehending the truth of scriptural authority and show that it is not a matter of logical deduction or reasoning: "Proof needs not here," the poet insists. Human reason grasps the superior truth of Scripture intuitively as soon as a comparison is presented to it:

> . . . for whether we compare
> That Impious, Idle, Superstitious Ware
> Of *Rites, Lustrations, Offerings,* (which before,
> In various Ages, various Countries bore)
> With *Christian Faith* and *Vertues,* we shall find
> None answ'ring the great ends of humane kind
> But *This one Rule of Life: That* shews us best
> How *God* may be *appeas'd,* and *Mortals blest.*
>
> [ll. 126–33]

Reason itself can see that the religion produced by the "Reason of the far greatest part of mankind, is," in Glanvill's words, "but an aggregate of mistaken phantasms." [37] It is "Superstitious Ware" which cannot be used in bartering for God's appeasement. The essentials of "this one Rule of Life," moreover, were made known to man long before the historical date of the Incarnation. These essentials were implanted in the ground of human reason, in the world, at the time of Creation:

> Whether from length of *Time* its worth we draw,
> The *World* is scarce more *Ancient* than the *Law:*
> Heav'ns early Care prescrib'd for every Age;
> First, in the *Soul,* and after, in the *Page.*
>
> [ll. 134–37]

37. See Willey, p. 184.

The complement of this idea is expressed a few lines later when the poet tells us that the Scriptures reproduce the force of God's very *first* words which began the creation of the world and, more specifically, endowed it with natural light:

> Then for the *Style; Majestick* and *Divine,*
> It speaks no less than God in every Line:
> *Commanding words;* whose *Force* is still the same
> As the first *Fiat* that produc'd our Frame.
>
> [ll. 152–55]

This conception of a universal revelation of natural light, preceding scriptural revelation and providing pre-Christians or non-Christians with a necessary minimum of guidance in the ground of human reason—in their part of the world (their "Hemisphere")—is a large part of the raison d'être of the first half of the poem.

When the deist objects that there are many "who never saw the Light" of scriptural revelation because they lived in unknown parts of the world, we remember that the poet has already prepared an answer to fit the terms of the objection. The deist says,

> No *Supernatural Worship* can be *True:*
> Because a *general Law* is that alone
> Which must to *all,* and every *where* be known:
> A Style so large as not *this* Book can claim
> Nor ought that bears *reveal'd* Religions *Name.*
>
> [ll. 169–73]

We saw before that this objection is the immediate occasion for the poet's concluding discussion of the ancients (ll. 184–211). There he answers, with the help of St. Paul, that God provided for their salvation in the capacity of human reason; so that it is in their power to raise their candle, to lift "high their Natural Light," and, by following the paths of "Reasons Dictates," travel up to "see their Maker's Face."

This answer to the deist is reinforced by its context. The deist raises his objection to the "Majestick and Divine" style of Scripture, which, he argues, was known to few. But the poet has already intimated that the other hemisphere—the whole "World" (l. 135)—was given a revelation in another "Style": this is the style of the "first Fiat" which "produc'd our Frame" (l. 155) and endowed it with "Natural Light" (l. 209). Dryden's argument for truths which were pre-scribed "First, in the Soul, and after, in the Page" thus has much the same force as the similar expressions of the Cambridge Platonists. Though Dryden carefully distinguishes between rational syllogistics and faith, he emphasizes, by means of an unashamed innatist metaphor, that faith itself has been graciously lodged in man's higher reason or understanding: "Faith," he says, "is the Seal of Heaven impress'd upon our humane understanding." [38] Dryden claims, like Whichcote, for example, that the truths of Scripture "are Truths of first Inscription; and these have a deeper Foundation, greater Ground for them, than that God gave the Law on Mount Sinai; or that he did after ingrave it on the Tables of Stone; or that we find the Ten Commandments in the Bible. For God made Man to them, and did write them upon the Heart of Man, before he did declare them upon Mount Sinai, before he ingraved them upon the Tables of Stone, or before they were writ in our Bibles; God made Man to them, and wrought his Law upon Mens Hearts; and as it were, interwove it into the Principles of our Reason." Dryden, like Whichcote, uses the traditional inscription metaphor with full consciousness of its metaphorical nature. Whichcote's interpretation of "first Inscription" (and that of most of the other Cambridge men)[39] issues in a dispositional account of innate ideas: the truths which were later set down in the Bible were *interwoven* by God into "the Principles of our Reason." The burden of this

38. Preface to *Religio Laici*, ll. 101–02.
39. Cf. the discussion of this point in chap. 4.

account is carried, as we have noted, by the pervasive light metaphors of the Cambridge group.

"God," wrote Whichcote, "hath set up Two Lights; to enlighten us in our Way: The Light of Reason, which is the Light of his Creation; and the Light of Scripture." [40] The universe of *Religio Laici* depends upon the light of the first fiat and the light of Scripture fully as much, in my view, as does the universe of the Cambridge Platonists. It differs from their world only in that, since the construction of its details was supervised by a poet, it is more closely ordered and observes a stricter economy in thought and language than their system. Dryden's own "Two Lights" are efficiently coordinated in a dynamic relationship which always guarantees men a sufficient quantity of illumination.

The divine mechanism or "automaton" depicted in the exordium, which allows the light of reason to fade when the light of revelation becomes stronger, also increases the light of reason when the light of revelation grows dimmer. Such a mechanism, made up of divine parts and operated by Providence, was uniquely fitted to the needs of a humanistic Christian standing on the threshold of the Clockmaker's Universe. The idea for its adjustable design probably came from the Cambridge Platonists' dispositional form of innatism and their creative use of candle and light imagery to guide those who have not seen the light of revelation. Dryden and Burthogge were building on flexibly formulated accounts of man's spiritual state, such as the following striking passage from More:

> among . . . many Lights which God makes to appear to man, there are two more eminent by far then the rest. The greater of which two has his dominion by day, and is a faithful guide to those which walk in the day, that is, that work the works of Righteousnesse. And this greater Light is but one, but does, being added, mightily

40. See Whichcote, *Moral and Religious Aphorisms*, nos. 109 and 916.

invigorate the former day-light man walked by, and it is a more full appearance of the *Sun of Righteousnesse;* which is an hearty and sincere *Love of God and a mans neighbour.* The lesser of these two great Lights has dominion by night, and is a rule to those whose inward mindes are held as yet too strongly in the works of darknesse; and it is a Principle weak, and variable as the Moon, and is called *Inconstancy of Life and Knowledge.* There are also an abundance of other *little Lights* thickly dispersed over the whole Understanding of man, as the Stars in the Firmament, which you may call *Notionality,* or *Multiplicity of ineffectual Opinions.*

But the worst of all these are better then down-right Sensuality and Brutishnesse, and therefore God may well be said to set them up in the *Heavenly* part of man, his Understanding, to give what light they are able to his *Earthly* parts.[41]

Dryden improved on formulations of this kind, not only in structure of thought, but in the efficient and significant use of language as well. He succeeds, where the Cambridge men failed, in developing a poetic language, even while he escapes the charge of using false imagery, because his metaphors precipitate out of and melt back into the "ground" of abstract "Discourse." [42] The reader hardly notices the insinuation of

41. Henry More, *Conjectura Cabbalistica. Or, A Conjectural Essay of Interpreting the mind of Moses* (London, 1662), p. 31. The resemblances between this passage and the parallel passages in *Causa Dei* (London, 1675) suggest that Burthogge may very well have known *Conjectura Cabbalistica* itself, especially because More's account appears in the section of his book concerned with the "Moral Cabbala" and Burthogge emphasizes similarly that his description pertains to "the *Moral* world" (p. 195). (On the extent and limit of Milton's relation to the *Conjectura Cabbalistica* and cabbalistic learning in general, see Marjorie H. Nicolson, "Milton and the *Conjectura Cabbalistica,*" *PQ,* VI, 1927, 1–18 and R. J. Zwi Werblowsky, "Milton and the *Conjectura Cabbalistica,*" *JWCI,* XVIII, 1955, 90–113.)

42. See Price, p. 29.

"our Hemisphere" in the exordium or the extent of the comparison in the "first Fiat that produc'd our Frame." It is a controlled achievement in modulation which gradually converts theological dispute into something very like a ratiocinative vision of the love that moves the sun and other stars.

Charitable Reason

In a chronological account of man's spiritual history, such as that outlined in the poet's Preface, the consideration of deism should have come after Roman Catholicism and Protestantism. But such an account is not the main concern of the poem. The meaning of *Religio Laici*, as I understand it, emerges from the poet's attempt to indicate the spiritual role of reason in two different, though related, situations: one in which no formal revelation is available to man's soul; the other in which revelation is available, although its authority and interpretation have become dangerously obscure. The deist's unfortunate situation is neither of these, but borders on both. His perversity and presumption have thrust him into a position where he is blind to the authenticity of any revelation; yet, since he has been presented with revelation, his reason is not that of the ancients, "those Gyant Wits" (l. 80), who could lift "high their Natural Light" (l. 209), but that of a "poor Worm" (l. 93). If he is to be saved it is only because, the poet intimates, even foes may claim pity from God's Nature (l. 190). In a poem which proceeds by indicating the abuse of reason in man's two situations, the deist serves as a useful transition figure: his "Systeme" in the realm of "unaided" reasoning and his "Objection" to revelation carry us from one phase of the poem to the next.

The objection allows the poet to conclude his consideration of man's first situation by asserting the efficacy of human reason where no revelation is available. God has made the reason of benighted man effective through His mercy (ll. 188 and 196). The same mercy, we learn, saves man, through his reason, from the obscurity of recorded revelation: in this second phase too, "God wou'd not leave Mankind without a way" (l. 296). The complement of God's mercy-in-action is man's charity-in-understanding. Man can understand God's merciful provision for men in all situations through his charitable reason. The four hundred and fifty-six lines of the poem are poised on this point. To make it unmistakably clear is the chief function of the bold digression on Athanasius.[43] After affirming the possibility of salvation for Heathens, the poet writes:

> Nor does it baulk my *Charity,* to find
> Th' *Egyptian* Bishop of another mind:
> For, though his *Creed Eternal Truth* contains,
> 'Tis hard for *Man* to doom to *endless pains*
> All who believ'd not all, his Zeal requir'd;
> Unless he first cou'd prove he was inspir'd.
> Then let us either think he meant to say
> *This Faith,* where *publish'd,* was the onely way;
> Or else conclude that, *Arius* to confute,
> The good old Man, too eager in dispute,
> Flew high; and as his *Christian* Fury rose
> Damn'd all for *Hereticks* who durst *oppose.*
>
> [ll. 212–23]

The Athanasian creed threatens to "baulk"—to block with an obstacle—the "path" of reason which his charity "has try'd" (cf. l. 224). Although the poet acknowledges that Athanasius has stated some truths that partake of divine qualities—that contain "Eternal Truth"—he is able to dismiss the Bishop's

---

43. Roscommon apparently believed that Dryden's remarks on Athanasius were a significant part of the total meaning of *Religio Laici.* Thirty-six of the fifty-four lines of his commendatory poem, "On Mr. Dryden's *Religio Laici,*" concern the importance of Dryden's objection to the creed of "the Egyptian patriarch": cf. *Works of John Dryden,* x, 34–35. Harth feels that Dryden's objection to Athanasius's view is a "gratuitous suggestion" (p. 171).

condemnation of the heathen on the same basis as he dismissed the systems of the ancients and the deist. Athanasius
deserted the ground of his human reason; he "flew high" in
an effort to comprehend an infinite subject (the "endless pains"
of eternal punishment) which his unaided reason (uninspired
mind) could not grasp. Athanasius's reason was clouded by
zeal, which led him to the un-Christian extremity of fury. It
was the failure of his reason which prevented him from
seeing what St. Paul and others, among them the poet, have
been able to see: God's mercy may "find ev'n for those be-
wildred Souls, a way." The creed of the "good old Man"
applies only where Scripture has been revealed; only there can
it be "the onely way." In other places, the same reason which
helps the poet to see what Athanasius could not, will also
provide a way for be-wildred heathen souls.

The assertion of charity in the use of human reason is
also used as a point of departure for the discussion of the
role of reason in relation to the Scriptures:

> Thus far my Charity this path has try'd;
> (A much unskilfull, but well meaning guide:)
> Yet what they are, ev'n these crude thoughts were bred
> By reading that, which better thou hast read,
> Thy Matchless Author's work: which thou, my Friend,
> By well translating better dost commend.
>
> [ll. 224–29]

These lines reinforce significant echoes from earlier parts of
the poem. The poet's charity has traveled a "path" of human
reason to discern the "way" for heathens, which is described in
the Scriptures (e.g., by St. Paul). This path of reason, used in
apprehending the word of God in the Scriptures, pertains to
reason in the second phase outlined in the exordium, where
reason's function is, as in the parenthesis above (l. 225), "not
to assure our doubtfull way, / But guide us upward to a better
Day." For those who have heard the word of God, the funda-

mentals of religion do not have to come from reason; nor should they think, like the deist, that their wit bred the God-like notions involved in the worship of God. Reason and its works can, however, breed useful thoughts concerning the true meaning of Scripture.

The process of finding a necessary minimum of gospel truth for the layman has now reached a crucial point. We have seen that God has provided for both the non-Christian and the Christian in the innate capacity of human reason, but the more precise nature of that reason and its function in obtaining a sufficiency of religious truths are yet to be described. To this end the poet considers various aspects of reason's operation in relation to Scripture and faith. In every case he comes to a mixed conclusion: the potential of reason to discover or imaginatively "apprehend" divine truths is considerable, but its performance is seriously inadequate. Still, the poet is not willing to submit to a fideistic solution. The problem, we see again, lies not in the inadequacy of reason but in man's abuse of it. Human reason sees only in part, but this should be enough. Through a gradual shift in concern to urgent essentials, the poet indicates that men need not brawl over obscure questions. The degeneracy of human reason is shown to be the greatest enemy of the layman's salvation; for his salvation depends upon his reason. The reformation of that degeneracy is the ultimate concern of the poem.

Modes of Reason

Reason's role in the realm of guiding the Christian is considered under three heads: 1) its ability to indicate the authenticity of Scripture in general; 2) its usefulness in isolating problems of scriptural transmission; 3) its resourcefulness in providing the necessary minimum of scriptural truth in the face of textual corruption and obscurity. These three parts follow one another to form a powerful argument for the role of reason in the Christian world (the second phase) and parallel the argument for the role of reason in the non-Christian world (the first phase). By placing the deist's objection and the answer to him between the first and second parts of the linked argument of the second phase, the poet is able to indicate a common source for reason's capacity in both major phases. This is God's mercy as understood by man's charitable reason. The intervening section, continued from the first phase (ll. 168–223), also lessens the appearance of a prepared polemic and sustains the concessive form of open "sceptical" discussion. We have already examined the first part (ll. 126–67) of reason's role in guiding us "upward" insofar as it relates to the deist's objection and to the answer to him which concludes the consideration of the first phase.[44] We must now see that this first part also performs a significant function in the progress of the poem's argument and in the evolution of its metaphorical structure.

The purpose of lines 126–67, beginning "Proof needs not here," is to help define the sphere of reason's work in apprehending Scripture and to differentiate between the manner of human and divine thought. The first lines emphasize the natural character of the Scriptures: they are shown to be the very opposite of human religious "Ware" which has been constructed by "Superstitious" imagination (l. 127) and they are closely identified with the creation of nature—the "World"—itself. Whether we look "on the Writers, or the written Book" (l. 139), we find a mixture of similarity and difference between the workings of reason and the revelation of the infinite. We see, for example, that men who were "unskill'd in Arts" and who were born in "several Ages" and "several parts" of the earth have been able to offer the same historical accounts (ll. 139–42). The poet's reason can also see the operation of a nonhuman logic in the renovation of the commercial re-

---

44. See Appendix B for a discussion of scriptural authority (the first part of the second phase in the structure of the poem) in relation to traditional Anglican views.

lationship: the inspired writers of the Book offered to endure
"Pains," though "unask'd," and to give "Advice" though they
were not thanked for it. Their only "gain" was "Starving";
their only "Price" was "Martyrdom" (ll. 140–45). The Book
itself is also susceptible to confirmation by "humane Sense"
and by man's knowledge of nature's laws:

> Concurrent Heathens prove the Story *True:*
> The *Doctrine, Miracles;* which must convince,
> For *Heav'n* in *Them* appeals to *humane Sense:*
> And though they *prove* not, they *Confirm* the Cause,
> When what is *Taught* agrees with *Natures Laws.*
>
> [ll. 147–51]

The words of the Book are the same in force as those which
gave man natural light; yet they are also far removed from
any words which he can invent: they speak "no less than God
in every line." The doctrine of revelation is open to the
scrutiny of human reason, though its rationale and the cause
of its successful propagation escape man's logic:

> All Faiths *beside,* or did by *Arms* ascend;
> Or *Sense* indulg'd has made *Mankind* their *Friend:*
> This *onely* Doctrine does our *Lusts* oppose:
> Unfed by Natures Soil, in which it grows;
> Cross to our *Interests,* curbing Sense, and Sin;
> Oppress'd without, and undermin'd within,
> It thrives through pain; its own Tormentours tires;
> And with a stubborn patience still aspires.
> To what can *Reason* such Effects assign
> Transcending *Nature,* but to *Laws Divine?*
> Which in that Sacred Volume are contain'd;
> Sufficient, clear, and for that use ordain'd.
>
> [ll. 156–67]

Human reason, we learn, can apprehend the reality of Scripture through its "Effects" which flourish on a plane of reality

coinciding with the ground of reason; but the doctrine of
Scripture is not fed by the same ground: its nutriments are of
a different character; it abhors pleasure and thrives on pain.
Man can apprehend the part of Scripture which is accessible to
his reason. The Scriptures, however, ascend and aspire to a
plane beyond earthly reason; they transcend Nature. Man can
perceive that the Bible is authentic because part of its miraculous quality "agrees with Natures Laws" (l. 151), but another
part of it can only be understood according to "Laws Divine"
(l. 165). These are above human reason, but we rest assured
that they are somehow "sufficient" and "clear."

The poet does not, at this point, identify the source of
this assurance. Since the questions of sufficiency and clarity are
obviously of great importance in a poem occasioned by a
work attacking the textual reliability of Scripture, we wonder
at first why he has dropped the matter so suddenly. The
answer lies, it would seem, in his strategy of abeyance. By
treating two related problems (salvation for heathens and
the sufficiency of Scripture in its present form) at the same
time, the poet can suggest solutions by mere proximity of
materials. The question of the present-day sufficiency of Scripture is not raised, much less answered, at this point. Instead,
God's mercy to righteous heathens, shown in the endow-
ment of their reason, is asserted and then the usefulness of
reason in locating problems of scriptural transmission is ap-
plauded. When the question of sufficiency is finally made
explicit (ll. 276 ff.), the reader finds that the basis for an
answer already exists in the previously prepared associations
of ideas and metaphors.

Plodding on to Heaven

The poet's "Charity" (ll. 212 and 224), which has helped
him understand God's mercy to righteous heathens, was inspired by Simon's work. In the further commendations of the
translator, his author, and the *Critical History* itself, reason's

offices in finding scriptural truth are shown to be considerable.
Says the poet to Dickinson, the young translator,

> Those youthfull hours which, of thy Equals most
> In *Toys* have *squander'd,* or in *Vice* have *lost,*
> Those hours hast thou to Nobler use employ'd;
> And the severe Delights of Truth enjoy'd.
> Witness this weighty Book, in which appears
> The crabbed Toil of many thoughtfull years,
> Spent by thy Authour, in the Sifting Care
> Of *Rabbins* old Sophisticated Ware
> From Gold Divine; which he who well can sort
> May afterwards make *Algebra* a Sport.
> A Treasure, which if *Country-Curates* buy,
> They *Junius,* and *Tremellius* may defy:
> Save pains in various readings, and Translations;
> And without *Hebrew* make most learn'd quotations.
> A Work so full with various Learning fraught,
> So nicely pondred, yet so strongly wrought,
> As Natures height and Arts last hand requir'd:
> As much as Man cou'd compass, uninspir'd.
> Where we may see what *Errours* have been made
> Both in the *Copiers* and *Translaters Trade:*
> How *Jewish, Popish,* Interests have prevail'd,
> And where *Infallibility* has *fail'd.*

> [ll. 230–51]

Dickinson is praised for employing his time in a way that
suits the best natural aspects of reason and closely imitates the
Scriptures. He has shunned the artificial vanities of young
people—their "Toys"—and, following the teaching of the
Bible, he has escaped "Vice." The deist thought he could find
divine truths "of a Nobler kind" (l. 67) with his own reason.
Dickinson does not presume so far. He accepts revelation as
the source of divine truths in this world and employs his
reason in the "Nobler use" of guiding us to a clear appre-

hension of those truths. His "severe Delights" come from study-
ing a doctrine which "does our Lusts oppose." Simon's *Critical
History* is described as being "weighty" in order to indicate
the kinship between it and the other Book which when
thrown "in equal ballance" with all the other books was
shown to be the most weighty (ll. 123–25). The "crabbed Toil"
of Simon's reason succeeded in elucidating supernatural truths
where the thorny, barren, "toyl" (ll. 31–32) of the ancients
failed, because in "our Hemisphere" the Bible has been
planted in "Natures Soil, in which it grows" (l. 159)—because,
in the larger argument of the poem, an adjustment in the
natural light of reason has been made that permits Scripture
to flourish and to be apprehended on the plane of human
reason. Simon, like Dickinson at a younger age, is not fooled
by the artificial creations of man's reason, represented here
by "Rabbins old Sophisticated Ware": the phrase catches up
the "Superstitious Ware" (l. 127) of man's mystical imagination as well as the "leaky Vessels" (l. 35) of the ancient system-
makers who abused their reason with sophistical thinking.

Simon improves on the deist who cries εὑρεκα like Archimedes
when he discovered a way to differentiate between gold and
baser metals. Simon has truly found a way to sift "Gold
Divine" from its alloys. Such a work of reason, the poet indicates, is superior to the mathematical achievements of Archi-
medean algebra.[45] Simon's reason, in its effort to lead us to a
revelation which is within our range, can reach much higher
than the ancients did toward knowledge of supernatural
truths. Their "Lamp" (l. 12), we recall, could go as high as
"Natures secret head" (l. 13) but not to any knowledge of the
Being "incompassing this Ball" (l. 16). Simon's reason, still
"uninspir'd" but operating in "our Hemisphere" (l. 9), can
"compass" or apprehend divine truths at "Natures height"—
at the height of reason's power. With the help of his reason,

45. Archimedes was associated with the origin of algebra: cf. John
Wallis, *Opera Mathematica* (Oxford, 1693), II, 20–23.

Simon can see where "Trade" and "Interests" have infringed on the dissemination of the divine word. He can see the "wounds" and "dimnesse" of reason, as Culverwel put it,[46] with the help of reason.

Even before the problem of sufficiency is raised explicitly, the poet is quick to exclude a fideistic solution. He does so by denying that even Simon, a Roman Catholic priest, could accept the absolute authority of the Roman Church as a modern-day source of tradition:

> For some, who have his secret meaning ghes'd,
> Have found our Authour not too *much* a *Priest:*
> For *Fashion-sake* he seems to have recourse
> To *Pope,* and *Councils,* and *Traditions* force:
> But he that *old* Traditions cou'd subdue,
> Cou'd not but find the weakness of the *New.*
>
> [ll. 252–57]

The fideist proceeds on the assumption that there must be an infallible authority somewhere: if it is not in the accuracy of the Bible it must be in the Church.[47] The poet sees no need for such a "recourse." He accepts the reality that, at the point where Scripture depends on human reason—in transmission—imperfection has crept in. Nor is there any cause for believing that later human reason (uninspired, in the poet's view) should be able to tell us more about the text than earlier:

> If *Scripture,* though deriv'd from *heav'nly birth,*
> Has been but carelessly preserv'd on *Earth;*
> If *God's own People,* who of *God* before
> Knew what we know, and had been promis'd more,
> In fuller Terms, of Heaven's assisting Care,

46. *An Elegant And Learned Discourse,* p. 4.
47. See Bredvold, *The Intellectual Milieu of John Dryden,* p. 80, for a still-useful account of conventional fideistic strategy.

And who did neither *Time,* nor *Study* spare
To keep this Book *untainted, unperplext;*
Let in gross *Errours* to corrupt the *Text:*
Omitted *paragraphs,* embroyl'd the *Sense;*
With vain *Traditions* stopt the gaping Fence,
Which every common hand pull'd up with ease:
What Safety from such *brushwood-helps* as these [i.e. "New
    Traditions"]?
If *written words* from time are not secur'd,
How can we think have *oral Sounds* endur'd?
Which *thus* transmitted, if *one* Mouth has fail'd,
Immortal Lyes on *Ages* are intail'd:
And that some such have been, is prov'd too plain;
If we consider *Interest, Church,* and *Gain.*

[ll. 258–75]

The Scriptures were planted in "Natures Soil" (l. 159); they
were committed to the care of human reason which was to
see that they were "preserv'd on Earth" (l. 259). But man
could no more protect the absolute perfection of scriptural
reliability than he could maintain the ground of human reason. The "Fence" and "brushwood-helps" improvised by man's
reason were of little avail: "Interest" and "Gain" exist in the
Church as in all institutions subject to human reason. Human
reason could not preserve the area of infallibility in times
gone by; we should not expect it to do so in 1682.

Now the problem of sufficiency can be postponed no
longer. The poet puts the question in the mouth of the
fideist, whose assumptions the reader has already been prepared to reject:

Oh but says one, *Tradition* set aside,
Where can we hope for an *unerring Guid?*
For since th' *original* Scripture has been lost,
All Copies *disagreeing, maim'd* the *most,*
Or *Christian Faith* can have no *certain* ground,

> Or *Truth* in *Church Tradition* must be found.
>
> [ll. 276–81]

The fideist presents an exaggerated case which harps on the "lost," "disagreeing," "maim'd" state of "All Copies" of the text.[48] This exaggeration, coupled with unjustified reliance on new traditions (ll. 256–57 and l. 281), gives rise to the poet's ironic answer which attacks the logical basis of the fideist's apologetic:[49]

> Such an *Omniscient* Church we wish indeed;
> 'Twere worth *Both Testaments,* and cast in the *Creed:*
> But if *this Mother* be a *Guid* so sure,
> As can all *doubts resolve,* all *truth secure,*
> Then her *Infallibility,* as well
> Where Copies are *corrupt,* or *lame,* can tell;
> Restore *lost Canon* with as little pains,
> As *truly explicate* what still *remains:*
> Which yet no *Council* dare *pretend* to doe;
> Unless like *Esdras,* they cou'd *write* it new:
> Strange Confidence, still to *interpret* true,
> Yet not be sure that all they have explain'd,
> Is in the blest *Original* contain'd.
>
> [ll. 282–94]

48. There seems to me no compelling reason for assuming, as Harth does (p. 205), that the "one" who speaks here is to be understood as Simon. The only evidence for assigning the later Catholic interjection, at lines 305 ff., to Simon's presence in the poem is the printed marginal note. The present, earlier Catholic objection, which defends *some* appeal to tradition rather than fideistic reliance on papal infallibility, is not accompanied by such a specific label. Coming as it does immediately after a passage in which the poet differentiates between Simon and truly orthodox Roman Catholics, it is difficult to understand why Harth insists that we hear Simon speaking in this place too. In addition, we should recall (as Harth, pp. 173–78, notes himself) that Simon's *Critical History* is remarkable for *not* developing a fideistic attack. Harth interprets Simon as Dryden's "adversary" (p. 201) in the second half of the poem.

49. An analysis of ll. 282–83 in context thus supports recent objections to Bredvold's interpretation of these lines that does not allow for any trace of irony. See Fujimura, p. 211.

If the Church is truly omniscient it should be able to restore "lost Canon." The fact that it does not engage in such restorations, although it continues to interpret the text in its present state, suggests both that the Church is not omniscient and that even *it* considers the text adequate in its present state and not impossibly "corrupt, or lame." The fideist's argument concerning the "lost" state of the text is thus refuted, and the poet is also brought to the assertion which is of greater concern to him than the mere refutation of the fideist:

> More Safe, and much more modest 'tis, to say
> *God wou'd not leave Mankind without a way:*
> And that the *Scriptures,* though not *every where*
> Free from Corruption, or intire, or clear,
> Are uncorrupt, sufficient, clear, intire,
> In *all* things which our needfull *Faith* require.
>
> [ll. 295–300]

The fideist objected that, without an omniscient Church, "Christian Faith can have no certain ground" because the reliability of the text is in doubt. His objection, like that of the deist in relation to the heathens, presumes a knowledge of the limits and workings of God's mercy. But God could "find ev'n for those be-wildred Souls, a way" (l. 189) in the other hemisphere, where no supernatural light has shown, by providing for the possibility of their salvation in their reason. The poet stated the problem of transmission and the fideist's objection concerning sufficiency in terms of reason's "ground" metaphors (l. 280)—"Or Christian Faith can have no certain ground, / Or Truth in Church Tradition must be found"— so that the same answer would now become immediately relevant. In our hemisphere, too, we are not lost. When "supernatural Light" is obscured, God's mercy provides a "way" for the Christian layman in the same capacity of reason, enabling him to guide himself upward to the "better Day"—which may mean, among other things, all the parts of Scripture "which

our needfull Faith require." The poet's charity helps him see
that God's mercy is extended to all Christian sects so that each
man is ultimately responsible for finding the essentials of
revelation by his own reason:

> If *others* in the *same Glass better* see
> 'Tis for *Themselves* they look, but not for *me:*
> For *MY* Salvation must its Doom receive
> Not from what *OTHERS,* but what *I* believe.
>
> [ll. 301–04]

The poet has cited the "great Apostle" (l. 199) as an authority
in favor of salvation for those heathens "who follow'd Reasons
Dictates right" (l. 208). Here again he uses a passage from
St. Paul to reinforce his conviction that individual human
reason has been endowed by God's mercy to help Christians
reach scriptural truth, although the Scriptures can only be
partially known. The text alluded to is I Corinthians 13:12–
13: "For now we see through a glass, darkly; but then face to
face: now I know in part; but then shall I know even as also
I am known. And now abideth faith, hope, charity, these
three; but the greatest of these is charity." "Supernatural
Light" is today obscure so that the Christian now knows
Scripture only in part—he sees through a glass darkly. But
this will give him all the knowledge which is required of him
for winning salvation.

The two-part structure of the poem's argument is especially
valuable at this point. Paul's opinion (cf. ll. 200–06) is more
explicit in relation to the problem of the heathen than it can
be in relation to the dilemma of the modern Christian. For
this reason the poet can only allude to Paul in the second case
and suggest that this is the apostle's meaning here also. But
the parallel development of the poet's arguments in relation to
heathen and Christian laymen enables him to reap the benefits of the second text as well. Paul's theme of charity, as we
noted before, is the point on which the argument of the poem

depends. It is asserted repeatedly as a major premise just as
the first half of the argument concludes and the second half
is resumed (cf. ll. 198, 212, and 224). Paul's mention of "face
to face" is also exploited. The poet, having told us before that
the heathens who followed the paths of their reason would
"see their Maker's Face" (l. 210), now implies that Christians
will not be granted any less through God's mercy.

The poet's assertion that his private reason is adequate to
help him determine his own belief concerning the essentials
of Scripture must be extended to include the most ignorant
Christian layman. This extension involves an implicit assertion
(cf. ll. 208–11) of the essentially regenerate state of man's
nature, which in turn puts the poet in a position bordering
on heresy. He therefore raises Simon's more conservative objections to furnish still another concessive step in his argument
and to steer himself away from heresy, although he does not
alter the substance of his opinions:

> Must *all Tradition* then be set aside?
> This to affirm were Ignorance, or Pride.
> Are there not many points, some needfull sure
> To saving Faith, that Scripture leaves obscure?
> Which every Sect will wrest a several way
> (For what *one* Sect Interprets, *all* Sects *may*:)
> We hold, and say we prove from Scripture plain,
> That *Christ* is *GOD;* the bold *Socinian*
> From the *same* Scripture urges he's but *MAN.*
> Now what Appeal can end th' important Suit;
> *Both* parts *talk* loudly, but the *Rule* is *mute?*
>
> [ll. 305–15]

The poet dissociates himself from the "boldness" of one of
the most feared heresies of his time. He can do this without
elaborate protest because he has already posited Christ's incarnation as an axiom in the workings of God's mercy (cf. ll.
107–10 and ll. 192–95). The need for grace is implicit in the

poet's description of God's mercy but, like the Cambridge Platonists, the poet of *Religio Laici* treads "seldom in the deep, dark ravines, where . . . redemption is found a vital need." [50] God is liberal in dispensing his mercy. Thus, although the poet disapproves of the Socinian's boldness, he is not willing to say that he is damned for his views—that his "way" (l. 309) cannot lead to salvation. In the poet's overview of theological dispute, the Anglican Church is no more than a sect itself. There is no denying Simon's contention that the "Rule is mute." The question of whether "all Tradition" must then be "set aside" admits of no easy answer.

This momentarily abortive attempt to find an outside court of appeal for "needfull," obscure, points leads the poet to reiterate the action of God's mercy in the capacity of the layman's reason:

> Shall I speak plain, and in a Nation free
> Assume an honest *Layman's Liberty?*
> I think (according to my little Skill,
> To my own Mother-Church submitting still:)
> That many have been sav'd, and many may,
> Who never heard this Question brought in play.
> Th' *unletter'd* Christian, who believes in *gross,*
> Plods on to *Heaven;* and ne'er is at a loss:
> For the *Streight-gate* wou'd be made *streighter* yet,
> Were *none* admitted there but men of *Wit.*
> The few, by Nature form'd, with Learning fraught,
> Born to instruct, as others to be taught,
> Must Study well the Sacred Page; and see
> Which Doctrine, this, or that, does best agree
> With the whole Tenour of the Work Divine:
> And plainlyest points to Heaven's reveal'd Design:
> *Which* Exposition flows from *genuine Sense;*
> And which is *forc'd* by *Wit* and *Eloquence.*
>
> [ll. 316–33]

50. See Carpenter, *The Church in England,* p. 383.

In this passage, which is central to his view of reason and religion, the poet elaborates the meaning of the two earlier lines which deal with the heathen's salvation:

> Heav'ns early Care prescrib'd for every Age;
> First, in the *Soul,* and after, in the *Page.*
>
> [ll. 136–37]

The Christian layman who is "unletter'd"—like the heathen who has no direct knowledge of the "Page" (l. 328)—has also been provided for by Heaven's mercy. The light of his reason, shining in his soul, shows him the way to apprehend sufficient scriptural truth to win salvation. As the good man of pre-revelation times follows the "Natural Light" of "Reasons Dictates" and so looks up to see his "Maker's Face," the Christian layman "Plods on to Heaven" on the ground of his reason which accepts, "in gross," the whole scriptural text. There is no "unerring Guid" (l. 277) or "certain ground" (l. 280) in the Christian's present situation, where "Supernatural Light" (l. 11) is obscure. But man's God-illuminated reason can, on its own ground, "guide us upward" (l. 7) even though it is not unerring or certain or assured. The light of reason provides different kinds of sufficiency for the non-Christian and the Christian, but in both cases it is God's mercy, his "early Care" continued in "every Age" (l. 136), which saves the ordinary man. That the poet can see these truths is no wonder. He sees them with the help of his "little Skill"—his "much unskilfull, but well meaning guide," which is charity following the path of reason (cf. ll. 224–25).

"Through a Glass, Darkly"

The poet has now described the manner in which the "bewildred" heathen and the "unletter'd" Christian can obtain a necessary minimum of religious knowledge through the operation of private reason. He recognizes, however, that the life of the Christian layman cannot and should not be com-

pletely independent of historical and social forces because
private reason and public action constantly interact. Dryden's
poem, like the writings of the Cambridge Platonists, not only
asserts the efficacy of divinely endowed individual reason but
also, in my view, proclaims the necessity of an environment
in which private reason is given sanctuary and, most important,
in which the motive of religion has been freed of venal considerations. The poem builds gradually to an assertion of
embattled moral action—to an expression, as More formulated
it, of "Love of God and a mans neighbour"—which is related
to the very core of the religious life as the poet understands it
and of which the poem itself, as a public act, is a prime exemplum. Verrall's concern for the progressive disappearance
of religious content from the poem and Ward's feeling that the
concluding lines are "somewhat anticlimactic" do not,[51] it
seems to me, take into account these larger purposes and the
development of ideas which helps to achieve them. The same
series of assertions and de-emphases—held together by the
same faith in the innate spirituality of human reason—that
we saw in chapter 4 in relation to the Cambridge Platonists
is reproduced in the unfolding of *Religio Laici.* We must be
able to see that the final statement in the argument of the
poem, "Common quiet is Mankind's concern" (l. 450), represents a culmination of related ideas rather than, as Nichol
Smith would have it, a "call of expediency." [52]

The central assertion in the movement of *Religio Laici* is
that of universal salvation for all good men. Once this has
been compassed the other elements in the system that the poet
has adopted fall into place. Scriptural interpretation and the
teachings of tradition are thus both placed in the realm of
the desirable but unessential. The "Streight-gate" (l. 324) has
been widened through God's mercy—even for those who travel

51. Verrall, *Lectures on Dryden,* p. 155 and Ward, *Life of John Dryden,*
p. 191.
52. Smith, *John Dryden,* p. 62.

by the way of unexceptional reason, even to men of little "wit": the textual "play" (l. 321) of "men of Wit" (l. 325), like Simon's "Sport" (l. 239), is not required activity for the layman. This does not mean that more gifted men cannot employ their powers of reason to the advantage of religion:

> The few, by Nature form'd, with Learning fraught,
> Born to instruct, as others to be taught,
> Must study well the Sacred Page.
>
> [ll. 326–28]

But the "written word of God," as Whichcote put it, "is not the first or only discovery of the duty of man": they know it "first, in the *Soul.*" [53] Simon's work is a notable example of the beneficial activity of the "few." His book, "with various Learning fraught" (l. 244), was "wrought, at Nature's height" (ll. 245–46): in pointing most plainly to "Heaven's reveal'd Design" it exemplifies the highest form of rational activity. But his writings cannot "assure our doubtfull way" (l. 6); they can only decide which of many suggested expositions seem most plausible. In a similar way, the poet does not say that tradition must "be set aside," but he notes that it, like the original text of Scripture, has been subject to the abuses of human reason. The poet emphasizes that he does not mean to discard tradition where it has survived intact. Yet he assigns tradition, in its best present form, only a secondary role:

> Not that Traditions parts are useless here:
> When general, old, disinteress'd and clear:
> That Ancient Fathers thus expound the Page,
> Gives *Truth* the reverend Majesty of *Age:*
> *Confirms* its force, by biding every *Test;*
> For best Authorities, next Rules, are best.[54]
>
> [ll. 334–39]

53. See Powicke, *The Cambridge Platonists,* p. 31.

54. In this one instance I have departed from Kinsley's text which reads, "For best Authority's next Rules are best." Kinsley's version has

Tradition confirms and gives "reverend Majesty" to interpretations which have been formulated by reason's apprehension of Scripture. In its pristine form—the form we no longer possess—it would come closest to the original "Rule." It would actually approach the well-spring of supernatural light—the flow of illumination which the ancients could trace only to "Natures secret head" (l. 13), not to the "God-head" (l. 78), but which the deist thought he had found (ll. 43–44):

> And still the nearer to the Spring we go
> More limpid, more unsoyl'd the Waters flow.
> Thus, *first Traditions* were a proof alone;
> Cou'd we be *certain* such they *were,* so *known.*
>
> [ll. 340–43]

But the poet has already told us that when we "consider Interest, Church, and Gain" in the transmission of "oral Sounds" (ll. 271–75) we realize that this approach to the spring of revelation has been largely lost to man through the abuses of human reason straining beyond its proper sphere of activity. The metaphor of the unreachable spring reminds the reader that the final stage of the exordium (the advent of supernatural light and the dissolution of lesser forms of spiritual cognition in that light) is not possible at the present time. This is reflected in a deft shift in metaphor from the incline instrumental to the flow of a spring to a declivity of deterioration. The poet's description of the actual transmission of tradition mixes the faint outline of a downward slope ("long descent," "Rouls down") in the overall image of generative inheritance ("descent," "descends"):

> But since some Flaws in long descent may be,
> They make not *Truth* but *Probability.*

---

total textual authority but its sense is less clear. I have adopted Christie's version which conforms to the context: when the "Rule is mute," those traditions which are "general, old, disinteress'd and clear" are best: *The Poetical Works of John Dryden,* ed. W. D. Christie (London, 1874).

> Even *Arius* and *Pelagius* durst provoke
> To what the *Centuries preceding* spoke.
> Such difference is there in an oft-told Tale:
> But Truth by its own Sinews will prevail.
> *Tradition written* therefore more commends
> *Authority,* than what from *Voice* descends:
> And this, as perfect as its kind can be,
> Rouls down to us the Sacred History:
> Which, from the *Universal Church receiv'd,*
> Is *try'd,* and *after,* for its *self* believ'd.

[ll. 344–55]

Taken in the abstract, the passage reminds us that the finite, imperfect capacity of man's reason can only communicate a partial account of infinite perfection. To the same effect, tradition's offices have been described as "parts" (l. 334), and the disagreeing sects as "parts" which "talk loudly" (l. 315). But partial knowledge does not discourage the poet. He accepts it as included in the idea of human imperfection. Even the church fathers, Arius and Pelagius, differed from each other. The allusion to these heresiarchs, taken together with the attack on Arius's antagonist (Athanasius) and the hesitating condemnation of the "bold Socinian" (l. 312), represents a liberalization of attitude toward heresy which is one more step in the poem's movement toward the essentials of the religious life. The choice of these particular heresiarchs also contributes to the meaning of the poem by putting their opinions, which (as the seventeenth-century reader would have realized immediately) are in some ways close to the position of the poet,[55] in a less severe light. Like the poet, they were

55. Arius, like Dryden, opposed Athanasius on the restriction of salvation (cf. l. 220). The points of similarity between *Religio Laici* and Pelagius's views, as they were understood in Dryden's time, are evident in a comparison of the poem with the following account of Pelagius's position in Moreri's *Great Historical, Geographical, Genealogical and Poetical Dictionary* (London, 1701): he held "that there were three ways of

unwilling to damn man for partial knowledge. The poet, in the apostle's words, is satisfied, in the present state of revelation, to "know only in part" and to see with his *own* human reason "through a glass darkly." The rationalist's faith that truth will eventually be victorious, that "Truth by its own Sinews will prevail" (l. 349), is made part of the poet's faith that man's God-inspired reason is able to arrive at gospel truth, while it also helps dispel the bogie of heresy. "A man may be suffer'd," Dryden writes in the Preface, "to quote an Adversary to our Religion, when he speaks Truth" (ll. 304–05). The powers of human reason, though restless "rowling Fires" (l. 4), are sufficient to roll "down to us the Sacred History" and to "try" it so that partial, but true, knowledge of the Scriptures may be apprehended and then "for its self believ'd."

Theological Economics

The discussion of parts and partial knowledge revives a pattern of metaphor that has a key function in the development of the poem. I have postponed a discussion of earlier appearances of this pattern to the present place because it is here that its full force is felt. The poet's early objection to the ancients' and the deists' confusion of different planes of reality and reason—of the finite ground of human reason with the infinite ground of divine "Reasons" (cf. ll. 40, 114 and 196) and of human conceptions of "Justice in the last Appeal" with "His Justice" (ll. 95 and 49)—is merged, as the reader will have noticed, with a long series of commercial metaphors. The conclusions which the deist announces (ll. 44–61) are not, as we noted, false in themselves. What is false is the belief that

---

Salvation, *viz.* By the Law of Nature, Law of *Moses,* and Law of *Christ;* That the Works of the Heathen were truly good and acceptable to God, though performed without the Assistance of Grace. He confounded Grace with the Power of Nature, and extended it to the revealed Will of God, with a certain inward Illumination of the Mind, which was given for a Help."

they follow from the logic of commercialism in which no
absolute distinctions are recognized and in which all things are
exchangeable—in which all things can be bartered for vary-
ing quantities of stuffs. The deist reasons that:

> some *Rules* of Worship must be given,
> Distributed alike to all by Heaven:
> Else *God* were *partial,* and to *some* deny'd
> The Means his Justice shou'd for *all* provide.
> This *general Worship* is to *PRAISE,* and *PRAY:*
> One part to *borrow* Blessings, one to *pay:*
> And when frail Nature slides into *Offence,*
> The *Sacrifice* for *Crimes* is *Penitence.*

[ll. 46–53]

It is the deist's confusion of the finite realm of human reason
with the infinite world of the divine which forms the basis of
the poet's censures.[56] Dryden emphasizes that the confusion is

56. Harth has given us much valuable information about deism in the
London of the 1670s, but he seems unable to understand *Religio Laici*
as a self-modifying argument in which the elements of the poem help to
qualify and define each other. He insists on Dryden's categorical rejection
of deistic views as well as the principles of the Cambridge Platonists,
which he seems to identify with a naïve theory of innate ideas (cf. p.
127 and p. 130, n. 52). He rejects Ward's and others' accounts of the
probable influence on Dryden of the liberal theology inspired (during
his undergraduate years) by the Cambridge Platonists (cf. p. 17). Like
Bredvold, but in a different cause, he denies Dryden's innatist tendencies
in the passages from *The Life of Plutarch* and the preface to *Sylvae* by
restricting the applicability of Dryden's statements to a few "wise men"
(pp. 135–36). Never, Harth says, does Dryden show the "least sympathy"
for the view which makes "natural religion a matter of common notions
easily available to all mankind" (p. 134).

Harth is too intent on supporting his theory of a specific deist adversary
in the poem. His interpretation becomes inflexible and overstated:
"Dryden confronts the Deist's argument," he tells us, "not by denying
natural religion, but by insisting on its essentially a posteriori and in-
ductive character which, by limiting its availability to a restricted few,
would make it an unacceptable substitute for revelation" (p. 129). Dryden,
we recall, was not willing to discard "Indian Souls, and Worlds discover'd New": "by their Conscience" and "Natural Light," he decides,

caused by the materialistic imagination. The deist views religion as a transaction governed by merchants' "Rules." His vocabulary is that of a shopkeeper rather than a divine; his notions of equitable distribution require that the same "Means" be provided for all. God is viewed by him as a great lender from whom blessings are borrowed and to whom payment is made in the currency of praises and prayers. When the borrower breaks the rules and commits some "Offence" he is fined in "Penitence." The shallow character of the deist's thought is signalized by the casual use of *sacrifice* which here carries no consciousness of the Incarnation and Crucifixion.[57] Since, for the deist, all things differ only quantitatively and relatively—since he has no conception of abstract, qualitative differences—he blithely reasons from the part to the whole: God cannot be "partial"; the truth must be known to all. Because the universe must be founded on a notion of justice that is the same, he believes, as earthly models of "sovereignty," the deist feels competent to extrapolate from a part of reality, in which vice triumphs and virtue suffers, to the "future State" (l. 23) that escaped the reason of the ancients:

> . . . since th' Effects of Providence, we find
> Are variously dispens'd to Humane kind;
> That *Vice Triumphs,* and *Vertue suffers* here,
> (A Brand that Sovereign Justice cannot bear;)
> Our Reason prompts us to a *future* State:
> The *last Appeal* from *Fortune,* and from *Fate:*

---

they must be "condemn'd or freed." "Charity bids hope the best" (cf. ll. 179–209). It is true, as we have noted, that Dryden (like most of the Cambridge Platonists) rejected the naïve theory of innate ideas, but this theory, as we have seen, was a small part of contemporary innatist doctrine. It is remarkable that in an investigation which attempts to elucidate the meaning of Dryden's poetry, Harth can dismiss the traditional inscription formulations of Hooker and St. Paul as "no more than a metaphor" (p. 166). The crucial question remains: no more than a metaphor for what?

57. Price (p. 67) makes a similar point about the deist's use of *sacrifice.*

> Where God's all-righteous ways will be declar'd;
> The *Bad* meet *Punishment,* the *Good, Reward.*
>
> [ll. 54–61]

The deist can predict the "last Appeal" and its outcome because heaven and chancery cannot differ.

What the ancients initiated in aboriginal misapprehension of the relations of God and man the deist has elaborated into a more genteel arrangement. The ancients did not prescribe "Remorse, to Expiate Sin,"

> But slew their fellow Creatures for a Bribe:
> The guiltless *Victim* groan'd for their Offence;
> And *Cruelty,* and *Blood* was *Penitence.*
>
> [ll. 85–88]

Man, in short, has no business with infinity. When he tries to transcend the limits of his reason he only abuses his clear perceptions. The poet denies the validity of all arrangements made according to man's measurements of the value of infinity or its price (l. 113). The chasm between man's finite, imperfect existence and the infinite perfection of Heaven can only be bridged by God:

> For granting we have Sin'd, and that th' offence
> Of *Man,* is made against *Omnipotence,*
> Some Price, that bears *proportion,* must be paid;
> And *Infinite* with *Infinite* be weigh'd.
> See then the *Deist lost: Remorse* for *Vice,*
> *Not* paid, or *paid, inadequate* in price.
>
> [ll. 111–16]

The deist could never win salvation if left to the resources of his own reason. His reason deals in the finite; his salvation requires infinite payment for infinite offense.

Following this assertion of God's generosity, the poet asks,

> What farther means can *Reason* now direct,
> Or what Relief from *humane Wit* expect?

> *That* shews us *sick;* and sadly are we sure
> *Still* to be *Sick,* till *Heav'n* reveal the *Cure.*
>
> [ll. 117–20]

The immediate answer to this question, as we noted above, is that reason aids us even in pointing to our malady and in directing us to heaven's aid. But there is also a less obvious and more important answer which does not become clear until the poem approaches its conclusion. Because "Heav'ns early Care prescrib'd for every Age"—because a sufficiency of spiritual knowledge is available to unabused private reason—the discourse of the poet, as he ultimately tells us, can describe sacred truth (ll. 454–55) and even find some of the relief (l. 443) which once seemed unobtainable by "humane Wit." The function of the commercial metaphors is not only to present, as Hoffman correctly notes, "the mean departures from and venal corruptions of the relationship rendered initially in the borrowing of light lent from above," [58] but also, I think, to discover and cure the affliction of human reason with its "Corporeal Malady of Imagination" of which these "departures" and "corruptions" are symptomatic. The "Sacred Truth" toward which the poem has been moving is obtained and stated clearly when, in the last hundred lines, the scarifying work of these metaphors intensifies and joins forces with the de-emphasis of theological unessentials and the assertion of the divinely endowed sufficiency of human reason.

The full weight of the commercial metaphor is applied to the Roman Catholic Church and the Sectarians. The poet begins by renewing the recognition of the central failing in commercialistic reasoning. The papists, like the deist, repudiate partial and finite knowledge—the plain truths granted to human reason—and, like him, would make themselves "the last Appeal" (ll. 59 and 95) by arrogating powers of transmission and interpretation:

---

58. Hoffman, p. 69.

> The partial *Papists* wou'd infer from hence
> *Their* Church, in last resort, shou'd Judge the *Sense.*
> But first they wou'd assume, with wondrous Art,
> *Themselves* to be the *whole,* who are but *part*
> Of that vast Frame, the Church; yet grant they were
> The handers down, can they from thence infer
> A right t' interpret? or wou'd they alone
> Who brought the Present, claim it for their own?
> The *Book*'s a *Common Largess* to *Mankind;*
> Not more for *them,* than *every* Man design'd:
> The *welcome News* is in the *Letter* found;
> The *Carrier*'s not Commission'd to *expound.*
> It *speaks* it *Self,* and what it does contain,
> In all things *needfull* to be *known,* is *plain.*

[ll. 356–69]

Discontent with the limits of reason leads the papists to abuse
their own reason and that of others. There must be, according
to their way of thinking, an earthly "last resort" to the infinite.
Their partiality to themselves prompts them to set themselves
up as "Justice in the last Appeal"; they fail to see that "that
vast Frame, the Church"—"the Universal Church" (l. 354)—
was endowed for all men by "the first Fiat that produc'd our
Frame" (l. 155) and by the event of Incarnation, by "God
descending in [a] Humane Frame" (l. 107). When they look in
the "same Glass" darkly they should not assume "Themselves
to be the whole." It is "for Themselves they look, but not for
me" (ll. 301–02)—not for each private man who must find the
way to his salvation (l. 303) through his own silent judgment
of the sense of Scripture, which is plain in "all things needfull
to be known."

The abuses of the Roman Church are dwelt upon in order
to bring together the arguments of the poem concerning the
issues of commercialized, "gainfull" theology, unessential,
rusted theological machinery, and neglect of individual human

reason—the layman kept low, kept from plodding on to
heaven:

> In times o'ergrown with Rust and Ignorance,
> A gainfull Trade their Clergy did advance:
> When want of Learning kept the *Laymen* low,
> And none but *Priests* were *Authoriz'd* to *know:*
> When what small Knowledge was, in them did dwell;
> And he a *God* who cou'd but *Reade* or *Spell;*
> Then *Mother Church* did mightily prevail:
> She parcel'd out the Bible by *retail:*
> But still *expounded* what She *sold* or *gave;*
> To keep it in *her Power* to *Damn* and *Save:*
> *Scripture* was *scarce,* and as the Market went,
> Poor *Laymen* took *Salvation* on *Content;*
> As needy men take Money, good or bad:
> *God's* Word they had not, but the *Priests* they had.
> Yet, whate'er *false Conveyances* they made,
> The *Lawyer* still was *certain* to be paid.
> In those dark times they learn'd their knack so well,
> That by long use they grew *Infallible.*
>
> [ll. 370–87]

By means of key allusions, the poet summons up previous contexts and brings them to bear on the crisis which preceded the
Reformation. "Gold Divine" (l. 238) does not "rust," but this
is not the case with "Idle, Superstitious Ware" (l. 127) and
"old Sophisticated Ware" (l. 237). These are the accretions
of abused reason with which the papists are associated. They
plied their wares in order to advance themselves toward the
status of the infinite while they kept the layman low. Like the
deist, they presumed to godlike status with their "small Knowledge" so that their "Authoriz'd" position tended to turn them
into authors of the Scripture: in the end, the layman could
not tell "If they the Book, or That did them inspire" (l. 389).

The manner in which Mother Church mightily prevailed recalls the previous description of

> what *Errours* have been made
> Both in the *Copiers* and *Translaters Trade:*
> How *Jewish, Popish,* Interests have prevail'd
> And where *Infallibility* has *fail'd.*

[ll. 248–51]

The commercialistic interest and trade of the papists, through
which they wish to advance to knowledge and control of the
whole (l. 359)—to omniscience in expounding and omnipotence
in damning and saving—have the effect of destroying the
wholeness of Scripture and reducing it to parts by *parceling*
it out. Their "retail" dealings "cut up" (Fr. *retailler*) the
original instead of delivering it in a whole-sale, "in *gross*" (l.
322). Their "Infallibility has fail'd" in religious matters but
they have learned to do their business to perfection.

Factious Debate

The intensification of commercial metaphors and the com-
pounding of arguments concerning sufficiency and unessentials
point up the need for reforming the materialistic mode of
human reason. The Protestant Reformation is described as an
attempt to answer this need. The words *parcel'd* and *retail*
(in its etymological sense) may be intended to carry faint outlines of a land metaphor which are subtly renewed in the layman's rediscovery of the ground of his own reason and its use
in apprehending scriptural truth:

> At last, a knowing Age began t' enquire
> If *they* the *Book,* or *That* did *them* inspire:
> And, making narrower search they found, thô late,
> That what they thought the *Priest*'s, was *Their* Estate:
> Taught by the *Will produc'd,* (the written Word)
> How long they had been *cheated* on *Record.*

Then, every man who saw the Title fair,
Claim'd a Child's part, and put in for a Share:
Consulted Soberly his private good;
And sav'd himself as cheap as e'er he cou'd.

                                        [ll. 388–97]

With the coming of the Reformation, the layman suddenly
realized that revelation had been given equally to all mankind: the interpretation of Scripture was each individual
soul's "Estate." But the individual was not content to use his
reason only for apprehending the truth necessary for salvation.
He too confused the finite ground of his reason with the divine
ground of revelation: like the papist, he split the Scripture
into parts and shares in an effort to buy salvation at a bargain,
to the exclusion or neglect of others. He lacked an understanding of the mercy of God operating in the innate capacity of
human reason, which makes fighting over parts of the text
unnecessary.

In reality, therefore, though the poet's description of the
freehold rationale of the Reformation contributes an extreme
position which helps determine the poem's final synthesis—
the unpresuming ground of reason—he notes that little change
in the materialism of human reason was brought about by
the Reformation itself. Where the rediscovery of the universal
intent of revelation should have led to greater reliance on
God's mercy and the capacity of individual reason to guide
man "upward," the Reformation instead encouraged each man
to become a public disputant and a greedy claimant:

'Tis true, my Friend, (and far be Flattery hence)
This good had full as bad a Consequence:
The Book thus put in every vulgar hand,
Which each presum'd he best cou'd understand,
The *Common Rule* was made the *common Prey;*
And at the mercy of the *Rabble* lay.
The tender Page with horney Fists was gaul'd;

And he was gifted most that loudest baul'd:
The *Spirit* gave the *Doctoral Degree:*
And every member of a *Company*
Was of *his Trade,* and of the *Bible free.*
Plain *Truths* enough for needfull *use* they found;
But men wou'd still be itching to *expound:*
Each was ambitious of th' obscurest place,
No measure ta'n from *Knowledge,* all from *GRACE.*
Study and *Pains* were now no more their Care;
Texts were explain'd by *Fasting,* and by *Prayer:*
This was the Fruit the *private Spirit* brought;
Occasion'd by *great Zeal,* and *little Thought.*

[ll. 398–416]

John Smith's observation that a fundamental purpose of the
Cambridge group was to teach man not "too zealously to
propugne the Dogmata of any Sect" [59] well describes the attitude of *Religio Laici.* The public dispute and disturbance
which the Reformation initiated represent, as the poet suggests, continued manifestations of degenerate human reason
and its "Notionality, or Multiplicity of ineffectual Opinions"
(to use More's phrase). Insofar as Simon's *Critical History* contributes to such disturbance it too is marked for censure and
not flattered. Even the most unlearned layman should be able
to find "Plain Truths enough for needful use" through his own
reason, which has been endowed by God's mercy; there is no
need for a feverish concern with "Grace." [60] But each man is

59. *The Cambridge Platonists,* ed. Campagnac, p. 88.
60. We can now turn profitably to the statement of Elias J. Chiasson,
"Dryden's Apparent Scepticism in *Religio Laici,*" p. 215, that Dryden,
"like most Anglicans," rejects the "precise point . . . that the common
notions (rationally derivable) can perform a function which Dryden . . .
restricts to a very special economy—the economy of grace, the only
known centre of which lies in the mystery of the Incarnation." Dryden's
whole poem can be viewed as a complex comment on the technicality which
Chiasson disposes of in a parenthesis: what does "rationally derivable"
mean in a system where man's reason is divinely endowed and grace is

"ambitious of th' obscurest place" in the infinitely distant
ground of revelation. The collective vanity and arrogance of
ambitious individuals tends to invert man's true relationship
to the divine: such men subject the Scriptures to their mercy
(l. 403) and, like the deist, impose their rules of trade on the
divine. Their commercialistic thinking, however, represents a
far greater threat than deism because it incorporates the zeal
(l. 416) of Athanasius and the papists which damns "all for
Hereticks who durst oppose" (ll. 216–23 and l. 379). In his
pride, the deist thought that his wit bred "God-like Notions,"
that the truths of revelation were the product of his mind (ll.
65–66). The poet's allusion to the recent experiments (with
blow-flies) of Francesco Redi, who had destroyed the myth of
"spontaneous generation," evidently exposes the vain and
fraudulent "inspiration" of the sects that do not really discover
anything new:

> While Crouds unlearn'd, with rude Devotion warm,
> About the Sacred Viands buz and swarm,
> The *Fly-blown Text* creates a *crawling Brood*;
> And turns to *Maggots* what was meant for *Food.*
> A *Thousand daily Sects rise up, and dye;*
> A *Thousand more the perish'd Race supply.*[61]
>
> [ll. 417–22]

The association of the word *Sects* with insects characterizes the

---

associated with God's bountiful mercy (l. 196)—shown even to heathens—
rather than, as in the negative example at line 412, with doctrinal
formality?

61. Dryden's debt in these lines is twofold. The immediate source was
undoubtedly Samuel Butler's *Hudibras,* III, ii, 7 ff., where a line-by-line
resemblance can be noted. Dryden's more profound debt, however, was
to the Italian scientist whose experiments with blow-flies and spontaneous
generation were made known by the Royal Society in 1670 (cf. *Philosophical Transactions of the Royal Society,* London, 1809, I, 429–32). Butler's
lines, written shortly after 1670, also seem to make use of an allusion to
Redi's work, but it is only for the purpose of representing the unthinking
destructiveness of the sects.

dehumanization of reason which commercial ambition for the "obscurest place" produces. The sects range themselves like ignorant armies clashing endlessly and to no purpose. Like the abusers of reason who came before them, they are (to use Dryden's phrase in *the Apology for . . . Poetic Licence*) "cozened by the fiction" of an earthly "image" which they are pleased to believe *is* the divine reality. They populate a spectacle of chaos from which no one is exempted:

> So all we make of Heavens discover'd Will
> Is, not to have it, or to use it ill.
> The Danger's much the same; on several Shelves
> If *others* wreck *us,* or *we* wreck our *selves.*

> [ll. 423–26]

Not only is the well-spring of supernatural light unavailable to us, but we also lose access to the available sufficiency of natural light through abuse of the ground of reason—"several Shelves." Either "others wreck us" by transmitting a corrupt text so that we do not have it; or "we wreck our selves" by not following reason to apprehend "Plain truths enough for needfull use."

The "Sun of Righteousnesse"

The account of "those dark times" (l. 386) was placed so late in the poem because the thinking and practices of the papists recapitulate, as we have seen, in intensified form, the abuses of reason which have been previously represented and because, according to my view, the account of the ensuing Protestant revolt furnishes an impulse for reform and resynthesis. The historical reformation turned out to be a delusion— "This good had full as bad a Consequence" (l. 399)—in that the degeneracy of human reason only changed its outward form: the yoke of the Church was thrown off but men still confounded trade and revelation (l. 408).

Yet the poet does not waste the energies of bitter disappoint-

ment. He despairs of public reform of the abuses of reason—
thousands of warring sects have accomplished nothing—but
he does not lose hope for the potential of the individual reason
to reform itself; there have been some "who follow'd Reasons
Dictates right" (l. 208) and others for whom martyrdom was
the only price or reward expected (l. 145). The poet's final
exhortation, therefore, is to the individual and concerns individual belief and actions, just as the last six lines of the
poem are a defense of individual expression. A tone of genuine
"last resort" (l. 357) is adopted which, in its laboring seriousness, contrasts sharply with the easy *quod est demonstrandum*
manner of the deist and the papists:

> What then remains, but, waving each Extreme,
> The Tides of Ignorance, and Pride to stem?
> Neither so rich a Treasure to forgo;
> Nor proudly seek beyond our pow'r to know:
> Faith is not built on disquisitions vain;
> The things we *must* believe, are *few,* and *plain.*
>
> [ll. 427–32]

The "last Appeal" of the poet does not presume on comprehension of the infinite. With his private reason he appeals to
the private reason of other individuals to reform the abuses of
reason. He speaks as one lonely traveler (l. 2) to another and
may intend in "Tides" that we recall the opening image of the
poem—the energy of the moon as reason (ll. 1–3)—when he
creates his final metaphor of reformation. The tides of ignorance—of not having revelation—and of pride—of using it ill
—are produced by the moon of reason at its *extremes.* These
extremes, however, can be avoided and the light of the moon
itself can serve as a useful guide in making our way upward
(l. 7). If we "stem" the tides and preserve the ground of reason
unabused—if we do not try to rise above this ground by reasoning or building on "disquisitions"—we can apprehend the
"things we must believe." The allusion to "Treasure" seems to

reflect the work of reformation which the poet intends: the word refers most directly perhaps to the "Gold Divine" (l. 238) of God's written word; but it may also allude to the "Cœlestial Wealth" of God's mercy (ll. 105–06), which has paid for man's sins and endowed his reason so that he can find a treasure (l. 240) of knowledge by his own power. This quest for abstract spiritual treasure reforms the "materious" commercial abuse of reason that proudly seeks "beyond our power to know" and restores the relationship in which man is satisfied with the true conceptions that God permits him to *borrow* (l. 1).

The relationship of the individual to a church is shown to be only of secondary importance for salvation. The essentials of "needfull Faith" (l. 300) are plain to each man's reason. The problem is not one of sufficient knowledge. "We want not," said Smith in this connection, "so much means of knowing what we ought to doe, as Wills to doe that which we may know." [62] Men's wills are perverse: they "will believe more than they need; / And every man will make himself a Creed" (ll. 433–34). The Church was once closest to knowledge of the infinite but now it is a guide in unessentials and keeps the individual will from dangerous errors in its search for the unnecessary: "In doubtfull questions"—those matters which are not "plain" and, therefore, do not concern "things we must believe" (l. 432)—

> 'tis the safest way
> To learn what unsuspected Ancients say:
> For 'tis not likely *we* shou'd higher Soar
> In search of Heav'n, then *all the Church before:*
> Nor can we be deceiv'd, unless we see
> The *Scripture,* and the *Fathers disagree.*
>
> [ll. 435–40]

Contrary to Verrall's and Nichol Smith's suggestions, I do not think that there is any indication here of a view that private

62. John Smith, *Select Discourses*, p. 15.

beliefs should be altered for the sake of politics or expedience. The reason of the individual, "lonely" (l. 2) as it may be, remains sacred and sufficient for private salvation:

> If after all, they [the Church Fathers] stand suspected still,
> (For no man's Faith depends upon his Will;)
> 'Tis some Relief, that points not clearly known,
> Without much hazard may be let alone.
>
> [ll. 441–44]

Reason, not will, apprehends the essential truths of Scripture which faith must absorb. The "doubtfull questions" upon which will ranges and the Church comments are unnecessary for salvation and should be ignored altogether when conflict arises: the Church's view of essentials should neither be accepted privately nor disputed publicly when it seems mistaken to the individual. Public peace is more important than unessential, obscure points:

> . . . after hearing what our Church can say,
> If still our Reason runs another way,
> That private Reason 'tis more Just to curb,
> Than by Disputes the publick Peace disturb.
> For points obscure are of small use to learn:
> But *Common quiet* is *Mankind's concern.*
>
> [ll. 445–50][63]

In the end, therefore, no external authority is designated as absolute in matters of salvation. The reliance on the Church which the poet suggests is clearly of secondary importance in

63. These same ideas, together with an emphasis on charity, occur in *An Essay on Man,* ed. Maynard Mack (London, 1950), III, 305–10:

> For Modes of Faith, let graceless zealots fight;
> His can't be wrong whose life is in the right:
> In Faith and Hope the world will disagree,
> But all Mankind's concern is Charity:
> All must be false that thwart this One great End,
> And all of God, that bless Mankind or mend.

relation to essential questions. The layman is told to "curb" the public expression of his private reason, not to change his convictions.[64] The poet speaks here of what is "just" to mankind, not of what God requires for salvation.

His belief in the innate power of man's Candle of the Lord or ground of reason has carried him far, just as it did the Cambridge Platonists. In the course of developing its ramifications he has, like them, opposed absolute reprobation, deemphasized the fall of man, decreased his dependence on scriptural interpretation, adopted a more tolerant attitude toward heresiarchs, and, most important, sought to pacify religious dispute by emphasizing communal tranquility. Like Boehme, he has emphasized that "the Being, Essence, or Substance of God, so far as he is called God, is understood to be *without* ground, place and time . . . he is no Image, nor needeth any place to dwell in, neither should man seek for him in any place, but only in his formed out-spoken or expressed word, viz. in the Image of God in Man himself. . . . And this is the right and neerest way to God; for the Image of God to sink down in it self from all imprinted Images: and forsake all Images Disputation and Contention." [65] The poet stops just short of the secularized disintegration of religious feeling— of man's relation to God—toward which the Platonists were moving unawares.[66] Their confidence in the Candle of the Lord and their desire for a concrete expression of man's regenerate nature drew them more and more from *theoria* to *praxis*. The inevitable result of this in their disciples was a diminution of consciousness of the divine and of the ultimate Christian goal, spiritual salvation.

In the development of natural religion at the beginning of the eighteenth century, the illumination of the God within

the law of public should take place, they breed disturbance" (*Laws*, I, xvi, 6).

64. When men follow "the law of private reason," said Hooker, "where
65. *Concerning the Election of Grace*, p. 7.
66. Cf. Lichtenstein, *Henry More*, pp. 156–205.

would soon be reduced to conscience. In *Religio Laici,* however, the movement from religion to practical morality is not
open-ended or uncontrolled. The poet never deserts the God-
infused idea of *caritas* for mere philanthropy. Divine Charity
(ll. 212 and 224) as manifested in God and man, we have seen,
is at the center of the poem where it preserves an order of dis-
abused reason or imagination that is truly sympathetic. The
conclusion of the argument, "Common quiet is Mankind's concern," calls for a tangible expression of reformed private reason. The poet's willingness to commend freely the theological
researches of a man whose church he must still condemn is
one such expression. But the poem avoids preoccupation with
practical morality for its own sake. The only *praxis* spoken
of is that which flows directly from the restoration of unam-
bitious, self-sufficient private reason and which is a condition
of its further unhampered operation in apprehending the
truths of "needfull Faith" (l. 300) in God. We need no longer
wonder, I hope, what has become of religious concerns by the
time the poet concludes his argument.

Religio Laici turns inward. Its subject, reason, is its method,
and its method is its achievement. Ratiocination is used to
purify Discourse (l. 71) so that by the end of the poem Discourse (l. 454) can once again be the instrument of divinely
endowed reason that it was meant to be—an instrument for
finding sacred truth.[67] Such it is in the hands of the poet:

> Thus have I made my own Opinions clear:
> Yet neither Praise expect, nor Censure fear:
> And this unpolish'd, rugged Verse, I chose;
> As fittest for Discourse, and nearest Prose:
> For, while from *Sacred Truth* I do not swerve,

67. The remark by Lamprecht, "Innate Ideas in the Cambridge
Platonists," p. 571, concerning the Cambridge Platonists applies equally
to the close of *Religio Laici:* "the seeming secularization of the foundation
of theological doctrine is offset by the . . . reiteration of the semi-divine
nature of the voice of reason."

Tom Sternhold's, or *Tom Shadwell's Rhimes* will serve.

[ll. 451–56]

Having left himself "no right," as he tells us in the Preface, "to interpret obscure places . . . because whatsoever is obscure is concluded not necessary to be known" (ll. 142–45), the poet has stepped into the arena of "points obscure" (l. 449) in order to stop the fight. He has made a public statement that public dispute must cease because the regeneration of reason must begin with a confrontation of degenerate forces. He has ventured into the chaos of dispute—much as he will enter into an "abyss" in *The Hind and the Panther* (I, 66)—to retrieve private reason *through* private reason. He rests assured that his poem is not merely one more bawling cry (cf. l. 405) because his reason is free of materialistic taint: like the "men unskill'd in Arts" who spoke divine truth, though "Unask'd their Pains, ungratefull their Advice, / Starving their Gain, and Martyrdom their Price" (ll. 140–45), the poet has spoken yet he neither expects "Praise," nor fears "Censure." His verse is "nearest Prose," the vehicle best suited for stating truth. As long as he adheres to the abstract vision of sacred truth furnished by his divinely endowed discourse,[68] as long as he does not "swerve" from the path of his private reason, even

68. G. M. Turnell's interesting study, "Dryden and the Religious Elements in the Classical Tradition," *Englische Studien,* LXX (1935–36), 244–61, depended too heavily on Bredvold's argument for Dryden's early Roman Catholic and Pyrrhonistic tendencies. Turnell, following Bredvold's interpretation of *Religio Laici,* attempts to use Dryden's poetry as proof for the argument that "classicism stands for outside authority, romanticism for the authority of the 'inner voice'" and that the "classical artist is regarded not as a seer" (pp. 246 and 254). *Religio Laici* cannot, it seems to me, be enlisted as evidence for such generalizations, which will not even be found convincing in relation to Horace—Dryden's classical model in *Religio Laici* (Preface, ll. 345–46). William K. Wimsatt, Jr. has remarked, for example, that Horace's poetry offers "evidence that the poet's divine inspiration was still a current concept"; see William K. Wimsatt, Jr. and Cleanth Brooks, *Literary Criticism: A Short History* (New York, 1957), p. 92.

the monotonous "Rhimes" of Sternhold and Shadwell[69]—
types of unskilled artists and men of little wit—can be used
to plod on to Heaven. Vaughan understood that Dryden was
using "reason's light" to disabuse reason,[70] that with God's
help reason was finding its way back to reason. In his un-

69. The particular choice of Sternhold and Shadwell is not easily explained. Dryden does say in the Preface to the poem that he has
"studied" Horace, not merely "read" him, and that he hopes "the style
of his Epistles is not ill imitated here" (ll. 345–46). It would seem quite
clear that line 454 especially asks us to keep Horace in mind. In 1697,
Dryden showed how powerfully the epigraph of *Religio Laici* (taken from
Manilius, *Astron.* iii, 39) was bound up with his conceptions of Horace:
he tells us that Horace's "*Satires* and *Epistles,* being intended wholly for
instruction, required another style: *Ornari res ipsa negat, contenta doceri:*
and therefore, as he himself professes, are *sermoni propiora,* nearer prose
than verse" (*Essays of John Dryden,* ed. W. P. Ker, Oxford, 1900, II, 214–
15).

One feature of Horace's *Epistles* which may have especially appealed to
Dryden is the allusions of the *Epistles* to characters in the *Satires* and
Odes. (See Jacques Perret, *Horace,* trans. Bertha Humez, New York, 1964,
pp. 103–04, for a discussion of this practice.) Dryden's satire of Shadwell,
Mac Flecknoe, had appeared in print only a short while before *Religio
Laici.* The freshness of the satire in the public mind may have suggested
itself to Dryden, it seems to me, as an opportunity for imitating Horace's
method of using allusion to heighten the tone of conversational, proselike
reality. The same observation may apply to the choice of Sternhold and
the linking of Sternhold with Shadwell: in Dryden's contribution to the
Second Part of *Absalom and Achitophel,* published almost simultaneously
with *Religio Laici,* he called Shadwell and Elkanah Settle (Og and Doeg)
worse rhymers than even Sternhold and Hopkins (ll. 402–11) and at line
488 Shadwell is again associated with poor translation of the Psalms. The
specific suggestion for linking Shadwell with Sternhold may have come,
as has been previously suggested, from Settle: in the *Preface to Ibrahim*
(reprinted from the edition of 1677, intro. Hugh Macdonald, Oxford,
1947), p. 10, Settle calls Shadwell "Our Hopkin Rhimer" in answer to
Shadwell's charge, in the preface to *The Libertine,* that Settle was "a
rough hobling, rhymer"; cf. Macdonald's introduction, p. iv, and Kinsley,
vol. IV, 1925, for his comment on line 403 of the Second Part of *Absalom
and Achitophel.* Samuel Woodford might have added that, as a poet of
religious truth, it was perfectly appropriate for Dryden to be so sensitive to poor paraphrases upon the Psalms of David.

70. *Works of John Dryden,* x, 35.

glamorous effort on behalf of the peace of mankind, the poet leaves behind the moon of inconstant knowledge and the stars of ineffectual opinion to act in accordance with divine "Light" —the "hearty and sincere Love of God and a mans neighbour." *Religio Laici* has finally created a ratiocinative "Sun of Righteousnesse."

7

Transversion, Conversion, and Revision: *The Hind and the Panther*

Of all Dryden's original poems, *The Hind and the Panther* is not only the longest but the least understood. The high quality of its verse has often been recognized, but no one has been able to speak of its mixture of beast fable and polemics as a unified whole. It was first published in the spring of 1687 when the country, Dryden tells us, was in high "Ferment." [1] Second and third editions were called for in the same year, but then its popularity suddenly waned. The religious controversies which had made it a subject of popular attention came to an end: as Scott noted, the poem was left "a disregarded wreck, stranded upon the shores which the surges once occupied." [2] But changes on the religious and political scene cannot, by themselves, account for the eclipse in interest which the work suffered. The poem, it may be noted, soon came to be considered poetically unworthy. Dryden's opponents had braced themselves for an onslaught of irresistible force but were relieved to find that, as the world thought, the mighty poet had nodded for the space of twenty-six hundred lines. Shortly after the poem made its appearance, one of Dryden's more moderate assailants, Thomas Heyrick, wrote:

When the Pamphlet of the Hind *and the* Panther

1. *The Hind and the Panther,* "To the Reader," l. 1.
2. *Works of John Dryden,* x, 97.

came out under so celebrated a Name, . . . I read it with as much eager desire as Curiosity could possibly create, reasonably supposing, the utmost could be said for the Cause of the Hind *was there. . . . But it cannot be imagined what a surprize I was in to find, that all the seemingly dreadful Host prov'd no more than that ridiculous Army drawn up upon the Mountains, which once made even* Alexander *stand, but was afterwards with laughter found to be but Troops of Apes.*[3]

This is, of course, the contemporary reaction of one whose judgment was primed to find fault. But from that time to this no one, even among the poet's appreciators, has offered any substantial argument for the fighting power of Dryden's "dreadful Host."

"This Constitutional Absurdity"

The opinion of Dr. Johnson, whose own judgment was perhaps "a little bribed" against the subject,[4] confirms the negative appraisals published in the late 1680s and has become standard:

The scheme of the work is injudicious and incommodious; for what can be more absurd than that one beast should counsel another to rest her faith upon a pope and council? . . . The original incongruity runs through the whole: the king is now Cæsar, and now the Lyon; and the name Pan is given to the Supreme Being.[5]

3. Thomas Heyrick (brother of Robert Herrick), *The New Atlantis. A Poem, In Three Books. With some Reflections upon the Hind and the Panther* (London, 1687), sig. [2πr].

4. Johnson felt that because Pope was a Roman Catholic his "judgement was perhaps a little bribed by the subject." He tells us that Pope "used to mention this poem as the most correct specimen of Dryden's versification."—Samuel Johnson, *Lives of the English Poets,* ed. George Birkbeck Hill (Oxford, 1905), I, 443.

5. Ibid., I, 442–45.

Johnson insists that the failure of the poem is to be ascribed
not to incidental details but to a blunder in fundamental conception: the poem suffers from "ridiculousness of . . . first
elements," "original impropriety," and "constitutional absurdity." [6] He tells us that

> This absurdity was very properly ridiculed in *The City
> Mouse and the Country Mouse* of Montague and Prior;
> and in the detection and censure of the incongruity of
> the fiction chiefly consists the value of their performance.[7]

Perhaps no other anti-poem in English has been as de-
vastating in its effects as *The Hind and the Panther Transvers'd to the Story of The Country Mouse and the City-Mouse*
(1687). It was immediately hailed as an epitome of just parody
and has since become a time-honored reference in introduc-
tions to Dryden's poem. It is said to have launched Montague
and Prior in their careers,[8] while it effectively ended that of
The Hind and the Panther. As an artistic creation, the satire-
of-the-satire is worse than mediocre, but as a catalogue of
alleged faults, which have become the stock in trade of sub-
sequent criticism of the poem, it is extremely useful. No defense of *The Hind and the Panther* can succeed without turning aside its major thrusts; for it strikes at the very heart of
the poem.

6. Ibid., I, 446. Notable among modern dismissals of the poem are those
of Sir Herbert Grierson, who condemned it for its extreme "want of
spiritual content" (*Cross Currents in English Literature of the xviith
Century*, London, 1929, p. 317), and C. S. Lewis, who asked, "what are we
to say if not that the very design of conducting in verse a theological
controversy allegorized as a beast fable suggests in the author a state of
mind bordering on aesthetic insanity?" (*Rehabilitations and Other
Essays*, London, 1939, pp. 8–9).

7. Ibid., I, 443.

8. See *The Literary Works of Matthew Prior,* ed. H. Bunker Wright
and Monroe K. Spears (Oxford, 1959), II, 831–32. All citations from
Montague and Prior in my text are to this edition.

Montague's animadversions on "the General Design" sum up the most serious hits of the parody:

> *Is it not as easie to imagine two* Mice *bilking Coachmen, and supping at the* Devil; *as to suppose a* Hind *entertaining the* Panther *at a* Hermits Cell, *discussing the greatest Mysteries of Religion, and telling you her son* Rodriguez *writ very good Spanish? What can be more improbable and contradictory to the Rules and Examples of all Fables, and to the very design and use of them? . . . Fables carry a double meaning; the Story is one and intire; the Characters the same throughout, not broken or chang'd, and always conformable to the Nature of the Creatures they introduce. They never tell you that the Dog which snapt at a shadow, lost his Troop of Horse, that would be unintelligible; a piece of Flesh is proper for him to drop, and the Reader will apply it to mankind; they would not say that the Daw who was so proud of her borrow'd Plumes lookt very ridiculous when* Rodriguez *came and took away all the book but the* 17th, 24th, *and* 25th *Chapters, which she stole from him: But this is his new way of telling a story, and confounding the* Moral *and the* Fable *together. . . .*
>
> *What relation has the* Hind *to our Saviour? or what notion have we of a* Panther's *Bible? If you say he means the* Church, *how does the Church feed on Lawns, or range in the Forest. Let it be always a Church, or always the cloven-footed Beast, for we cannot bear his shifting the scene every Line.*[9]

These are well-aimed blows. Dryden's choice of emblems appears to be both adventitious and incongruous. Scott understood these charges but offered that "perhaps . . . it is sufficient for the fabulist, if he can point out certain original and leading features of resemblance betwixt his emblems and that

9. Preface, ll. 9–33.

which they are intended to represent, and he may be permitted to take considerable latitude in their further approximation." As precedent for this practice, he cites Spenser's *Mother Hubberd's Tale* (to which Dryden himself appeals for authority at line 8 of the Third Part) and Chaucer's *Nun's Priest's Tale*.[10] Earl Miner has further argued that Dryden was building on typological, zoögraphic, and exegetical conventions of the Middle Ages and the Renaissance.[11] But we must remember that neither Spenser's nor Chaucer's animals represent divine creatures and that there is no apparent reason for us to accept readily Dryden's representation of the Hind as supernatural. Miner's annotations have not provided any compelling or specific precedents to counter what must seem the essential truth of Prior's overstatement: "The C: of R: is no more like a Hind than 'tis like an Elephant, & the Rhinoceros is as good a representation of the C. of E. as the Panther."[12] In a tradition so heavily dependent on specific sacred iconography, novel, random symbolizing must seem gauche and ridiculous. Where objects of faith are concerned, one cannot expect a willing suspension of disbelief.

The complaint that in fables "the Story is one and intire; the Characters the same throughout, not broken or chang'd" and the observation that Dryden confounds "the Moral and the Fable together" are, of course, related. They are "first elements" in the "ridiculousness" Johnson saw in the sparring of two animals that ends in one advising the other "to rest her faith upon a pope and council." Miner's explanation of Dryden's "deliberate purpose in his choice of . . . discontinuous metaphor" contains much of value,[13] but it does not dispel the charge of fundamental absurdity which generations of readers—trained, perhaps, in the classroom of Montague

10. *Works of John Dryden*, x, 93–94.
11. Earl Miner, *Dryden's Poetry* (Bloomington, Ind., 1967), pp. 144–205.
12. Prior, II, 833.
13. Miner, pp. 151 ff.

and Prior—have felt to be just. Miner, I believe, begs the question when he writes:

> Has not his sensibility somehow got dissociated by critics unable to believe that Dryden might jest on serious occasions and at his work as it proceeds? A sense of humor is not among the things Dryden was required to give up at conversion. Such passages are, in short, to be enjoyed for their absurdity and especially, as so often with our poet, for the added point given to what has (in its very absurdity) a special claim to attention.[14]

No one, I think, would deny that Dryden employs humor and sarcasm to win his points. The passages that Miner cites in illustration of his argument (II, 18–30, 52–60) are of this kind. But this controlled humor must not be confused with the absurdity that threatens the dignity of the Hind as a symbol of the divine and, in fact, endangers the high seriousness of the poem as a whole.

Montague and Prior point out that the beast fable itself offers two more difficulties. First, Dryden "confounds" not only moral and fable but also man and beast. We hear the following exchange between Bayes (Dryden) and his interlocutors, in which he describes another beauty in his rag-bag poem.

> *Bayes.* . . . come, Gentlemen, let us return to our Business, and here I'le give you a delicate description of a Man.
>
> *Smith.* But how does that come in?
>
> *Bayes.* Come in? very naturally. I was talking of a *Wolf* and that supposes a Wood, and then I clap an Epithet to 't, and call it a *Celtic Wood:* Now when I was there, I could not help thinking of the *French Persecution,* and I'gad from all these Thoughts I took occasion to

14. Ibid., p. 148.

rail at the *French King,* and show that he was not of
the same make with other Men.[15]

It is difficult to find a defense against this imputation of
stream-of-consciousness chaos. How does a lengthy description
of the unique qualities of man, or *a* man, fit into a fable in
which men and their institutions are being represented by a
beast fable?

Second, Montague and Prior object that the plot of the
fable is truncated and pointless.

> *Bayes.* . . . Well Gentlemen! Thus far I have followed
> Antiquity, and as *Homer* has numbered his Ships, so I
> have rang'd my Beasts. Here is my *Boar* and my *Bear,*
> and my *Fox,* and my *Wolf,* and the rest of 'em all
> against my poor *Mouse.* Now what do you think I do
> with all these?
>
> *Smith.* Faith I don't know, I suppose you make 'em fight.
>
> *Bayes.* Fight! I'gad I'd as soon make 'em Dance. No, I do
> no earthly thing with 'em, nothing at all, I'gad: I think
> they have play'd their Parts sufficiently already; I have
> walk'd 'em out, show'd 'em to the Company, and
> rais'd your Expectation. And now whilst you hope to
> see 'em bated, and are dreaming of Blood and Battels,
> they sculk off, and you hear no more of 'em.[16]

Even Saintsbury, a defender of *The Hind and the Panther,*
registered similar criticism in noting that the poem "is so entirely desultory that it could not prove anything; . . . [it]
ends abruptly." [17]

Montague and Prior were quick to suggest a reason for this
seeming truncation and later commentators have repeated

15. *The Hind and the Panther Transvers'd,* ll. 268–77.
16. Ibid., ll. 228–39.
17. George Saintsbury, *Dryden* (New York, 1881), pp. 79 and 97.

their suggestion. They took their cue from Dryden's own remark in the preface:

> *About a Fortnight before I had finish'd it, His Majesties
> Declaration for Liberty of Conscience came abroad:
> which, if I had so soon expected, I might have spar'd
> my self the labour of writing many things which are con-
> tain'd in the third part of it.*[18]

In the parodists' hands this becomes an admission of frustrated
purpose.

> *Bayes.* Wars! why there had bin bloody Wars, tho' they
> were pretty well reconcil'd now. Yet to bring in two
> or three . . . fine things . . . , I don't tell you the
> Lyon's Peace was proclaim'd till fifty pages after, tho
> 'twas really done before I had finish'd my Poem.[19]

Although Dryden tells us that his effort to persuade the Church
of England to remove the Penal Laws and the Test was only
"one Design of the poem," [20] Scott also was willing to say
that the "change of political measures, which took place
while the poem was composing, has greatly injured its unity
and consistence." [21]

Conversion and Revision

The weapon of transversion was especially effective against
The Hind and the Panther because it could be used to suggest that Dryden's adventitious, easily altered prosopopoeia
reflected the fickleness and insincerity of his Roman Catholic
conversion. There is more than a hint of this charge, for example, in the exchange between Bayes and Smith concerning
the "predestinating ears" (I, 165) of the Presbyterians:

18. "To the Reader," ll. 59–62.
19. *The Hind and the Panther Transvers'd*, ll. 170–73.
20. "To the Reader," ll. 64–65.
21. Scott, *Life of John Dryden*, ed. Kreissman, p. 278.

> *Smith.* Pray Mr. *Bays,* if any of 'em should come over to
> the *Royal Party,* would their Ears alter?

> *Bayes.* Would they? Aye, I gad, they would shed their
> *Fanatical Lugs,* and have just such well-turn'd *Ears* as
> I have; mind this *Ear,* this is a true *Roman Ear,* mine
> are much chang'd for the better within this two years.

> *Smith.* Then if ever the Party should chance to fail, you
> might lose 'em, *for what may change, may fall.*[22]

The last five words are quoted from the Hind's own criticism
of the Panther's changeability:

> There chang'd your faith, and what may change may fall.
> Who can believe what varies every day,
> Nor ever was, nor will be at a stay?
>
> [II, 35–37]

Without prompting, Dryden realized that his recent conversion left him open to the very same charge: in fact, the disparity between the poet's acknowledged record of faith-changes
and his desire for an immutable faith—"immortal and unchang'd" (I, 1)—provides much of the interest that his voice
holds for us. Lines 68–77 of the First Part are (among other
things) a *confessio* of convertibility: they describe the poet's
own changeable "nature" and his "shame." His acute consciousness of this charge is also apparent in the Panther's
attack on the Hind's recent converts:

> who unfed
> Have follow'd you for miracles of bread;
> Such who themselves of no religion are,
> Allur'd with gain, for any will declare.
>
> [III, 195–98]

The Hind's defense argues that it is a desire to endure which
is their real motive:

22. *The Hind and the Panther Transvers'd,* ll. 192–98.

My Proselytes are struck with awfull dread,
Your bloudy Comet-laws hang blazing o're their head.
The respite they enjoy but onely lent,
The best they have to hope, protracted punishment.

[III, 380–83]

It has not been noted before that Dryden's procedure in
The Hind and the Panther is designed to avoid the imputation
that his new faith represents a venal conversion from "no
religion." He takes great pains to indicate that his change of
faith is a *conversion* in the best sense: that is, that he has not
simply discarded his old faith or acquired a new one *ex nihilo,*
but that he has reviewed and revised what were before de-
voutly held convictions. Poetry, especially poetry with a Neoplatonic bias, is admirably suited to representing such revision.
Having converted in his heart, he proceeded to convert his
poetic vision. It must be laid to the credit of his genius for
decorum, subtlety, and poise that the process which unfolds
before us never becomes a mere extrusion of emotional viscera,
but rather is expressed in terms of delicate remodulations of
the metaphors which were central to his first religious poem,
Religio Laici. The readjustment is so carefully managed that
Dryden succeeded in creating an impression of unbroken continuity or even inherent inevitability in the development of
his opinions.[23]

In our investigation of *Religio Laici* we found that the
moonlight of reason, though reflected and dim, is the best
last resort of a layman in his quest for salvation. In 1682, at
least, Dryden believed that reason's "borrow'd beams" could
"guide us upward to a better Day" (l. 7), just as the heathens
who "lifted high their Natural Light; / With Socrates may
see their Maker's Face" (ll. 209–10). We noticed also that

23. Bredvold, *The Intellectual Milieu of John Dryden,* p. 121, misapplied
his appreciation of this continuity to assert a fallacious identity of the
ideas in the two poems. Harth, *Contexts of Dryden's Thought,* pp. 264 and
284, notes some of the specific resemblances in imagery.

Dryden's final image of control is a carefully managed extension of the moon metaphor: the tides of ignorance, of not having revelation, and of pride, of using it ill, are caused by the moon of reason at its "extremes." These extremes, the poet of *Religio Laici* suggested, could be avoided and the light of the moon itself could serve as a useful guide, if only we would stem the tides and preserve the ground of reason (cf. ll. 424–28). The poet's views in *The Hind and the Panther* represent a studied redaction of the materials of his earlier vision. If the Anglican Church, he tells us, would keep her place in the divine system, she would retain her spiritual power.

> Thus is the *Panther* neither lov'd nor fear'd,
> A mere mock Queen of a divided Herd;
> Whom soon by lawfull pow'r she might controll,
> Her self a part submitted to the whole.
> Then, as the Moon who first receives the light
> By which she makes our nether regions bright,
> So might she shine, reflecting from afar
> The rays she borrow'd from a better star:
> Big with the beams which from her mother flow
> And reigning o'er the rising tides below.
>
> [1, 497–506]

This might have been the case, but the Anglican Church and the use of reason that the poet imputes to her could not be satisfied with a place second to God's revealed word:

> Can I my reason to my faith compell,
> And shall my sight, and touch, and taste rebell?
> Superiour faculties are set aside,
> Shall their subservient organs be my guide?
> Then let the moon usurp the rule of day,
> And winking tapers shew the sun his way.
>
> [1, 85–90]

The "Tapers" of *Religio Laici* (l. 8) are acknowledged, but
now they are "winking" and now, instead of guiding us to
the sun, they presume to guide the sun itself. The attempted
usurpation results in reason's degeneracy and disqualification
as an instrument of divine knowledge.

Nor does the poet simply discard his earlier image of God
as a "Spring of Good" (*Religio Laici*, l. 44), a flow of bounty
and light. The Hind repeatedly insists on her association with
"the fountain of eternal grace" (II, 627), the "fountains head"
(III, 123), the "immortal spring" (III, 807), and the "limpid
stream drawn from the native source" (II, 614). But Dryden
does reject one major aspect of the metaphorical design we
found in *Religio Laici*: the fragile affiliation of a "ground"
metaphor with a minimum of divine truth accessible to
ordinary human reason is explicitly discarded, while the metaphor of "lineal course" (II, 615) or fountain-head (II, 616) is
represented as "unconfin'dly spread" (II, 617) and becomes
one of the major images associated with the Hind in the poem.
The unfathomed deep, with its powerful tides and endless
expanse, ceases to be an image of chaos (as it was in *Religio
Laici*) and becomes a symbol of God's mystery and glory which
demands total immersion in the divine.

> Thus one, thus pure, behold her largely spread
> Like the fair ocean from her mother bed;
> From East to West triumphantly she rides,
> All shoars are water'd by her wealthy Tides.
>
> [II, 548–51]

Dryden took the materials for his revision from at least
one other earlier vision besides *Religio Laici*. Twenty years
before, in the "Digression concerning Shipping and Naviga-
tion" of *Annus Mirabilis*, he had foreseen a brilliant future
for his nation of the sea.

> Then the bold *English* none more fame have won:

Beyond the Year, and out of Heav'ns high-way,
    They make discoveries where they see no Sun.

But what so long in vain, and yet unknown,
    By poor man-kinds benighted wit is sought,
Shall in this Age to *Britain* first be shown,
    And hence be to admiring Nations taught.
. . . .
Instructed ships shall sail to quick Commerce;
    By which remotest Regions are alli'd:
Which makes one City of the Universe,
    Where some may gain, and all may be suppli'd.

Then, we upon our Globes last verge shall go,
    And view the Ocean leaning on the sky:
From thence our rolling Neighbours we shall know,
    And on the Lunar world securely pry.

                      [ll. 638–56]

Now, with echoes of the earlier poem ironically rebounding, he reviews the subject:

Here let my sorrow give my satyr place,
To raise new blushes on my *British* race;
Our sayling ships like common shoars we use,
And through our distant colonies diffuse
The draughts of Dungeons, and the stench of stews.
Whom, when their home-bred honesty is lost,
We disembogue on some far *Indian* coast:
Thieves, Pandars, Palliards, sins of ev'ry sort,
Those are the manufactures we export;
And these the Missionaires our zeal has made:
For, with my countrey's pardon be it said,
Religion is the least of all our trade.

                      [II, 556–67]

This is the noxious cargo of materialistic exploitation that the poet has jettisoned in order to escape from a tawdry

market prediction into a truly universal vision of a gospel
"ocean."

> The Gospel-sound diffus'd from Pole to Pole,
> Where winds can carry, and where waves can roll.
> The self same doctrine of the Sacred page
> Convey'd to ev'ry clime in ev'ry age.
>
> [II, 552–55]

The Panther reinforces the Hind's metaphorical identification with the sea when she says,

> Our penal laws no sons of yours admit,
> Our *Test* excludes your Tribe from benefit.
> These are my banks your ocean to withstand,
> Which proudly rising overlooks the land.
>
> [III, 829–32]

The Hind's response to this fixes the identification of the
Panther with the land or *ground:*

> Your care about your Banks, infers a fear
> Of threatning Floods, and Inundations near;
> If so, a just Reprise would only be
> Of what the Land usurp'd upon the Sea;
> And all your Jealousies but serve to show
> Your Ground is, like your Neighbor-Nation, low.
>
> [III, 860–65]

Elsewhere we are told that the Panther's party claims "all
the land" (III, 768) and seems to walk "as on inchanted
ground" (III, 722), but her doctrines are "unstable sands"
(II, 589). When her followers attempt to interpret Scripture for
themselves, "with full sails," they themselves run "upon the
shelf" (II, 257).

The Panther was once pure like the Hind: she too belonged to the fountain and the gospel ocean (cf. II, 552). But
now that the Panther is "a creature of a double kind" (I, 402),

she has no real home. Dryden employs this metaphor of aliena-
tion in his powerful exhortation near the beginning of the
poem:

> Why chuse we then like *Bilanders* to creep
> Along the coast, and land in view to keep,
> When safely we may launch into the deep?
> In the same vessel which our Saviour bore
> Himself the Pilot, let us leave the shoar,
> And with a better guide a better world explore.[24]
>
> [I, 128–33]

But with this much information we must admit that it is
still far from clear how the vast beast allegory called *The
Hind and the Panther* might represent Dryden's approach to
the divine "deep."

"The Majestick Turn of Heroick Poesie"

On one point modern judgment has parted company with
Montague and Prior, though even here the disagreement has
by no means been to the poet's advantage. This concerns
Dryden's well-known description of the poem's three styles
corresponding to its three parts:

24. John Vaughan's commendatory verses to Dryden on the publication
of *Religio Laici* elaborated the metaphor of avoiding the "shelves of ruin"
and applied it to the author:

> The only free enriching port God made,
> What shameful monopoly did invade?
> One factious company engrossed the trade.
> Thou to the distant shore hast safely sailed,
> Where the best pilots have so often failed.
> Freely we now may buy the pearl of price;
> The happy land abounds with fragrant spice,
> And nothing is forbidden there but vice.
> Thou best Columbus to the unknown world!
>
> [*Works of John Dryden*, x, 36]

These lines may have helped Dryden crystallize in his own mind the
work that remained to be done in *The Hind and the Panther*.

> *The* first part, *consisting most in general Characters and*
> *Narration, I have endeavour'd to raise, and give it the*
> *Majestick Turn of Heroick Poesie. The* second, *being*
> *Matter of Dispute, and chiefly concerning Church Author-*
> *ity, I was oblig'd to make as plain and perspicuous as pos-*
> *sibly I cou'd: yet not wholly neglecting the Numbers,*
> *though I had not frequent occasions for the Magnificence*
> *of Verse. The* third, *which has more of the Nature of Do-*
> *mestick Conversation, is, or ought to be more free and*
> *familiar than the two former.*[25]

Montague and Prior were content to deride this as a kind of
Peri Bathous:

> *Bayes.* . . . And then I'le tell you another thing, 'tis not
> every one that reads a Poem through. And therefore I
> fill the first part with Flowers, Figures, fine Language,
> and all that; and then I'gad sink by degrees, till at
> last I write but little better than other People.[26]

Later critics have been inclined to treat the entire description of three styles as something of a fiction. In the first part
of the poem, Johnson noted, the "character of a Presbyterian,
whose emblem is the Wolf, is not very heroically majestick"
and the

> general character of the other sorts of beasts that never
> go to church, though spritely and keen, has, however
> not much of heroick poesy. . . . The second and third
> parts he professes to have reduced to diction more famil-
> iar, and more suitable to dispute and conversation; the
> difference is not, however, very easily perceived: the first
> has familiar, and the two others have sonorous, lines.[27]

25. "To the Reader," ll. 92–99.
26. *The Hind and the Panther Transvers'd,* ll. 243–46.
27. Johnson, *Lives,* I, 444–45.

Scott noted, "with Johnson, that [Dryden's] distinctions of style are not always accurately adhered to." [28]

At the core of Johnson's rejection of the "three styles" account is an objection of great seriousness. Johnson complains that Dryden's satiric penchant cost him the goal of heroic poetry which he had set for himself:

> perhaps he might have executed his design not unsuccessfully had not an opportunity of satire, which he cannot forbear, fallen sometimes in his way.[29]

This remark raises the spectre of the splenetic satirist which the nineteenth century was so willing to believe hovered over much Augustan verse. It casts doubt on Dryden's ability to subordinate part to whole. And the doubt persists. One critic has recently argued, for example, that the fable of the swallows in the Third Part is an aberration of this kind:

> Dryden obviously disliked Father Petre (the Martin) and disapproved of the inflexible policies in which he was encouraging James, but that alone does not explain why he allowed the Anglican Panther, who tells the fable, so polished an exposure of the folly of Catholic hopes. The Hind is almost out of patience when she marks 'the malice of the Tale', but such malice as there is in the tale is Dryden's own.[30]

This is a serious charge; so too are the other objections of generations of Dryden's readers—sympathetic and unsympathetic—that we have reviewed. A great deal seems very wrong with this *longum opus* written, if we may judge by the Killigrew *Ode* and the *Song for St. Cecilia's Day* which bound it,

28. *Works of John Dryden*, x, 96. See Clarence H. Miller, "The Styles of *The Hind and the Panther*," *JEGP*, LXI (1962), 511–27; cf. Miner, p. 339.

29. Johnson, *Lives*, I, 444.

30. *Dryden's Satire*, ed. D. R. Elloway (New York, 1966), pp. xliii–xliv. Elloway feels that "the animal myth is quite ineffective as a means of adding imaginative conviction to the debate."

at the height of Dryden's poetic powers. Either the poem is
a gross anomaly or we have really understood even less of
the poem's content than we have previously recognized. In
relation to this latter possibility, it may be that Dr. Johnson's
intuition of our ignorance is the most useful of all the remarks which three centuries of criticism have bestowed on the
poem:

> Some of the facts to which allusions are made are now
> become obscure, and perhaps there may be many satirical
> passages little understood.[31]

We must now attempt to illuminate some of these obscure
facts.

31. Johnson, *Lives,* I, 446.

8

The Hind and the Legend of Saint Chad

In the Roman Hind's invitation to the Anglican Panther to enter

> her lowly roof, (a shed
> With hoary moss and winding Ivy spread,
> Honest enough to hide an humble Hermit's head,)
>
> [II, 697–99]

Dryden is employing one in a series of allusions to the legend of Saint Chad, Bishop of Lichfield. The fullest version of that legend survives in the well-known *Monasticon Anglicanum* (London, 1655–73) compiled by Roger Dodsworth and Sir William Dugdale.[1] The scene is seventh-century England.

---

1. Dodsworth and Dugdale indicate (II, 119) that they took their account from Cotton MS Otho A. 16. This manuscript was destroyed in the Cottonian fire of 1731. Thomas Smith, *Catalogus Librorum Manuscriptorum Bibliothecæ Cottonianæ* (Oxford, 1696), p. 69, described the manuscript as "Passio SS. Ulfadi et Ruffini, filiorum Wlferi Regis, Fundatoris istius domus, quorum passio erat occasio fundationis." A brief version of the legend survives in MS Cotton Nero CXII, fols. 181 ff. and has been published in *Altenglische Legenden,* ed. C. Horstmann (Heilbronn, Germany, 1881), pp. 308–14. A useful modern version of the legend (based on the *Monasticon*) is available in R. Hyett Warner, *Life and Legends of Saint Chad* (London, n.d.), pp. 75–94. See also Thomas Dunham Whitaker, *The History and Antiquities of the Deanery of Craven* (London, 1805), p. 383 and *The Life of St. Chad,* ed. R. Vleeskruyer (Amsterdam, 1953), pp. 12–18 for related background information. The basic outline of the legend is also to be found on the first page of John Leland's . . . *De Rebvs Britannicis Collectanea* (London, 1770). For general

King Wulfer, ruler of the Mercians, had forsaken his baptismal
oaths to root out pagan idolatry and extend the faith of
Christ. Under the influence of his evil councilor, Werebod,
an "alter Achitophel," Wulfer reapproached paganism: "penè
in apostasiam lapsus," the chronicler tells us, "à fide retrorsum
abiit." Just at this time, too, Chad had retreated to a hermit's
existence in the forest where he sustained himself "radicibus
herbarum et fructibus arborum silvestrium." One day, Prince
Wulfad, son of Wulfer and "Sanctæ Reginæ Ermenildis," [2]
was "seized with the desire to hunt wild animals," but instead
"he was shot by the hunters of the Lord, and taken off for
salvation." The story continues:

> Quadam namque die, dum venatum pergeret, offendit
> cervum miræ magnitudinis, quem fugientem diuciùs solus
> solum insequebatur, sociis dispersis, ac nutu divino fati-
> gatis: Cervus opaca silvarum irrumpens, ad habitaculum
> viri Dei *Ceddæ* infra nemoris condensa supra cujusdam
> fontis marginem constructum pervenit, seque in eundem
> fontem latitando lascitudinem requie refrigerioque re-
> creando projecit. Famulus Christi *Cedda* misericordiæ
> visceribus affluens erga creaturas Dei; frondibus et foliis
> arboreis cervum occultando et refrigerando contexit;
> quoniam ut in fine rei claruit, aliquid divinitus actitari
> per ejus obsequium intellexit.[3]

---

comment on the use of deer images in the seventeenth century, see Don
Cameron Allen, *Image and Meaning: Metaphoric Traditions in Renaissance Poetry* (Baltimore, 1960), pp. 93–114.

It is possible that Dryden was personally acquainted with Dugdale. In
the summer of 1680 Jacob Tonson wrote to Luttrell, "Mr. Dryden is in
Staffordshire at Sᵣ Ch Woolslys & Mr Dugdale at Stafford": see Osborn,
John Dryden: Facts and Problems, pp. 200–01. The letter is now in the
library of All Souls College, Oxford (MS 181, No. 63).

2. *Monasticon*, II, 120.

3. For the reader's convenience, I have included an essentially literal
translation of selected passages. I am indebted to James Hutton for his
aid in preparing footnotes 3–10, 12, and 16. The imperfections which
remain are mine alone.

Prince Wulfad, "è vicino terens vestigia cervi," approaches
Chad and asks where the stag has gone. While the animal
gathers food in the forest ("pabula carpenda in silvas"), Chad
answers the prince with an elaborate disquisition on the
"ministry of the stag."

> *Nunquid custos cervi tui sum ego? Non curo, non custodio
> feras silvarum seu pecora campi, vel volucres cœli, set
> agnovi et suscepi ductorem salutis tuæ ministerio cervi.
> Voluntas enim Domini præparantis cervos revelavit tibi
> condensa sacramentorum suorum, ut credas in nomine
> ipsius, et baptizeris in remissionem peccatorum tuorum.
> Perpulcro prænostico, immo indicio certi præsagii por-
> tendit et præostendit tibi cervus demersus in fontem
> salutaris baptismi lavacrum, quatinus ex sententia discere
> possis illud Daviticum, Quemadmodum desiderat cervus
> ad fontes aquarum, ita desiderat anima mea ad te, Deus,
> sitivit anima mea ad Deum fontem vivum, quando
> veniam et apparebo ante faciem Dei?* [4]

"For one day, while pursuing the hunt, he came upon a stag of
marvelous size, whom, fleeing alone, he alone followed for a very long
time. His comrades were dispersed and fatigued by divine will. The stag,
breaking through the dense forest, came to the hut of the man of God,
Cedda, which was built within a dense grove just on the edge of a
fountain, and he threw himself into this fountain to hide and revive
himself by rest and cooling. The servant of Christ, Cedda, rich in the
bowels of mercy for the creatures of God, covered the stag with leaves
and branches of trees to hide and cool him; since, as was clear at the
end of the matter, he understood that through his compliance something
was being brought to pass by divine will."—Ibid., II, 120.

4. Ibid., II, 120–21: "Am I the keeper of your stag? I do not protect, nor
do I guard the wild animals of the forest, nor the cattle of the field,
nor the birds of the heavens, but in the ministry of the stag I have recognized and received the guide of your salvation. The will of God, who
makes provision of stags, has revealed to you the hidden things of his
sacraments, that you might believe in his name, and be baptized for the
remission of your sins. By a beautiful foreknowledge, nay, even a sure
indication of presage, the stag by plunging into this spring portends and
reveals to you the font of saving baptism, that you may come to know in

The chronicler paraphrases the remainder of Chad's words on this point:

> Perplura eciam peroravit Sanctus, persuadens et docens qualiter in misterio irrationalium animalium misteria sua revelare dignata sit divina sapientia in salutem fidelium. Nempe *Noe* nunciavit post suum naufragium, mundi reparatricem siccitatem, per columbam, et ore subjugalis Asinæ prophetæ cohibuit insipientiam, et obsequio Corvi prophetam eximium pavit *Helyam.* Jure verò dominus prophetarum tendens *Jerosolimam* ascendere dignatus est Asinam et pullum, in conversionis utriusque populi figuram. Narravit nichilominus ei quod de beato *Eustachio* legitur, qualiter in specie Cervi ei apparere Dominus dignabatur; et multa subjunxit quæ in gestis beatorum *Martini Jeronimi* et aliorum sanctorum patrum patrata signa de brutis animalibus inveniuntur.[5]

In this way Chad establishes the identity of the stag as a guide to God's sacraments, an agent of baptism, a minister of salvation, and, most important, a converter of whole peoples. Wulfad is soon converted (or reconverted) and spends

---

its [true] meaning the statement of David: Just as the stag longs for the fountain of waters, so does my soul long for you, Lord, and thirsts for the living fountain of God. When shall I come and appear before the face of God?"

5. Ibid., II, 121: "The Saint spoke many things more, persuading and teaching, how in the ministry of irrational animals divine Wisdom has deigned to reveal its mysteries for the salvation of the faithful. For it [Divine Wisdom] announced to Noah after his shipwreck the reappearance of dry land through a dove, and by the mouth of a beast of burden, an ass, it [Divine Wisdom] restrained the foolishness of the prophet, and by the service of a raven it fed the great prophet Elijah. Justly indeed the Lord of the prophets, on his way to Jerusalem, deigned to mount upon an ass and her foal, as a figure of the conversion of two peoples. He told him no less what is said about the blessed Eustachius, how the Lord condescended to appear to him in the form of a hart; and he subjoined the numerous signs given by brute beasts in the records of blessed Martin, Jerome, and other saintly fathers."

the night with Chad in his cell, while the stag remains unfrightened even by other animals:

> Et quoniam advesperascebat et inclinata erat jam dies, pater sanctus secum filiolum pernoctare fecit, et cibo corporalis et spiritualis alimoniæ, prout potuit, illius utrumque hominem refecit. Perpulchrum simul spectaculum ibidem apparebat; sicut sanctus *Cedda* cum sancto *Wlfado* manebat, sic Cervus cum jumento, agreste animal cum domito in omni mansuetudine stabat, accubabat, fœnum carpebat.[6]

We recall that Dryden's Hind, who "fed on the lawns," also "fear'd no danger" (I, 2–4) and also attempted to reconvert a whole people through an evening's and a night's talk in her cell with the Anglican Panther:

> The Western borders were with crimson spread,
> The moon descending look'd all flaming red,
> She thought good manners bound her to invite
> The stranger Dame to be her guest that night.
> . . . .
> . . . what plain fare her cottage cou'd afford,
> A hearty welcome at a homely board
> Was freely hers; and, to supply the rest,
> An honest meaning and an open breast.
>
> [II, 668–78]

Through Wulfad's influence, his brother prince, Ruffinus, is also converted. Ruffinus sets out in the morning with a

6. Ibid., II, 121: **"And** since it was becoming evening and the day was already declining, the holy father made his dear son spend the night with him and, to the best of his ability, with the bread of corporeal and spiritual nourishment, he refreshed both his [Wulfad's] inner and outer man. At the same time appeared there a very beautiful sight. Just as the holy Chad abode with holy Wulfad, so the hart with the horse stood, the wild animal with the tame, all peaceably stood, lay down, and cropped the hay."

brace of hounds, "cum canibus quasi venatum," and soon
finds the stag, which leads him to Chad and throws itself
into Chad's baptismal font.

> ut patenter daretur intelligi, quod indicio, quo poterat,
> puerum perduceret ad vitalis fluenta baptismi. Referunt
> plures sanctissimum *Ceddam* fontem illum de terra suis
> precibus perduxisse, qui usque in hodiernum diem vocatur
> *Fons sancti Cedde.*[7]

Dryden's Hind, as we have seen, repeatedly insists on her
association with "the fountain of eternal grace" (II, 627), the
fountains head" (III, 123), the "immortal spring" (III, 807),
and the "limpid stream drawn from the native source" whose
"head" spreads "unconfin'dly" (II, 614–17).

In the Chad legend, baptismal vows are violated and the
story takes a tragic turn when the evil Werebod inflames the
king against his "spotless" sons (*inmaculatos*) by convincing
him that their "Christ worship" is intended as irreverence
and insolence toward the king. Wulfer, according to the
proverb, "sicut fremitus leonis, sic ira Regis," roars like a
lion, "et tempore commotionis suæ fera ferocior ferâ furi-
bundus." [8]

In his wrath the "lion" murders his sons. Wulfer tries to keep
the crime a secret, but Werebod, the "perjur'd foe" (cf. *The
Hind and the Panther*, I, 16) of the young martyrs, no sooner
reaches the courtyard of the royal residence than the blood
of the boys becomes "vocal" (cf. *The Hind and the Panther*,
I, 15–16) in him and he is forced to cry out:

7. Ibid., II, 122: ". . . so that it might be clearly given to be understood that, by means of all that as a stag he could do, he was leading
the boy to the streams of life-giving baptism. Many say that he, most
holy Chad, produced that fountain from the earth by his prayers which
even today is called the fountain of St. Chad."

8. Ibid., II, 122–23: "and, at the time of his disturbance, was a furious
beast more savage than a wild animal."

> Manus enim suas et brachia propriis dentibus dilaniabat; et quicquid per sui ipsius funestam instigationem in filios pater cruentus commiserat, vociferans in auribus omnium vocibus inconditis divulgabat. Spiritus verò domini malus illum tamdiu non cessabat vexare, quoad usque compelleret eum spiritum fœtidum exhalare.[9]

Like the lion of *The Hind and the Panther*, which has two aspects or incarnations, one "furious" (i, 351) and the other protective of the Hind (i, 531), Wulfer soon does penance under Ermenilda's direction and is reconverted by the ministry of the stag which leads him to Chad and the baptismal font. Finally, the cleansing and conversion of the entire nation is accomplished:

> Beato *Cedda* commonente, et cooperante sancta *Ermenilda*, rex infra temporis spacium totum regnum suum ab omni spurcitia idolatriæ purgavit, et quicquid sanæ fidei adversum agnoscere poterat eliminare curavit. Ecclesias congruis in locis exstruxit, aut extrui fecit; Monasteria utriusque sexus plura et præclara ædificavit, amplisque possessionibus locupletavit.[10]

Dryden's fable of conversion represents a conflation of principal elements in the Chad legend. In the proselytizing Hind we find not only the saintly bishop and the miraculous

9. Ibid., ii, 123: "For he tore his hands and arms with his own teeth and whatever the bloody father had committed by his own wicked instigation against his sons, he divulged, shouting into the ears of everyone in a tumult of words; but an evil spirit of the Lord did not cease to torment him until it forced him to breathe forth his foul spirit."

10. Ibid., ii, 125: "With the advice of blessed Chad and the cooperation of holy Ermenilda, the king in a short space of time cleansed his entire kingdom of every filthiness of idolatry and, whatever he could recognize as opposed to the wholesome faith, took pains to eliminate. He built, or caused to be built, churches in suitable places. He built many beautiful monasteries for both sexes and enriched them with many possessions."

stag—who both sustain themselves on the fruits of the forest
—but also the holy mother Ermenilda who looks after the
remains of her martyred sons. The Hind, Dryden tells us, is
not killed by her enemies, but

> Not so her young, for their unequal line
> Was Heroe's make, half humane, half divine.
> Their earthly mold obnoxious was to fate,
> Th' immortal part assum'd immortal state.
> Of these a slaughtered army lay in bloud,
> Extended o'er the *Caledonian* wood,
> Their native walk; whose vocal blood arose,
> And cry'd for pardon on their perjur'd foes;
> Their fate was fruitfull, and the sanguin seed
> Endu'd with souls, encreas'd the sacred breed.
>
> . . . .
>
> With grief and gladness mixt, their mother view'd
> Her martyr'd offspring, and their race renew'd;
> Their corps to perish, but their kind to last,
> So much the deathless plant the dying fruit surpass'd.
>
> [I, 9–24]

In the Chad legend, Wulfad and Ruffinus, who are in Wulfer's
"sanguinis linea," [11] are said to be made "more brotherly by
means of a happier seed"—faith and martyrdom.

> eos gratia regenerationis in fide atque sanguinis effusione
> feliciori germine germaniores reddit.[12]

They are part of Ermenilda's "deathless plant": "ex sanctissima
Regum orientalium Anglorum stirpe originem duxerat." [13]
The spirit of her "slaughtered army" is described as being that

11. Ibid., II, 119.
12. Ibid., II, 120: "the grace of regeneration in faith and in the
shedding of blood made them more brotherly by means of a happier
seed."
13. Ibid., II, 120.

of a "recruit" or "athlete": "animus tironis Christi"[14] and "athletæ Christi."[15] After their blood is shed in the English wood and becomes "vocal" in "perjur'd foes," the holy mother views their martyrdom and secures their immortality:

> ad locum martyrii eorum accessit, et corpora colligens illorum, in uno saxeo sarcophago simul honorificè sepelivit. Et congruè Domino disponente, . . . in pace sepulta sunt corpora eorum, quorum animas introduxit Dominus in splendoribus Sanctorum, ut vivant nomina eorum libro vitæ inscripta in secula seculorum.[16]

In at least one version of the Chad legend, the stag is replaced by a hind: as in this account—published while Dryden was composing his poem—by Robert Plot, one of Dryden's successors as historiographer-royal:

> St *Ceadda* . . . came at first . . . as into a private place, *in secretum locum Staffordiensis provinciæ* . . . where he lived (as the *Legend* says) only upon the milk of a *Doe*, which being hunted by *Wlfade* son of *Wlfere* King of *Mercia* brought him to the Cell of St *Ceadda*, who first converted him to the Christian faith, and his brother *Ruffine* after.[17]

We can see, then, that in the fable of the "Milk white Hind" Dryden was depending on an allusive complex of national-epic proportions. Nothing less than the ultimate

---

14. Ibid., II, 121.

15. Ibid., II, 123.

16. Ibid., II, 124: "she went to the place of their martyrdom and, gathering their bodies, buried them with honor together in one stone sarcophagus, and the Lord assenting, . . . their bodies were buried in peace, whose souls the Lord introduced in among the splendors of his Saints, that their names might live inscribed in the book of life forever."

17. Robert Plot, *The Natural History of Stafford-Shire* (Oxford, 1686), p. 407.

spiritual salvation of England is projected in its outlines. But the Chad legend cannot, by itself, explain the fable of *The Hind and the Panther*. The largest part of Dryden's materials came from a better known and more sanctified source. If he understood what Dryden was about, Bishop Sprat should have been pleased to realize that Dryden had accepted not only his analysis of poetry's malady but also his prescription for a new "Foundation for Wit": the carefully wrought abstract mechanism of *Religio Laici* was an exquisite realization of the suggestion that the poet draw his images from "the Sciences, and Manners of Men, the several Arts of their hands, and the works of Nature"; while the allegory of *The Hind and the Panther* was built upon the "Civil History" of the poet's country and, what Sprat recommended more than anything else, the Bible.[18]

18. *History of the Royal Society*, pp. 413–14; cf. chap. 1. A compressed account of some of the materials presented in chapters 8, 9, and 10 has appeared in my article, "Dryden's 'Mysterious Writ' deciphered," *TLS*, April 3, 1969, p. 371, and my letter, *TLS*, May 22, 1969, p. 559.

9

The Hind and the Panther: I

Even before *The Hind and the Panther* was published, Dryden knew that many readers would either encounter or create difficulties in understanding his fable. In fact, it seems probable that an element of the esoteric was one of the conscious goals in the poem. We recall that the Third Part begins with the observation that

> Much malice mingl'd with a little wit
> Perhaps may censure this mysterious writ,
> Because the Muse has peopl'd *Caledon*
> With *Panthers, Bears,* and *Wolves,* and Beasts unknown.

But Dryden declines to explain the mystery. His prefatory remark that the poem is a "Satyr" of which the First Part, at least, has been given "the Majestick Turn of Heroick Poesie" only adds to our puzzlement.[1] As we have seen, it is precisely this mixture of satire and epic—of mock heroic or heroic mockery—which has caused so much perplexity.[2] How are these elements related to each other or, indeed, how can they be? This is an important question for a great deal of Augustan poetry; in *The Hind and the Panther* we are involved in a specific and, perhaps, specialized case.

Satire, Epic, and Daniel

We must try to understand the terms of the mixture or

1. "To the Reader," ll. 20 and 94.
2. Cf. *Works of John Dryden,* x, 95–96.

opposition as they occur here. Johnson, Scott, and later critics seem to have assumed that in the phrase "Majestick Turn of Heroick Poesie" Dryden referred only to characteristics of metre, idiom, or diction. This use of *turn* is common in Dryden's essays, but the word frequently has a more complex meaning, and may also refer to alterations of dramatic action and plot. In *Of Dramatic Poesy: An Essay* (1668), for example, Lisideius says of the French heroic plays:

> 'Tis a great mistake in us to believe the French present no part of the action on the stage: every alteration or crossing of a design, every new-sprung passion, and turn of it, is a part of the action, and much the noblest, except we conceive nothing to be action till they come to blows.[3]

By 1690, Neander was inclined to the same use and valuation of the term, for Dryden writes in the preface to *Don Sebastian*:

> Corneille writ an *Oedipus* after Sophocles; and I have designed one after him, which I wrote with Mr Lee, yet neither the French poet stole from the Greek, nor we from the Frenchman. 'Tis the contrivance, the new turn, and new characters, which alter the property and make it ours. The *materia poetica* is as common to all writers as the *materia medica* to all physicians.[4]

We must bear in mind that the major heroic constituent of *The Hind and the Panther* may depend on pre-existing material to which Dryden applies a "turn." If this is the case, it would be impossible for us to know the nature of the satiric-heroic complex without first knowing the *materia poetica*.

It is also important to remember that for Dryden the critic, satire and epic are not conflicting modes. He asserts, in fact, that satire is "undoubtedly a species" of "heroic poetry."[5] This is not an offhand statement. It is a conviction

3. *Of Dramatic Poesy*, ed. Watson, I, 52.
4. Ibid., II, 48–49.
5. Ibid., II, 149.

that is supported by the entire design of the lengthy essay, *A Discourse concerning the Original and Progress of Satire* (1693), in which it occurs. After an extended compliment to his patron, Dorset, Dryden begins his discussion with what he calls "a digression from satire to heroic poetry." [6] This digression, which we have examined in part earlier, is itself one of his most interesting critical productions. In a sense, it is for Dryden what the letter to Ralegh concerning *The Faerie Queene* is for Spenser, or the preface to *The Excursion* for Wordsworth; for Dryden here presents us with a plan for the poem he most desired to write, although for him, we have believed, the plan did not produce any semblance of its object. Dryden tells us that it is

> a rude draught of what I have been long labouring in my imagination, and what I had intended to have put in practice (though far unable for the attempt of such a poem), and to have left the stage, to which my genius never much inclined me, for a work which would have taken up my life in the performance of it. This, too, I had intended chiefly for the honour of my native country, to which a poet is particularly obliged. Of two subjects, both relating to it, I was doubtful whether I should choose that of King Arthur conquering the Saxons . . . or that of Edward, the Black Prince, in subduing Spain . . . . But being encouraged only with fair words by King Charles II, my little salary ill paid, and no prospect of a future subsistence, I was then discouraged in the beginning of my attempt; and now age has overtaken me; and want, a more insufferable evil, through the change of the times, has wholly disenabled me.[7]

This lament is perhaps the saddest passage in all of Dryden's

6. Ibid., ii, 85.
7. Ibid., ii, 91–92.

writings. It is his record of the frustration and finally the death of his fondest, lifelong ambition. But what he had been "long labouring in his imagination"—during, we must suppose, the recently closed period of satire, as well—was not completely wasted. In an essay on satire that acknowledges, for the first time, authorship of *Mac Flecknoe*, we are not surprised to find clues to another Dryden secret, his "mysterious writ."

Dryden's "rude draught" amounts to no less than a religio-poetic cosmology. It was meant to provide a Christian mythological structure for a natural epic, but, like the heathen mythologies it was intended to supplant,[8] it contains a thread of independent narrative and a more or less clear delineation of opposing forces. Dryden begins by noting that the French satirist and critic, Boileau, complained that:

> the machines of our Christian religion, in heroic poetry, are much more feeble to support that weight than those of heathenism. Their doctrine, grounded as it was on ridiculous fables, was yet the belief of the two victorious monarchies, the Grecian and Roman. Their gods did not only interest themselves in the event of wars . . . but also espoused the several parties in a visible corporeal descent, managed their intrigues, and fought their battles sometimes in opposition to each other.[9]

Dryden agrees:

> We cannot hitherto boast that our religion has furnished

8. Cf. ibid., II, 89

9. Ibid., II, 86–87. Dryden's English predecessors and successors in the general advocacy of Christian epic machinery have been enumerated by H. T. Swedenberg, Jr., *The Theory of the Epic in England, 1650–1800* (Berkeley, Calif., 1944), pp. 266–305. For commentary on the continental origins of the idea see *Critical Essays of the Seventeenth Century*, ed. J. E. Spingarn (Oxford, 1908–09), II, 332–34 and III, 310. Especially suggestive are Antoine Godeau's comments in his "Discours de la poésie chrestienne," *Œuvres chrestiennes* (Paris, 1635), pp. 17 ff. Cf. also Friedrich Brie, "Popes *Brutus*," *Anglia*, LXIII (1939), 151.

us with any such machines as have made the strength
and beauty of the ancient buildings.

"But what if I," he adds, "venture to advance an invention
of my own, to supply the manifest defect of our new
writers?" [10]

Dryden's resulting "draught" consists, in effect, of two related parts. One is a general plan for Christian epic machinery; the other is a specific suggestion which contains
characters and narrative, and which also lends scriptural
support to the larger design. The general plan is fashioned in
such a way that the Christian poet may oversee his plot without losing his impartiality.

> 'Tis a doctrine almost universally received by Christians,
> as well Protestants as Catholics, that there are guardian
> angels appointed by God Almighty as his vicegerents, for
> the protection and government of cities, provinces, king-
> doms, and monarchies; and those as well of heathens,
> as of true believers. All this is so plainly proved from . . .
> texts of Daniel that it admits of no farther controversy.
> The Prince of the Persians, and that other of the
> Grecians, are granted to be the guardians and protecting
> ministers of those empires. It cannot be denied that
> they were opposite, and resisted one another. St Michael
> is mentioned by his name as the patron of the Jews, and
> is now taken by the Christians as the protector-general of
> our religion. These tutelar genii, who presided over the
> several people and regions committed to their charge, were
> watchful over them for good, as far as their commissions
> could possibly extend. The general purpose and design
> of all was certainly the service of their Great Creator.
> But 'tis an undoubted truth that, for ends best known to
> the Almighty Majesty of Heaven, his providential designs
> for the benefit of his creatures, for the debasing and

10. Ibid., II, 88.

punishing of some nations, and the exaltation and tem-
poral reward of others, were not wholly known to these
his ministers; else why those factious quarrels, controversies, and battles amongst themselves, when they were
all united in the same design, the service and honour of
their common master? . . . how far these controversies
and appearing enmities of . . . glorious creatures may
be carried; how these oppositions may best be managed,
and by what means conducted, is not my business to shew
or determine: these things must be left to the invention
and judgment of the poet.[11]

This emphasis on the objectivity of the poet, even in the heat
of battle, and the feeling that the management of the oppositions themselves could not be presented in a blueprint, were
very important to Dryden. In the preface to *The Hind and the
Panther*—which he calls a "Satyr . . . aim'd only at the
refractory and disobedient on either side" [12]—we hear Dryden
strike very similar notes, and in much the same order:

> *The Nation is in too high a Ferment, for me to expect
> either fair War, or even so much as fair Quarter from a
> Reader of the opposite Party. All Men are engag'd either
> on this side or that: and tho' Conscience is the common
> Word, which is given by both, yet if a Writer fall among
> Enemies, and cannot give the Marks of* Their *Conscience,
> he is knock'd down before the Reasons of his own are
> heard. A* Preface, *therefore, which is but a bespeaking
> of Favour, is altogether useless. What I desire the* Reader
> *should know concerning me, he will find in the Body of
> the Poem.*[13]

Dryden's admission that he too is engaged on one side does
not constitute a violation of the heroic poet's objectivity, as

11. Ibid., II, 89–90.
12. "To the Reader," ll. 20–21.
13. Ibid., ll. 1–8.

he understands it: his general plan also provides for "the opposition of ill spirits to the good":

> they [the "ill spirits"] have also their design, ever oppo-
> site to that of Heaven; . . . this imperfect system, if I
> may call it such, which I have given, will infinitely ad-
> vance and carry farther that hypothesis of the evil spirits
> contending with the good. For being so much weaker since
> their fall than those blessed beings, they are yet sup-
> posed to have a permitted power from God of acting ill,
> as from their own depraved nature they have always the
> will of designing it.[14]

According to this provision, the poet by no means exceeds the
limits of his office in making moral judgments.

We have seen that Dryden finds support for his conception
of Christian epic machinery in the example of "guardian
angels" represented in the Book of Daniel.[15] We must remember that his specific suggestion for a mythological narrative
and dramatis personae also centers on Daniel:

> Christian poets have not hitherto been acquainted with
> their own strength. If they had searched the Old Testa-
> ment as they ought, they might there have found the
> machines which are proper for their work; and those
> more certain in their effect than it may be the New
> Testament is in the rules sufficient for salvation. The
> perusing of one chapter in the prophecy of Daniel, and

14. *Of Dramatic Poesy,* II, 90–91.
15. In *The Life of Plutarch* (1683) Dryden gives evidence of earlier
interest in guardian angels of the "Christian Platonist" type: he is drawn
to the subject, he tells us, "because it somewhat appertains to our own
country": see *Prose Works of John Dryden,* ed. Malone, II, 375–77. We
should also note that among the books purchased by a man named
Dryden in 1682 was *Officium angeli* (Antwerp, 1617) by the Jesuit George
Mayr. See T. A. Birrell, "John Dryden's Purchases at Two Book Auctions,
1680 and 1682," *ES,* XLII (1961), 195 and 211. See also the motto of
Britannia Rediviva (1688) and ll. 3, 52–53, 71–79, 146–51, 165, 198, and
222–27; cf. Scott's interesting remarks, *Works of John Dryden,* X, 285.

accommodating what there they find with the principles of Platonic philosophy as it is now Christianised, would have made the ministry of angels as strong an engine for the working up heroic poetry, in our religion, as that of the Ancients has been to raise theirs by all the fables of their gods, which were only received for truths by the most ignorant and weakest of the people.[16]

Dryden does not tell us which chapter of Daniel he means, or, indeed, if he means a specific chapter at all. Ker suggests that he is referring here to Dan. 10:13 ff. because of his later references to Michael and the princes of Persia and Grecia.[17] We note, however, that many parts of Daniel refer to the princes of Persia and Grecia. The vision of the ram and capricorn in chapter eight, for example, is explained by Gabriel to signify these powers:

> 20   The ram which thou sawest having *two* horns *are* the kings of Media and Persia.
>
> 21   And the rough goat *is* the king of Grecia: and the great horn that *is* between his eyes *is* the first king.[18]

Of special interest to us is another passage in Daniel which, according to traditional interpretation, is also an account of the Persian and Greek kingdoms, as well as the Babylonian and Roman. This occurs in chapter 7:

> 3   And four great beasts came up from the sea, diverse one from another.
>
> 4   The first *was* like a lion, and had eagle's wings: I beheld till the wings thereof were plucked, and it was lifted up from the earth, and made stand upon the feet as a man, and a man's heart was given to it.
>
> 5   And behold another beast, a second, like to a bear, and it raised up itself on one side, and *it had* three

16. *Of Dramatic Poesy,* II, 88–89.
17. *Essays of John Dryden,* ed. Ker, II, 280.
18. All citations from Daniel are to the King James Version.

      ribs in the mouth of it between the teeth of it: and
they said thus unto it, Arise, devour much flesh.

6   After this I beheld, and lo another, like a leopard,
which had upon the back of it four wings of a fowl;
the beast had also four heads; and dominion was
given to it.

7   After this I saw in the night visions, and behold a
fourth beast, dreadful and terrible, and strong ex-
ceedingly; and it had great iron teeth: it devoured
and brake in pieces, and stamped the residue with
the feet of it: and it *was* diverse from all the beasts
that *were* before it; and it had ten horns.

23   . . . The fourth beast shall be the fourth kingdom
upon earth, which shall be diverse from all kingdoms,
and shall devour the whole earth, and shall tread
it down, and break it in pieces.

There is an obvious superficial parallel, as Kinsley has observed,[19] between Daniel and *The Hind and the Panther* in
the concomitant use of a bear and a leopard (panther), but
the resemblance goes much deeper. Dryden's Panther also
succeeds "A Lyon old, obscene, and furious made" (I, 351):
for Daniel the lion is Nebuchadnezzar of Babylon, whose
madness turned him into a beast; for Dryden it is Henry VIII.
Like the winged leopard, the Panther is "a creature of a
double kind": "Her upper part of decent discipline" but the
"rest" is "disgrac'd" (I, 396–402). The unnamed fourth beast
is also not forgotten by Dryden. The other beasts "sought to
find / The ten-horn'd monster in the harmless Hind" (I, 536–
37). But the poet has told us that the forces of good are "Not
arm'd with horns of arbitrary might" (I, 266). Instead Dryden
associates the idea of a "deform'd . . . beast of Grace" (I, 162)
with the wolf. The fourth beast of Daniel is "diverse from all
the beasts that were before it" and destroys all previous king-

19. James Kinsley, "Dryden's Bestiary," *RES*, IV (1953), 334.

doms. Dryden's wolf "Did all the bestial citizens surprize" (I, 167) and "ruled awhile" (I, 168) in spite of "his innate antipathy to kings" (I, 177). The fourth beast *stamps* and Dryden's wolf *tramples down* "divine and humane laws" (I, 358). The beast has "iron teeth" and Dryden tells us that the wolfish art of Luther "In malice . . . began, by malice grows, / He sow'd the Serpent's teeth, an iron-harvest rose" (III, 642–43).

We recall that Dryden's suggestion that heroic poets should peruse "the prophecy of Daniel, . . . accommodating what there they find with the principles of Platonic philosophy as it is now Christianised," is accompanied by an outline for "the opposition of ill spirits to the good." [20] The details of this outline may ultimately help us to understand why Dryden decided to locate the Panther—"sure the noblest, next the Hind" (I, 327)—in the camp of evil forces and to conclude that "her hour of Grace was past" (III, 893). Dryden tells us in the *Discourse concerning . . . Satire* that what

> wicked spirits cannot compass, by the vast disproportion of their forces to those of . . . superior beings, they may by their fraud, and cunning carry farther, in a seeming league, confederacy, or subserviency to the designs of some good angel, as far as consists with his purity to suffer such an aid, the end of which may possibly be disguised, and concealed from his finite knowledge. This is indeed to suppose a great error in such a being: yet since a devil can appear like an angel of light; since craft and malice may sometimes blind for a while a more perfect understanding . . . I know not why . . . a fiend may not deceive a creature of more excellency than himself, but yet a creature; at least by the connivance, or tacit permission, of the Omniscient Being.[21]

20. *Of Dramatic Poesy*, II, 88–90.
21. Ibid., II, 91.

The Panther is described according to a similar formula which also depends on the Platonists. When the "Wolfe begins to share her wandring heart" (I, 338), Dryden remarks:

> If, as our dreaming *Platonists* report,
> There could be spirits of a middle sort,
> Too black for heav'n, and yet too white for hell,
> Who just dropt half way down, nor lower fell;
> So pois'd, so gently she descends from high,
> It seems a soft dismission from the sky.
>
> [I, 341–46]

But one cannot help wondering, at first, why Dryden the Roman Catholic, writing a poem in 1687 and an essay in 1693, should direct us to the Cambridge Platonists for poetic material of a heroic and theological nature. We recall that the Hind tells the Panther:

> Your sons of Latitude that court your grace,
> Though most resembling you in form and face,
> Are far the worst of your pretended race.
>
> [III, 160–62]

This question becomes even more puzzling when we realize that one of the main objects of the Cambridge Platonists' commentary on Daniel was to prove that the Bishop of Rome is Antichrist.

"Antichrist by Antichrist Expell'd"

The answer to this last question as well as the largest part of the solution to the mystery of the Hind's identity awaits us in the pages of seventeenth-century English interpretation of the apocalypse of Daniel.[22] We cannot know at this distance

22. Useful bibliographies of early Daniel commentaries are available in E. F. C. Rosenmüller, *Scholia in Vetus Testamentum* (Leipzig, 1832), pp. 42–48; R. Cornely, *Historica et Critica Introductio in U. T. Libros Sacros* (Paris, 1897), pp. 513–17; and James A. Montgomery, *A Critical and Exegetical Commentary on the Book of Daniel* (New York, 1927), pp. xv–xxvi.

the full extent of the influence of this body of writing on the
Restoration mind. There is no doubt, however, that the preoccupation of such men as Henry More and Isaac Newton with
technical problems of apocalyptic exegesis was not anti-
quarian or pedantic but rather an enterprise of the greatest
possible responsibility.[23] More, for example, insisted on the

> Necessity *incumbent upon us, to study the Prophecies of
> the Holy Scripture, and to endeavour after the attainment
> of the right sense of them, and more especially of* Daniel
> *and the* Apocalypse, *the Prophecies there so assuredly
> reaching into our Times, and so lively setting out the
> State of the Christian Church.*[24]

English popular interest in the interpretation of Daniel had
reached its height during the previous half-century in the
publication of such works as Thomas Brightman's posthumous
most Comfortable Exposition of . . . Daniel (London, 1644)[25]
and Thomas Parker's *Visions and Prophecies of Daniel Expounded* (London, 1646).

But formal commentaries tell only a small part of the story.
Throughout the century, and in many quarters, there was
manifest an almost obsessive desire to identify the Antichrist,
which (according to New Testament parallels) was forecast in
the Little Horn of Daniel 7:8 and 8:9. After the Reformation, the Pope became the obvious choice of Protestant po-
lemicists on the continent as well as in England. George
Downame's *Treatise Concerning Antichrist* (London, 1603),
Robert Abbot's *Antichristi Demonstratio, Contra Fabvlas*

23. For a fascinating glimpse of More's and Newton's daily involve-
ment in this work, see More's letter to John Sharp, 16 August 1680,
published in *Conway Letters: The Correspondence of Anne, Viscountess
Conway, Henry More, and their Friends, 1642–1684,* ed. Marjorie Hope
Nicolson (New Haven, 1930), pp. 478–79.

24. *A Plain and Continued Exposition Of the several Prophecies or
Divine Visions of the Prophet Daniel* (London, 1681), pp. xxiii-xxiv.

25. Published as part of *The Workes of . . . M^r. Tho: Brightman*
(London, 1644).

Pontificias (London, 1603), and Thomas Beard's *Antichrist the Pope of Rome: Or, The Pope of Rome is Antichrist* (London, 1625) are typical expositions of the papal Antichrist theory.[26]

By the end of the century a more generalized, less papal-centered interpretation of Antichrist became common in England and, although the Roman Catholic Church was not forgotten by its opponents, a looser symbolic language of beasts and horns—based largely on Daniel—was applied to other churches and sects. In England, this method of polemical exegesis of Daniel was already in evidence, in sophisticated form, in the first years of the Anglican Church. George Joye published such a work two years before the death of Henry VIII.[27] His *Exposicion of Daniel the Prophete* (London, 1545), which was publicly burned in 1546, presents *"A Prophecy diligently to be noted of al . . . kinges in these laste dayes."* Joye argues that lust and drunkenness are characteristic of "panthers or leopards (for both be one save the pardus is the male and the panther the female)" and that "the Gote" of chapter 8 "as afore the Leoparde" of chapter 7 "signifye the same king." He warns that "Noble Valeant princes" have been "deformed and destroyed in their owne fylthy dronken lecherose lustis" and he offers this taunt: "Whether ther be yet any siche Gotis let their fortune declare them and the clere eyed observe it." [28] Joye is carried away by his bitterness and his exegesis becomes vague, though still fascinating:

26. The strain of popular prophecy, represented by such works as *Strange and Remarkable Prophesies and Predictions Of the Holy, Learned, and excellent James Usher* (London, 1678), *The Most Strange and Wonderful Predictions of Cleombrotus an Heathen Jew* (London, 1679), or *The Strange and Wonderful History of Mother Shipton, . . . With an exact Collection of all her famous Prophecys . . . And large Explanations* (London, 1686), helped to accustom the public mind to contemporary applications of biblical prophecy.

27. See Charles C. Butterworth and Allan G. Chester, *George Joye: 1495?-1553* (Philadelphia, 1962), pp. 235-44.

28. Joye, fols. 128v-130r.

> The emprour hath the winges of the flying egle. . . . The
> other popisshe princes be beres winged swift speckled
> panthers. . . . here shal this fleinge egle be slayne upon
> the mountains of Israel / whyls he is in persecuting the
> chirche of cryste shall he be slayne with the breath and
> worde of this lyons mouthe cominge downe to iugement.[29]

Thus Dryden was clearly not the first to represent the enemies
of the true Church in the forms of Daniel's bear and panther.

The Fifth Monarchy controversy renewed the verbal currency of Daniel-Antichrist charges and enlarged the use of
theriomorphic imagery.[30] We should not wonder at Dryden's
newfangledness in describing a "bristl'd Baptist Boar" (I, 43)
or a Socinian "False Reynard" (I, 53) when we recall that the
Restoration was ushered in by such books as Richard Farne-
worth's *A Rod to drive out the Wilde Bores and Subtill Foxes
from amongst the Vines* (London, 1655) or William Aspinwall's *The Work of the Age: or, The sealed Prophecies of
Daniel opened and applied* (London, 1655) in which we are
told that "Charls Stuart is called a little Horn, because hee was
not his Fathers first born, but the younger brother" (p. 32).
The same politico-exegetical impulse which produced the
stream of David-Absolon applications which ultimately re-
sulted in Dryden's *Absalom and Achitophel* (1681)[31] also generated the literature of horn and beast applications which was
to eventuate, in complex ways, in *The Hind and the Panther*.
Sometimes, indeed, the two themes were even explicitly related and elaborated together, as in John Canne's *Time of the
End* (London, 1657):

> *It was told David, that Ahitophel was among the Con-
> spirators with Absolom.* Hee had but one *Ahitophel*
> with him, this *Horn* [i.e., Antichrist] will have many,

29. Joye, fols. 231r–233r.
30. See P. G. Rogers, *The Fifth Monarchy Men* (London, 1966).
31. See Richard Foster Jones, "The Originality of *Absalom and
Achitophel*," *MLN*, XLVI (1931), 211–18.

suttle and crafty foxes. . . . That hee perisheth under
the name of a *Beast,* though formerly a *Horn,* it shews
how little his death will bee pittied any where: No more
than if a bloudy Lyon, or crafty Fox had been killed by
hunters.[32]

The reactions of individual sects and churches to the annoy-
ing free-for-all use of the Antichrist charge helped create more
general conceptions of the doctrine and a more flexible set of
terms, metaphors, and images. Quaker apologiae, for example,
such as Richard Hubberthorn's *The Horn of the He-goat
Broken* (London, 1656) and George Whitehead's *The He-
Goats Horn Broken* (London, 1660) indicate the inclination of
the age to discard narrow identifications of the Antichrist.
Griffith Williams's Ὁ Αντιχριστος. *The Great Antichrist Revealed* (London, 1660) represents a fruition of this tendency.
As he announces to the reader in the extended title, his intention is to prove that Antichrist is *"neither Pope, nor Turk,
nor any Single Person, nor the Succession of any one Monarch,
or Tyrant in any Policie; But A collected pack, or multitude of
Hypocritical, Heretical, Blasphemous, and most scandalous
wicked men, that have fulfilled all the Prophesies of the Scriptures."*
Dryden's "pack" of enemies to the Church of Christ has
much to do, as we shall see, with such a conception. But first
we should recognize that even in the 1680s the imputation of
antichristianism to the Roman Catholic Church, in such works
as Robert Ware's *Hunting of the Romish Fox* (Dublin, 1683),
was still common. John Gother's widely read *Amicable Accommodation Of the Difference Between the Representer and
the Answerer* (London, 1686) brings together contemporary
antipopish charges in the mouth of a hypothetical "Zealous
Brother": such charges, as English Roman Catholics were

32. Canne, pp. 181 and 201

sensitively aware, were shot through with Antichrist beast images.[33]

Dryden's suggestion, in 1693, that poets should search for materials in "the prophecy of Daniel, . . . accommodating what there they find with the principles of Platonic philosophy as it is now Christianised" is certainly, in some sense, alluding to the Daniel commentary of the Cambridge Platonists. During the fourth quarter of the century no one else gave Daniel the systematic attention that they bestowed upon it; and no one else was as interested in the application of Platonic or Neoplatonic concepts to that prophet. But, we should point out, few other writers at that late date were also as vehement in their use of Daniel to prove that the Pope is Antichrist: "the Pope will be Antichrist," said More, in his Daniel commentary, "and no mortal man knows how to help it." [34] Dryden must have known that this was More's view. The Cambridge divine produced not one but a series of commentaries on Daniel, all of the same general anti-Roman import. More and his circle made it a point of their Christianity (as we saw in chapter 4) to put by "the weapons of controversy," but here was a violent departure from their calm creed. Aside from incidental comments on Daniel, which abound in almost all of More's writings, these works include *A Plain and Continued Exposition Of the several Prophecies or Divine Visions of the Prophet Daniel* (London, 1681), *An*

---

33. See Gother, pp. 33 ff. According to Joseph Gillow, *A Literary and Biographical History, or Bibliographical Dictionary of the English Catholics* (London, 1885–1902), II, 541, Gother's "literary style was greatly admired by Dryden." See also Victor M. Hamm, "Dryden's *The Hind and the Panther* and Roman Catholic Apologetics," *PMLA*, LXXXIII (1968), 413, on this point.

34. *Exposition Of . . . Daniel*, p. xliv. For Cudworth's similar views see *The Works of Ralph Cudworth*, ed. Thomas Birch (Oxford, 1829), III, 55–56. Cudworth's interest in Daniel was great: at the British Museum there are two enormous manuscript volumes of Daniel commentary in his hand (Sloane MS Add. 4986 and 4987).

Answer to Several Remarks Upon Dr. Henry More His Expositions of . . . Daniel (London, 1684), *Paralipomena prophetica* (London, 1685), and *An Illustration Of . . . the Book of Daniel* (London, 1685).[35]

Henry More and the Antichrist *Tsebi*

More's exegetical attack on the Pope and the Roman Catholic Church is, in the main, conventional. He tells us that the "little Horn" of Daniel 7:8 is the "Papal Polity or Hierarchy."[36] With an imaginative thoroughness which is More's hallmark as an interpreter, he explains that the eyes of the Horn—"eyes like the eyes of a man"—denote the "Papal Hierarchy how cunning and quick-sighted a Polity it has been":

> though this little Horn pretends to the only *sight* and *infallibility* in matters of Religion, as if it were inspired so from God that it cannot erre; yet the very character which the Prophecy gives it, doth advertise us, that this is but a bold boast among the rest, and that these are really but the *eyes* of a *man,* even of that *man of Sin* or *Antichrist,* that exalts himself above all that is called *God,* or worshipped.[37]

Similarly, he tells us that Daniel's description of the Horn's "Mouth speaking great things" signifies the Pope's

> Uttering great boasts of his own *Power* and *Infallibility.* . . . this speaking great things may more especially respect the great vaunts of the *Papal authoritive* Power, he being

35. Even after More died there was apparently still enough interest in what he had written to prompt the publication of a rebuttal to his Answer of 1684: the anonymous work is entitled *Remarks on D*ʳ. *Henry More's Expositions of the Apocalypse and Daniel, and Upon his Apology: Defended Against his Answer To Them* (London, 1690).

36. *Exposition Of . . . Daniel,* p. 38.

37. Ibid., pp. 39–40.

called by the Pontifician Polity, Our Lord God, *Optimum Maximum et Supremum Numen in Terris.*[38]

But, in his zeal, More is not satisfied with identifying the little Horn with the papal Antichrist of past and present. The single point on which he bestows greatest attention in his commentary is a prediction of the future based on 11:45. He prepares us for this in the preface:

> But as for what is to come, . . . as he is the best Hariolus that guesses well, so he the best Interpreter of Divine Prophecies that gives a rational account (whatever the Event may prove) touching such passages of them as concern things yet future. Which I speak in reference to my Expounding Dan. Ch. 11. vers. 45. of the taking of Rome by the Turk, which I heartily wish the Papal Hierarchy may prevent by a timely repentance of their Idolatry and bloud.[39]

Verse 45 of chapter 11 is as follows: "And he shall plant the tabernacles of his palace between the seas in the glorious holy mountain; yet he shall come to his end, and none shall help him." The Hebrew original of the phrase "glorious holy mountain" is *"Har Tsebi* [or *Sabi*] *Kodesh."* More's entire prophecy turns on the interpretation of the word *Tsebi* which occurs four times in Daniel and can mean 1) beauty, glory, or pleasantness; 2) a roe or hind; or 3) tumidity. These possibilities of alternate meaning were to lead to serious consequences. "As long as words a diff'rent sense will bear," Dryden noted, "And each may be his own Interpreter, / Our ai'ry faith will no foundation find: / The word's a weathercock for ev'ry wind" (I, 462–65).

In Daniel 8:9, the "little horn" (now of the Capricorn)

38. Ibid., pp. 40–41.
39. Ibid., pp. lxxxiv–lxxxv.

"waxes exceeding great toward the south, and toward the east, and toward the land of the Tsebi." More comments,

> The Hebrew word is [*Tsebi*][40] which signifies what is *beautifull, fair,* and *pleasant.* All interpreters understand it of the Land of *Judea,* this being the character of that Land in Holy Scripture, as *Psal.* 38. *The City of Jerusalem is* said to be *beautifull for situation, and the joy of the whole Earth;* and *Ezec.* 20.6. the Land of *Judea* is described as a Land flowing with Milk and Honey, and *as the glory of all Lands.*[41]

The word occurs three times in chapter 11. In verse 16 we are told that the king of the north "shall stand in the land of Tsebi," of which More says,

> *viz.* in *Judea.* The *Septuagint* do not venture to render the sense of [*Tsebi*] but retain the word, as if we should say, *And he shall stand in the land of* Sabi. Which I confess I suspect to be the name of the God of that Land, namely of the God of *Israel,* who is called the Lord of Hosts.[42]

Though More does not develop this suggestion any further, his comment is especially interesting in the light of his emphasis on intervening gods or guardian angels. It was this point, we recall, which attracted Dryden's attention in the *Discourse concerning . . . Satire.* More tells us in the preface to his *Exposition* that *"the affairs of men and of Kingdomes especially are carried on by the activity and ministry of Angels."* [43] Upon the occurrence of the word in verse 41, "He shall enter also into the land of Tsebi," More remarks,

40. The word *Tsebi* in brackets represents a transliteration of the Hebrew original in More's text.
41. *Exposition Of . . . Daniel,* p. 70.
42. Ibid., p. 174.
43. Ibid., p. vi.

(as Ch. 8.9.) signifies the land of *Judæa,* according to the general strain of Interpreters, by reason of the glory of the Temple and Divine Residence there.[44]

Yet when he comes to the word *Tsebi* in verse 45, More's antipapal feeling prompts him to develop another interpretation. He recognizes that

This Interpreters ordinarily understand of his [the king of the north's] entring into *Judæa,* because of the word [*Tsebi*] here used, which they make a character of the land of *Judæa,* and will have the Mountain Mount *Sion* and *Moria,* where the Temple stands, betwixt two Seas, the *Mediterranean* and *Mare Mortuum.*[45]

But More prefers to construct his interpretation on the view that *Tsebi*

is not necessarily a proper name of *Judæa,* but may be a Noun Appellative (though the *Seventy,* both here and also ver. 41 do not change it in their translation, but call it . . . *Sabi*) which signifies *rem tumidam, plenam, turgidam,* as *A Lapide* himself has noted.[46]

More decides that the "mountain" refers to the hills of Rome where, through the might of the Turk, the Antichrist Pope and the papal hierarchy will be destroyed. More asks, why may not "the mountain of *Tsebi,*"

which may seem to belong properly to *Judæa* and the Temple there, be applied to Antichrist *himself,* especially it hitting so fitly as it does in vertue of other significations of the word [*Tsebi*], it signifying as well a *tumid* excellency, as *solid* excellency; For so you may render [*Har Tsebi Kodesh*], either the *Hill of a tumid pompousness*

44. Ibid., p. 208.
45. Ibid., pp. 210–11.
46. Ibid., p. 211.

of Holiness, the Holiness of that Church consisting most-
what in outward pomps and shews, or, *The Hill of the
tumour and fastuosity of his Holiness* the Pope, . . . the
Hill of a very *tumid* though not solid *Supremum Numen
in terris.* . . . by [the] description in *Ezekiel,* what a *Zebi*
Antichrist is, that is, what a *turgid and tumid thing,* as
Cornelius à Lapide interprets the word, *swoln* and *puffed
up.*[47]

But, as More well knew, this was not all that Lapide had
to say about the word. The Anglican polemicist could not
have his way so easily. "While *sound* and *sound* a diff'rent
sense explains," Dryden observed sagaciously, "Both play at
hard-head till they break their brains" (II, 442–43). On the
occurrence of the word in Ezekiel 20:6, Lapide had noted:

> *tsebi,* id est præstantia, exsultatio, superbia, *q. d.* Terra
> Israel est excellentia et superbia, æque ac pulchritudo et
> deliciæ regionum. Vatablus: *Est desiderabilis et amabilis ut
> caprea,* quæ hebraice *tsebi* dicitur; . . . Quid proprie sit
> *tsebi* dicam *Daniel.* cap. VIII, 9.[48]

And on the appearance of the word in Daniel 8:9, Lapide
remarks:

> Proprie *tsebi* significat rem tumidam, plenam, turgidam,
> eminentem, crassam, pinguem, quæ alios in sui amorem
> et desiderium allicit. Hinc ulterius per catachresin *tsebi*
> significat id quod est pulchrum, amabile et inclytum, puta
> decus, gloriam, decorem, jucunditatem, delicias et capreo-
> lum, qui homini est in deliciis. Unde *tsebi* vel *tsebia*
> [feminine gender], . . . id est *dama,* vel caprea.[49]

47. Ibid., pp. 212–13.
48. Cornelius à Lapide (Roman Catholic commentator), *Commentaria
in Scripturam Sacram* (Paris, 1868), XII, 647.
49. Ibid., XIII, 105.

More self-consciously insists that in his interpretation of *Tsebi*
"no Grammatical or Critical violence is done to the Text by
thus expounding of it," [50] but we can see that Lapide, at least,
would not agree with him.

Tsebi and Hind

In fact, the catachresis that Lapide observes in understanding the word as both "beauty" and "hind" or "roe" was the
basis for a veritable subtradition in the exegesis of these passages in Daniel. On the continent—both early and late in the
century—we find examples of this fascinating interpretation
which has the effect of producing another animal in the
animal-laden mythology of Daniel. Thomas Malvenda's famous
De Antichristo (Rome, 1604) notes:

> *In terram gloriosam.* pro gloriosa, Hebraice est *Tsebi*,
> quae vox præter notum significatum capreæ vel capreoli,
> dicitur quoque significare Gloriam, decorem, desider-
> ium—., iucunditatem, amœnitatem, voluptatem, pulchri-
> tudinem.[51]

Eighty years later Martin Geier writes,

> Nomen [*tsebi*], qvod qvandoque etiam *capream* denotat,
> (vid. *Prov.* VI, 5.) idem est ac *ornamentum, decus.*[52]

Curiously enough, this interpretation enjoyed greater vogue
in England than anywhere else. Hugh Broughton's *Daniel His
Chaldie Visions and His Ebrew* (London, 1596), which went
through many editions in English and Latin, observes of 8:9.

> Israel, is the Tzeby of landes: the ornament, pleasure, and
> noblenes or as it were the Roe: so much Tzeby signifieth
> in Dan. 11. Daniel in this phrase, putteth Iudah in

50. *Exposition Of . . . Daniel*, p. 221.
51. Malvenda, p. 268.
52. *Prælectiones Academicæ in Danielem Prophetam* (Leipzig, 1684),
pp. 609–10.

minde of that oration which God maketh in Ezekiel [20].
[sig. G2v]

In the year of the Restoration, John Trapp, in his *Commentary or Exposition upon . . . Daniel* (London, 1660), says simply that the *Tsebi* of 8:9 must mean *"Judæa,* called here *Decus, Capreolus"* (p. 558). Edward Leigh's *Critica Sacra* (London, 1662) elaborates the same interpretation and refers his readers to Thomas Brightman for further illumination (II, 200). It was Brightman's *Comfortable Exposition of . . . Daniel,* mentioned earlier, which brought the "roe" or "hind" of Daniel to vivid life. On 11:41, Brightman expounds as follows:

> The first Countrie made mention of is the land of the *Roe,* or of delight and ornament, that is *Iudea* it self, as *Ezechiel* sheweth, calling it the land of the *Roe,* or of glory, which God sware to give to the *Israelites* after their delivery out of *Egypt,* and which hee gave them to possesse after forty yeeres wandring in the Wildernesse, *Ezech.* 20.6.15.
>
> But it may happily be doubted, what should be the reason of this appellation, whether it be so called from his inhabitants put to flight, and driven into banishment; as the *Roe* Bucks, leaving their wonted haunts, do run hither and thither, when the hounds and hunters do pursue them in the mountains. (*Erets hatsebi* [sic]. *Terra capreolæ.* So *Esay* speaks of *Babylon,* describing her exiled Citizens carried away; *for it shall be,* saith he, *as the chased Roe, and as the Sheep that no man taketh up,* Chap. 13.14. And, *Iudea,* whether we respect the first *Canaanites,* whom the land spued out for their horrible wickednesse, or the new dwellers, the *Israelites,* first carried away by the *Assyrians,* and after driven out of their Countrey by the *Romans,* and scattered thorow the whole earth, may worthily be called a chased *Roe.* But *Ezechiel,*

in the place aforesaid, seemeth to bring another notation
of this name: for he describing *Canaan* from the abound-
ing of milk and honey; as if it had borrowed his name of
this fruitfulnesse, saith: It is the *Roe,* or glory of all lands,
as if all lands did hunt, and seeke eagerly after this land,
as after the *Roe,* because of the felicity thereof, as if this
were the glory and delicious delight of all lands, for so is
tsebi often used. I think the spirit did use this word of set
purpose, thereby to comprehend both their expulsion, and
happinesse, lest their Citizens should despaire, and be
quite out of heart; but in the midst of her sorrowfull
exile they should think themselves to be Gods *tsebi,*
darlings, and delight.⁵³

This is catachresis elevated toward the condition of poetry.
It provides much of the material for Dryden's outcast Hind:

> Panting and pensive now she rang'd alone,
> And wander'd in the kingdoms, once Her own.
>
> [I, 25–26]

With the help of the Hind exegesis, Dryden could represent
the guardian angel of the Roman Catholic Church in an
heroic contest prophesied in Scripture and could deny the
identification of the Pope with a "tumid thing" or Antichrist.
The poet of *Religio Laici* left himself "no right to interpret
obscure places" of the Bible. The poet of *The Hind and the
Panther* silently and humbly asserts the power of human
reason to find saving truth in the crippled text of the Old
Testament. It was an act that represented welcome release
from the textual doubts torturing the poet of *Religio Laici.*
In her comment on the complexity of exegesis, the Hind hints
at her biblical identity; she is the *Tsebi* or Hind of Daniel,
chapters 8 and 11 persecuted by Antichrist, not the Antichrist
Tsebi which More would make her:

53. *The Workes of . . . Mʳ. Tho: Brightman,* pp. 923–24.

The sense is intricate, 'tis onely clear
What vowels and what consonants are there.
Therefore 'tis plain, its meaning must be try'd
Before some judge appointed to decide.[54]

[II, 385–88]

But the Panther does not understand. Her retort blunderingly
confirms the account of persecution—of the "chase"—which
the immortal Hind has just given her.

Your arguments an endless chase persue:
Produce this vaunted Leader to our view,
This might *Moyses* of the chosen crew.

[II, 391–93]

The Hind is left with no choice but to announce explicitly
that she is the guardian in question.

The Dame, who saw her fainting foe retir'd,
With force renew'd, to victory aspir'd;
(And looking upward to her kindred sky,
As once our Saviour own'd his Deity,
Pronounc'd his words—*she whom ye seek am I*.)
Nor less amaz'd this voice the *Panther* heard,
Than were those *Jews* to hear a god declar'd.

[II, 394–400]

Anglicans like More would make of the papal polity a *"Zebi
Antichrist"*—a "ten-horn'd monster" (I, 537). Dryden—no

---

54. Even in 1682 Dryden shows more than a superficial knowledge of
Hebrew names and etymologies. In the "Epistle To the Whigs," prefixed to
The Medall, Dryden recommends the author of "the Whip and Key"
in these words: *"I am charitable enough to doe him a kindness, that it
may be publish'd as well as printed; and that so much skill in Hebrew
Derivations, may not lie for Wast-paper in the Shop. Yet I half suspect
he went no farther for his learning, than the Index of Hebrew Names
and Etymologies, which is printed at the end of some* English *Bibles.
If* Achitophel *signify the Brother of a Fool, the Authour of that Poem
will pass with his Readers for the next of kin"* (ll. 106–13).

longer an adherent of the Platonists but still deriving inspiration from their work—reverses the situation. He *turns* the dangerous myth into "Heroick Poesie." The Hind is "chas'd with horns" (I, 5) which are, he implies, "horns of arbitrary might" (I, 266). According to this parallel, as Brightman suggested, the Hind and her offspring are like "Captive Israel," a "numerous Exile" with "grief and gladness mixt" (I, 19–21).

Dryden also uses the association of the Roman Catholic Church with Daniel's Hind or *Tsebi* to upset the traditional Protestant argument that, as More insisted, the Reformation was the fulfilling of the vision of the rising of the "Witnesses" who would testify to the antichristianity of the Pope and/or his Church.[55] Once the Roman Hind is seen in the position of being attacked by the little horn of Antichrist rather than being that horn, the image of a pack of antichristian beasts naturally falls to the Protestant sects, while the Protestants' own expositions of their witness capacity become the material of satire. More, for example, had berated the several sects for their

> *humour, fansifulness and partiality* . . . , *that they can hardly believe of themselves, that the Witnesses are risen, till Kingdomes, Nations, and Principalities of their own party rise into Political power, namely all* Episcopal, *all* Presbyterian, *all* Calvinists, *all* Arminians, *all* Socinians, *and so of* Anabaptists, Quakers *and* Famulists. *But they erre knowing not the Scriptures or the true meaning of them, nor rightly considering the Records of History, where they may find what was the testimony of these Witnesses who are predicted to rise in the Reformation, and to be warred against before by the Beast and cruelly persecuted.*[56]

55. *Exposition Of . . . Daniel*, p. lviii.
56. Ibid., pp. li–lii.

More insists that "at this very day our own Church of England
. . . gives the same testimony of the Church of Rome." [57] According to Dryden, these are the false witnesses who "sought
to find / The ten-horn'd monster in the harmless Hind" (I,
536–37). Dryden reveals the beastlike essence of these witnesses
when he slyly observes that the Panther should beware of her
associates because

> Some evil minded beasts might lye in wait;
> And without witness wreak their hidden hate.
>
> [II, 689–90]

The "weight of antient witness" (I, 62) shows us that the
Protestant sects are the impious, blasphemous race (I, 56) of
Antichrist who invert the image of the true Deity:

> Revers'd they view'd him lessen'd to their eye,
> Nor in an Infant could a God descry:
> New swarming Sects to this obliquely tend,
> Hence they began, and here they all will end.
>
> [I, 58–61]

The "graceless beast" (I, 54), in ways similar to Daniel's Ten-
Horned Monster, represents the culmination of the line of
destruction composed of the Independent Bear, the Quaking
Hare, the Atheist Ape, the Baptist Boar, and the "creature
of a double kind" spawned by a "furious" Lion. These
"monsters" (I, 292), "A slimy-born and sun-begotten Tribe"
(I, 311), are not Witnesses, Dryden tells us; they are themselves
the "pack" of Antichrist.

57. Ibid., p. liii.

10

The Hind and the Panther: II

More informs us that the Protestants' *"plain and simple testimony against the Church of* Rome *was this, That the Pope was that Man of sin or Antichrist, and their Church Idolatrous by reason of their adoration of the Host, invocation of Saints and worshipping of Images."* [1] It is the refutation of this "revers'd" testimony which occupies the polemical as well as aesthetic center of *The Hind and the Panther.* More himself, as we might expect, was not behindhand in supplying the specifics of what he considered the essential Protestant Witness. At the end of the book-length introduction to the *Exposition . . . Of Daniel* he notes that no one has attempted to refute his own proof of "the Antichristianity and Idolatry of the Church of Rome" published "at least fifteen years agoe" in his "Synopsis Prophetica." [2] More is referring here to the closing chapters of his *Modest Enquiry into the Mystery of Iniquity* (London, 1664) which attempted to deflect "all suspicions of Antichristianism" from the Church of England to the Church of Rome.[3] Five years later he felt compelled to repeat the same arguments—this time in a barrage aimed exclusively at the Roman Church—in *An Antidote against Idolatry* (London, 1669).

1. *Exposition Of . . . Daniel,* p. lii.
2. Ibid., p. lxxxvi.
3. Pages 459–78. The second part of the *Modest Enquiry* is entitled "*Synopsis Prophetica.*"

Henry More, John Walton, and
Roman Catholic "Idolatry"

More's assertion that no one attempted to answer his charges is quite remarkable. In 1672 he himself had penned *A Brief Reply To a Late Answer To Dr. Henry More His Antidote Against Idolatry* (London, 1672) in counter-rebuttal to *A Brief Answer To The Many Calumnies of Dr. Henry More, In His Pretended Antidote Against Idolatry* (n.p., 1672) by the Jesuit John Walton.[4] Walton's work has now almost totally disappeared and More apparently thought then that it was best to bury the controversy, for he decided not to include his own answer in his *Opera Omnia* (London, 1675–79); but we may suppose that English Catholics—especially those interested in Protestant, Platonic, anti-Catholic interpretations of Daniel— would have known of this lone cry of recusant resistance to More's charge of Catholic antichristianism.

Walton presents More with a Roman Catholic challenge on precisely the point which led Dryden to More's "accommodation" of Daniel "with the principles of Platonic philosophy as it is now Christianised"; it was this accommodation, we recall, which Dryden hoped could make "the ministry of angels as strong an engine for the working up heroic poetry, in our religion, as that of the Ancients has been to raise theirs by all the fables of their gods."[5] More's charge of idolatry against the Roman Catholic Church depended in large meas-

---

4. According to H. Foley, *Records of the English Province of the Society of Jesus,* Series 12 (London, 1879), v, 340, Walton was born in Lancashire in 1622 and died in 1677 or 1678. Walton's book is now very rare; it is not listed in the Wing index. There is a copy in the library of Heythrop College, Chipping Norton, Oxford. For help in finding this work, I am indebted to Antony Allison of the British Museum and to Thomas H. Clancy, S.J., of Loyola University in New Orleans who generously sent me a copy of his valuable—yet unpublished—list (compiled with the aid of Dr. David Rogers), "English Catholic Books, 1666–1700."

5. *Of Dramatic Poesy,* ed. Watson, II, 88–89.

ure on a comparison of Roman Catholic "invocation of Saints
and worshipping of Images" [6] with the idolatry of the pagans.
Walton examines More's elaboration of this point:

> The Idolatry of the Pagans, says the Doctor, consisted in
> this, viz. in that they either took something to be the
> supreme God, that was not, and worshipped it for such;
> or else worshipped the supreme God in an Image; or gave
> religious worship . . . and invoked such, as they them-
> selves knew not to be the supreme God, but either the
> souls of Men departed, or other demons, or else particular
> appearances or powers of nature. And concerning these
> demons, he adds . . . , That the Pagans demons ex-
> quisitely Answer to the Christian Saints and Angels, in
> this point; saving that this spiritual fornication is a rape
> upon our Saints and Angels, but single fornication in the
> Heathen with their impure demons. Thus far the modest
> Doctor. . . . Of all the Doctor's conclusions, there is none
> more intrinseck and fundamental to the subject now
> under debate [i.e. the charge of Roman Catholic idolatry]
> than this. . . . That the Pagans demons exquisitely an-
> swer to the Christians Saints and Angels.[7]

Further on Walton notes that:

> the Doctor falls foul upon the Council of Trent, for
> teaching, That the Saints raigning with Christ offer up
> their Prayers for Men; and that it is good and profitable
> humbly to invocate them. . . . This the Doctor terms
> making the Saints the more exactly like the Pagans Dii
> Medioxumi, and the Demons that negotiated the affairs
> of Men with the highest Deities.[8]

Walton's defense rests partly on patristic authority. He quotes
Saint Augustine who

6. *Exposition Of . . . Daniel*, p. lii.
7. Walton, pp. 11–12.
8. Ibid., p. 63.

renders it easily intelligible, how the Saints might . . .
relieve those that called upon them: Viz. *God omnipotent
and ever present hearing the Prayers of the Martyrs, and
granting to Men, by the Ministery of Angels those helps
—when he will, where he will, and how he pleaseth.*[9]

But the main burden of Walton's argument rests on two
assertions. First, he distinguishes between *latria,* the highest
form of Roman Catholic worship reserved for God alone, and
dulia, the lower form of worship addressed to saints and
angels.[10] Second, he *insists* on the legitimacy of artistic representation of divine subjects. "I would gladly know of the
Doctor," he asks,

> why he calls a Figure, or Image a symbolical presence,
> but only because the Image is a sign or token, signifying
> or representing the Person, whose image it is?
> . . . the honour done to the Image may be referr'd to
> the Prototype, though there be no personal similitude of
> figure betwixt the Image and the Person it represents. For
> besides the similitude of figure, there is another similitude,
> which the Doctor, if he please may call a similitude of
> signification; the Image signifying the dignity, quality, or
> other perfections of the Prototype: . . . it did actually so
> fall out in the images of the Angels or Cherubims over
> the Ark, which (if we regard personal similitude of figure
> and feature) were more like some material and terrestrial
> Beeings, then those incorporeal intelligences; and yet the
> honour done to them was referred to the Prototypes.
> . . . the Principles of the late revived Platonick Philos-
> ophy . . . allow unto Souls separated and discharged
> from these gross terrestrial Elements, the like Aerial or
> Ætherial Vehicles with Angels; and therefore under this

9. Ibid., p. 36.
10. Ibid., pp. 45 ff.

notion, either both, or neither of them, are capable of an imagery representation.[11]

Walton, of course, believed that according to "the principles of Platonic philosophy as it is now Christianised" (to use Dryden's comparable phrase) *both* angels and the "separated" souls of saints were perfectly capable of such "imagery representation." He believed this in an age when Thomas Sprat was saying that most poetical images "disgust the best things, if they come sound, and unadorn'd: they are in open defiance against Reason: professing, not to hold much correspondence with that; but with its Slaves, the Passions." [12] It was a time, we recall, of complaints like More's against the "Corporeal Malady of Imagination," a time of "exaggerated antipathy to metaphors" and of frantic "desire to make the word match the thing"—the *verba* match the *res*.[13] Dryden himself must have recalled quite vividly that, five years earlier, the poet of an Anglican *religio laici* had declared in his motto that *Ornari res ipsa negat,* and had summarily rejected the "Figurative way" as suited only "for the Passions." "A Man," the Anglican poet had said, "is to be cheated into Passion, but to be reason'd into Truth." [14] For Dryden, the allegorical poet of the Roman Catholic Church, Walton's qualifications on More must have been an object of substantial interest.

The main focus of Walton's rebuttal deals with the ultimate implications of the charge of Roman Catholic idolatry. More paraphrased the words of the Jesuit Costerus to indicate the centrality and the precariousness of the special image-worship involved in the adoration of the Host: *"if our Church be mistaken in the doctrin of Transubstantiation, we Ipso Facto*

---

11. Ibid., pp. 40 and 75–77.

12. See Sprat, *History of the Royal Society,* pp. 111–12; cf. chap. 9, n. 15.

13. R. F. Jones, "Science and Language in England of the Mid-Seventeenth Century," p. 155.

14. *Religio Laici,* Preface, ll. 350–55.

stand guilty of such a piece of idolatry, as never was before seen or known in this World." [15] Walton points out that these words are largely More's own and then treats of the "physics" involved in the miracle of transubstantiation. This was a step beyond the point where a poet could accompany a polemicist. Walton had come far in demonstrating the design of Roman Catholic image worship, though the ultimate Roman Catholic icon—the transubstantiated Host—lay beyond his discursive reach. Dryden would soon perfect the representation of the Roman Catholic design—and even integrate the miraculous icon—in an icon of his own creation.

Sign and Substance: Icon and Divinity

Dryden could go beyond Walton because he understood that the basis of the charge of Roman Catholic idolatry was essentially poetic. He realized that the priestly miracle of transubstantiation comprehended elements of word, thing, and image which represented, at one remove, a theological equivalent of the problem of *res et verba*. On the charge of image idolatry turned the holiness or antichristianity of the entire Roman Catholic faith. Dryden's poem is, therefore, designed as a vindication and assertion of the divine *poesis* of his adopted church. The Hind makes clear the centrality of this issue in her analysis of the Panther's difficulties with the Host:

> In doubtfull points betwixt her diff'ring friends,
> Where one for substance, one for sign contends,
> Their contradicting terms she strives to join,
> Sign shall be substance, substance shall be sign.
> A real presence all her sons allow,
> And yet 'tis flat Idolatry to bow,
> Because the god-head's there they know not how.
> Her Novices are taught that bread and wine

15. See Walton, p. 46.

Are but the visible and outward sign
Receiv'd by those who in communion join.
But th' inward grace, or the thing signify'd,
His bloud and body, who to save us dy'd;
The faithfull this thing signify'd receive.
What is't those faithfull then partake or leave?
For what is signify'd and understood,
Is, by her own confession, flesh and blood.
Then, by the same acknowledgement, we know
They take the sign, and take the substance too.
The lit'ral sense is hard to flesh and blood,
But nonsense never can be understood.

[1, 410–29]

The Anglican Panther's confusion about the "thing signify'd"
—the relation between the "substance" and the "sign," the
"thing" and the image or word—immediately endangers her
communion: the "inward grace" embodied in Christ's person
remains beyond her reach. Her inability to accept the priest's
word, which creates Christ's "flesh and blood" (1, 425) in the
mass, makes impossible the difficult union of Christ's body
with *men's* "flesh and blood" (1, 429). The Anglican's denial
of "lit'ral sense" in the Host—her theory of spiritual "nonsense"—is itself, Dryden suggests, blindness born of materialistic reasoning. "Certitude of sense," he tells us, is the Panther's
"guide in faith" (1, 540–41). If there is a "real presence" in
the Host, the demands of "sense" should be more than satisfied. There is a reality in the icon of the Host, Dryden insists,
which is a presensual or suprasensual apprehension of the
"body" of Christ imparted and confirmed by divine revelation:

For what my senses can themselves perceive
I need no revelation to believe.
Can they who say the Host should be descry'd
By sense, define a body glorify'd?

[1, 91–94]

Divine revelations were intended as a means of transcending sense and grasping the literalness of Christ's presence: they were the "means" of a "more deep design"—

> To prove the god-head of th' eternal Son.
> God thus asserted: man is to believe
> Beyond what sense and reason can conceive.
> [I, 115–19]

This is the way to the "mysterious things of faith" (I, 120). "Could He," Dryden asks,

> his god-head veil with flesh and bloud
> And not veil these again to be our food?
> His grace in both is equal in extent,
> The first affords us life, the second nourishment.
> And if he can, why all this frantick pain
> To construe what his clearest words contain . . . ?
> [I, 134–39]

For the Panther, the word and the image remain merely descriptive and figurative. She says that

> *Luther,* more mistaking what he read,
> Misjoins the sacred Body with the Bread;
> Yet, *Lady,* still remember I maintain,
> The Word in needfull points is onely plain.
> [II, 141–44]

She fails to understand that the word conveys more than doctrinal "points," and that, in fact, it *contains* (I, 139) the means of joining the man-made image with the divine substance.

The Hind explains to the fair Anglican that it is her vacillation and ambiguity on the question of the Eucharist which have determined the fundamental weakness of her Church:

> . . . to explain what your forefathers meant,
> By real presence in the sacrament,
>
> . . . .

Your *salvo* comes, that he's not there at all:
There chang'd your faith, and what may change may fall.
Who can believe what varies every day,
Nor ever was, nor will be at a stay?
. . . .
For *real,* as you now the word expound,
From solid substance dwindles to a sound.
Methinks an *Æsop's* fable you repeat,
You know who took the shadow for the meat:
Your churches substance thus you change at will,
And yet retain your former figure still.
. . . ev'ry hour your form
Is chop'd and chang'd, like winds before a storm.

[II, 31–57]

Because the Panther cannot discern the "substance" of Christ
in the Host, there is no substance—no enduring or mean-
ingful structure of belief—to her church.[16] Her "form" is, as
we were told earlier, "of a double kind" (I, 402). Like the
animal in Aesop's fable she takes "the shadow for the meat,"
the sign for the substance. The Panther repeats the Aesopian
fable in two ways: she reiterates Aesop's playing with sign
and substance and she reenacts the error of the beast. We
saw earlier that, in important ways, *The Hind and the Panther* represents a revision of the materials of *Religio Laici:*
as such, the later poem is not only a defense of a convert's
new faith, but also a vindication of his *process* of conversion.
In a still larger sense, the process of substantive revision and
conversion to the true faith of Christ offers a ritual of faith
which itself intimates and imitates the great mystery of deific
transubstantiation. Dryden's aim is to reclaim the "meat,"

16. Dryden's formulations of key theological problems resemble Swift's
in *A Tale of a Tub* in such obvious ways that, considering Swift's
explicit hostility to concealed allegory and to *The Hind and the
Panther,* it would be fascinating to know how much of Dryden's poem
Swift understood.

the "substance," or "flesh and blood" of Christ, represented by the true Church whose form is "immortal and unchang'd" (I, 1).

When he considers the possibility of "censure" against his "mysterious writ" which has "peopl'd Caledon/With Panthers, Bears, and Wolves, and Beasts unknown" (III, 2–4), he suggests that his poem is an "Æsop"-like response (III, 6)—as was Spenser's *Mother Hubberd's Tale* (III, 8)—to the monstrous aspects of contemporary life:

> Led by those great examples, may not I
> The wanted organs of their words supply?
> If men transact like brutes 'tis equal then
> For brutes to claim the privilege of men.
>
> [III, 12–15]

To those of "little wit" and "much malice" some of the animals in Dryden's poem are "beasts unknown"; his fable seems to them a "mysterious writ." Dryden implies that, to those who are better disposed toward his poem and who are possessed of more wit, the mystery is soon opened.

The Hind and the Panther is, as we have seen, an adaptation of allegorical Holy Writ—of the complex beast fable of Daniel. Dryden's role as Daniel-like poet causes him to adopt the tone of personal guilt and conflict of Daniel's prophetic voice. Daniel wrote in chapters 9 and 10:

> 4 And I prayed unto the Lord my God, and made my confession, and said, O Lord, the great and dreadful God, keeping the covenant and mercy to them that love him, and to them that keep his commandments;
>
> 5 We have sinned, and have committed iniquity, and have done wickedly, and have rebelled, even by departing from thy precepts and from thy judgments . . .

7 O Lord righteousness *belongeth* unto thee, but
    unto us confusion of faces . . .

8 O Lord, to us *belongeth* confusion of face . . .

9 To the Lord our God *belong* mercies and forgive-
    ness, though we have rebelled against him.

10:8 . . . I was left alone, and saw this great vision, and
    there remained no strength in me: for my come-
    liness was turned in me into corruption, and I
    retained no strength.

"Be thine the glory, and be mine the shame," writes Dryden
in the *confessio* near the beginning of the poem. This famous
passage has long been valued as one of the few personal
revelations in Dryden's work. It is also, I believe, Dryden's
allusive invocation of Daniel's prophetic knowledge:

. . . gratious God, how well dost thou provide
For erring judgments an unerring Guide?
Thy throne is darkness in th' abyss of light,
A blaze of glory that forbids the sight;
O teach me to believe Thee thus conceal'd,
And search no farther than thy self reveal'd;
But her alone for my Directour take
Whom thou hast promis'd never to forsake!
My thoughtless youth was wing'd with vain desires,
My manhood, long misled by wandring fires,
Follow'd false lights; and when their glimps was gone,
My pride struck out new sparkles of her own.
Such was I, such by nature still I am,
Be thine the glory, and be mine the shame.

[I, 64–77]

In his discourse "Of Prophecie," the Cambridge Platonist
John Smith explained that Daniel's "Fatigations" in chapter
10 are the mark of "true Prophesie entred upon the Mind as
a fire." This genuine prophetic spirit, he says, should be

sharply distinguished from the "False light which pretends to
Prophesie, but is not; as being seated only in the Imaginative
power." [17] Dryden's *confessio* serves as evidence of his own
"fatigations" and his own consciousness of having followed
"false lights" and "wandring fires." Now he has found the
true "sun" (I, 90); and, in opposition to Smith's coreligionist,
More, Dryden argues that the "Imaginative power" of the
Roman Catholic Church, *which he represents in his poem*,
is truly inspired and prophetic. Montague and Prior did not
(or would not) understand that his theological beast-fable
interchanges kinds of life and institutions (or polities)—men
and beasts; churches and animals; lions and kings—in the
same way that Daniel did. Even the absurdity of theology-
spouting brutes is seen in a new light when we recall that the
Antichrist beast in Daniel speaks "great words against the
most High" and wears "out the saints of the most High"
(7:25). Montague and Prior's jest at the lack of actual blows
and battles in the poem misses the essential point: the real
battle with the forces of Antichrist *is* a war of words and
ideas. The Hind hints at explicit consciousness of this aspect
of her encounter with the Panther when she puts words into
the mouth of a hypothetical Independent: "Shall she com-
mand," asks the Independent concerning the Panther, "who
has herself rebell'd?"

> Is *Antichrist* by *Antichrist* expell'd?
> Did we a lawfull tyranny displace,
> To set aloft a bastard of the race?
> Why all these wars to win the Book, if we
> Must not interpret for our selves, but she?
>
> [II, 279–84]

The war against the "great words" of Antichrist is encap-
sulated in the matched bird fables—or, perhaps, more precisely, vulture fables—found in the Third Part. These

17. John Smith, *Select Discourses*, pp. 191, 200, and 207.

prophecies of "future change in state" (III, 415) epitomize
Dryden's effort to upset the fabling designs of anti–Roman
Catholic forces even while he asserts the scripture-derived
fable—reinforced by an English saint's legend—of ultimate
Roman Catholic ascendancy. It is the Panther, Dryden emphasizes, who initiates the fable contest: "Perhaps," she says to
the Hind,

> you think your time of triumph near,
> But may mistake the season of the year;
> The *Swallows* fortune gives you cause to fear.
>
> [III, 417–19]

In making her prediction of Roman Catholic ruin, the
Panther exhibits acute awareness of seventeenth-century abuse
of apocalyptic modes. The Martyn, she tells us, claimed that

> He found a leaf inscrib'd with sacred rime,
> Whose antique characters did well denote
> The *Sibyl*'s hand of the *Cumæan* Grott:[18]
> The mad Divineress had plainly writ,
> A time shou'd come (but many ages yet,)
> In which, sinister destinies ordain,
> A *Dame* shou'd drown with all her feather'd train.
>
> [III, 487–93]

Even though the Panther is in the process of affirming the
Martyn's prediction, she pretends that she is above such
methods:

> Most prophecies are of a piece with these,
> Each *Nostradamus* can foretell with ease:[19]

18. In the decades preceding the publication of *The Hind and the
Panther* there had been considerable interest in sibylline writings. Cf.
especially David Blondel, *A Treatise of the Sibyls* (London, 1661) and
John Twysden, *A Disquisition Touching the Sibylls And the Sibylline
Writings* (London, 1662).

19. See *Poems on Affairs of State,* ed. George deF. Lord (New Haven,
1963,) I, 185–89.

> Not naming persons, and confounding times,
> One casual truth supports a thousand lying rimes.
>
> [III, 519–22]

Despite her supposed innocence of the methods of pseudo-prophets, the Panther slyly buttresses her prediction of Roman Catholic doom with a double allusion to the Antichrist battle of the Ram and the Capricorn (which produces the little horn) in Daniel 8. The Martyn, she tells us, foretells a time of peace at the sign of "the Ram" (III, 536); this is "accomplish'd" (III, 545), but then the sun is "enter'd into Capricorn" (III, 598) and the destruction of the swallows soon follows. The Hind is quick to note the Antichrist overtones in the Panther's story. She sees in it the repeated papal-beast charge of the Reformation—a charge which is itself antichristian.

> The patience of the *Hind* did almost fail,
> For well she mark'd the malice of the tale:
> Which Ribbald art their church to *Luther* owes,
> In malice it began, by malice grows,
> He sow'd the *Serpent's* teeth, an iron-harvest rose.
>
> [III, 639–43]

The Hind's countertale of the Doves, like Dryden's larger fable of the Hind herself, denies the charge of Roman Catholic antichristianity. In his controversy with Walton on the issue of idolatrous image worship, More wrote,

> A Dove may be the Hieroglyphick of [the Holy Ghost as easily] as that description of the Ancient of dayes in *Daniel* is an Hieroglyphick of God the father. But to do Divine worship toward such an Image of a Dove, it is absolutely the same Idolatry that was in so doing to the Image of God the Father, and of Christ.[20]

20. More, *An Appendix to the late Antidote against Idolatry* (London, 1673), p. 29.
It may be that Dryden is also alluding to folk traditions of deer-to-bird soul transmigration. See Lowry Charles Wimberly, *Folklore in the English and Scottish Ballads* (Chicago, 1928), pp. 51–58.

As if by way of satiric rejoinder to More's attack, Dryden
makes the pretentious Anglicans a "sort of Doves" (III, 946).
The Hind locates the evil of the pigeons, misled by an Anti-
christlike "Beast of a Bird" (III, 1013), in *their* attempt to
identify the Roman Catholics with Antichrist.

> An hideous Figure of their Foes they drew,
> Nor Lines, nor Looks, nor Shades, nor Colours true;
> And this Grotesque design, expos'd to Publick view.
> . . . .
> All so perverse a Draught, so far unlike,
> It was no Libell where it meant to strike:
> Yet still the daubing pleas'd, and Great and Small
> To view the Monster crowded Pigeon-hall.
>
> [III, 1042–51]

The Hind's tale of Anglican catastrophe implies the fulfill-
ment of the scriptural prophecy which describes the end of
Antichrist's reign: "Here ends the Reign of this pretended
Dove; / All Prophecies accomplish'd from above" (III, 1256–57).

Conclusion: "For Thou Shalt Rest"

In his discussion of the *Discourse concerning . . . Satire*
Johnson remarked that Dryden's plan for epic poetry built
on Daniel-like guardian angels was "the most reasonable
scheme of celestial interposition that ever was formed. . . .
That this poem was never written," said Johnson, "is reasonably to be lamented." [21] I have tried to show that this poem

21. *Lives of the English Poets,* ed. Hill, I, 385–86. Johnson thought that
he detected a major flaw in the conception: "In the scheme of Dryden
there is one great difficulty, which yet he would perhaps have had
address enough to surmount. In a war justice can be but on one side,
and to entitle the hero to the protection of angels he must fight in the
defence of indubitable right. Yet some of the celestial beings, thus
opposed to each other, must have been represented as defending guilt"
(I, 386). Dryden, as we noticed earlier, did have "address enough" to
solve the difficulty of which Johnson speaks. We recall that in the
Discourse concerning . . . Satire he anticipates Johnson's objection and

—or the core of it—was in fact written, and that it is a complex effort, to overturn the charge of Roman Catholic antichristianism and idolatry and to reaffirm the poetry of Roman Catholic iconic worship in a prophecy of inevitable English reconversion to the true faith. To accomplish this end, Dryden fused the allusive invocation of an English saint with the apocalyptic image of a Roman Catholic guardian angel— the poetically elaborated *"Tsebi"* or hind of Daniel—which itself does battle with the forces of Antichrist.[22]

The Book of Daniel ends with a refusal to explain its mysterious allegories and with a prophecy of "rest."

> 12:8   . . . then said I, O my Lord, what *shall be* the end
>   of these *things?*
>
>   9   And he said, Go thy way, Daniel: for the words
>   *are* closed up and sealed till the time of the end.
>
>   10   Many shall be purified, and made white. . . .

---

describes the solution which he actually employed in *The Hind and the Panther.* Some "celestial beings" can be "represented as defending guilt," Dryden suggests, because what "wicked spirits cannot compass, by the vast disproportion of their forces to those of the superior beings, they may by their fraud, and cunning carry farther, in a seeming league, confederacy, or subserviency to the designs of some good angel. . . . I know not why . . . a fiend may not deceive a creature of more excellency than himself, but yet a creature; at least by the connivance, or tacit permission, of the Omniscient Being" (*Of Dramatic Poesy,* II, 91). The Anglican guardian angel defends guilt when "The *Wolfe* begins to share her wandring heart. / Though unpolluted yet with actual ill, / She half commits, who sins but in Her will" (I, 338–40). She is like a spirit "of a midle sort, / Too black for heav'n, and yet too white for hell, / Who just dropt half way down, nor lower fell" (I, 342–44). By analogy, the pigeons do not commit any acts of rank evil until, as we saw, they are misled by the "Beast of a Bird" (III, 1013 ff.).

22. Although no important seventeenth-century analogue for *The Hind and the Panther*—as a whole—has been found, it is possible that the poem's significant elements had been brought together by someone before Dryden. (Lockier has left us the following unexplained comment: "the *Hind and the Panther* full of wit but a servile copy"—see Joseph Spence, *Observations, Anecdotes, and Characters of Books and Men,* ed. James M. Osborn, Oxford, 1966, I, 277.)

13 But go thou thy way till the end *be:* for thou shalt
rest, and stand in thy lot at the end of the days.

At the end of *The Hind and the Panther* the spotted Panther
is left—in a gesture of hope—in the hermit's proselytizing
cell, while the Hind goes her way to glorious rest. Apocalyptic predictions suddenly become unimportant; there will
be strife and tragic suffering, Dryden implies, but the outcome
will ultimately be sabbatic millennium.

> The Dame withdrew, and, wishing to her Guest
> The peace of Heav'n, betook her self to rest.
> Ten thousand Angels on her slumbers waite
> With glorious Visions of her future state.
>
> [III, 1295–98]

The transcendence implied in these lines should not surprise us. Already in *Religio Laici* the poet's reason, as we
have seen, was reaching beyond reason. Instrumental to the
functioning of the "great automaton" or abstract image which
moves that poem is the gracious assistance of suprarational
energy.[23] The poet could lower himself into the chaos of
dispute and still attain clear conceptions of divine truth because his reason was secured and elevated by celestial aid. In
addition, his conceptions could correspond to truth because
he achieved them without submitting to the materiousness of
imagination. From the Panther's point of view, his reason
succeeded in resisting the "Abyss of deep Idolatry" (II, 633).

The essential differences between *Religio Laici* and *The
Hind and the Panther* are not so much matters of doctrine as
differences in attitude toward metaphors and images which
correlate with, and perhaps even determine, differences in
epistemology and belief. For Dryden, Anglicanism and Roman
Catholicism came to represent distinct orders of imagination,
both of which, at their best, could succeed in imaging spiritual

23. Cf. chap. 6.

truth. The Anglicanism espoused by *Religio Laici* succeeds by virtue of its ability to mold intellectual abstractions into a dynamic outline of divine reality. The Roman Catholicism of *The Hind and the Panther* takes a different route: it avoids metaphor and false images by surrogating a dazzling monstrance of mystery. Like Daniel's visions, *The Hind and the Panther* had to remain "closed up and sealed." Dryden believed that satire in general should proceed "figuratively, and occultly";[24] and in *The Hind and the Panther,* particularly, the occult is of crucial importance. "O teach me to believe Thee," the Roman Catholic poet says to his God, "thus conceal'd" (I, 68),

> Beyond what sense and reason can conceive.
> And for mysterious things of faith rely
> On the Proponent, heav'ns authority.
>
> [I, 119–21]

Divine truth, he now emphasizes—even more than he did in *Religio Laici*—should be communicated mysteriously:

> what one Saint has said of holy *Paul,*
> *He darkly writ,* is true apply'd to all.
>
> [II, 344–45]

The Hind and the Panther makes a program of the mysterious. In it Dryden decided to "launch"—"In the same vessel which our Saviour bore / Himself the Pilot" (I, 130–32)—into the "abyss of light" (I, 66): he committed himself to the darkling revelations of divine truth which emerge from God's secret mercy to man's reason and from the occult symbol of tragedy and triumph which the poet's reason was allowed to create from the mysteries of Daniel and primitive English Christianity. In the "abyss of light" Dryden attained the final stage in the surrogation of light images for the divine essence. The metaphor of a "throne [of] darkness in th' abyss

24. *Of Dramatic Poesy,* II, 143.

of light" indicates a realm beyond metaphor; it creates an image beyond imagination, a conceit which defies concrete conceptualization. With this image—and in *The Hind and the Panther* as a whole—Dryden showed us that allusions need not be merely descriptive or definitive, that at their most striking they are powerfully invocative and infinitive.[25] In *The Hind and the Panther,* Dryden attempted to approximate the shape of the divine by creating immeasurable correspondences and resonances. He recognized that one of the things poetry and religion have most in common is a sense of intellectual infinitude.

Each of Dryden's religious poems is an act of faith; each renders a central imaginative process of its belief (as Dryden understood it) and each relies, for its own wholeness, on God's gracious aid. From a formalist point of view, we might say that it is the planned leap or gap itself—the architectonic void supported between proposition and conclusion—which gives these works much of their power. In *The Hind and the Panther,* indeed, Dryden found a way to import *infinite* spaciousness. But there is a cultural or spiritual dimension to both poems for which no formalism can account. In both, the poet's imaginative reason remains inadequate without revelation or illumination from without. In both, a vision of truth is impossible without first entering the chaos and trusting to a higher power. Dryden's forays into the abyss added two links to the concatenate enterprise of courageous artificers in all ages who have resolved to fend off the night. One thinks readily, as Dryden might have, of *Paradise Lost* and its "descent to light" (to use D. C. Allen's fine phrases), in which Milton joined "the procession, heathen and Christian, of

25. Maynard Mack has pointed out that we generally associate this latter quality with Romantic poetry: see " 'Wit and Poetry and Pope': Some Observations on his Imagery," p. 21. (It may be, for example, that Dryden's account of the immortal white Hind in the closing lines of the poem is meant to echo the description of the "Ancient of days" in Daniel 7:9–10.)

those who acted in the great allegory of faith, who descended to ascend, who entered the darkness to see the light." [26]

The millennial *dissolution* of rationalistic constructs presaged in the sea of "Supernatural Light" of *Religio Laici* (l. 11) was, for Dryden at least, realized in the "abyss of light"—the "fair ocean" (II, 549)—or "mysterious writ" (III, 2) of *The Hind and the Panther.* Even in 1693 he would only offer camouflaged hints to the vast unfathomed meaning of his culminating poetic-religious vision. In the last year of his life, he recalled with a sense of secret pride that Blackmore had pilfered the shell of an heroic poem from the *Discourse concerning . . . Satire*; but the core of his heroic idea presented in the same place remained beyond Blackmore's powers: "The Guardian Angels of kingdoms were machines too ponderous for him to manage; and therefore he rejected them, as Dares did the whirl-bats of Eryx when they were thrown before him by Entellus." [27] Dryden's biographers have been reluctant to credit the tradition that he wept upon reading *The Hind and the Panther Transvers'd*.[28] Perhaps we can now understand that Dryden might very well have wept: not for the insolence of two young puppies, but for the failure in culture—the vacuum in knowledge, sensibility, and religion—which their betrayal or ignorance represented.

26. "Milton and the Descent to Light," reprinted in *Milton: Modern Essays in Criticism*, ed. Arthur E. Barker (New York, 1965), p. 192.

27. *Of Dramatic Poesy*, II, 293; see also II, 178.

28. See *Lives of the English Poets*, ed. Hill, II, 182, and Scott, *Life of John Dryden*, ed. Kreissman, pp. 284–85. Malone believed that the story was essentially (though not literally) accurate: see *Prose Works of John Dryden*, ed. Malone, I, 199.

Appendix A

The Old Mystery of "A. W."
and the New Mystery of "W. A."

Our altered perspective on Dryden's early religious thought puts us in a better position to consider two pieces of evidence that have been, until recently, unknown quantities. The first has long been recognized as a mystery. The second has been no less a mystery, though less notice has been taken of it. Both are possibly of great significance to filling in the early years of Dryden's career.

In 1885, George Saintsbury reported that he had found "some curious and hitherto almost unknown matter concerning a supposed Deistical treatise of Dryden's." [1] He promised to include these materials in a later volume of Dryden's prose, but by the time he reached that volume, as he tells us, he had unfortunately lost the materials and could say only, "I remember nothing about it, except that the 'supposition' as far as I then examined it seemed to me to have very little, if any, strength." [2] We cannot be sure what materials Saintsbury had found but it seems likely that it was *A Summary Account of the Deist's Religion . . . and An Essay by the Celebrated Poet, John Dryden, Esq; to prove that Natural Religion is alone necessary to Salvation* (London, 1745). The editor of this book defended his attribution by saying that he was

1. *Works of John Dryden*, x, 9.
2. Ibid., XVIII, 310.

"credibly informed by a Gentleman of great Learning and Integrity [that the work] was penn'd by that Eminent Poet John Dryden, Esq."[3] The essay first appeared, as far as we know, in Blount's *Oracles of Reason* (1693). The *Oracles* were reprinted in Blount's *Miscellaneous Works* (1695). The 1745 edition differs from the 1693 and 1695 editions in that it omits the complimentary close, "I am, SIR, Your Friend without Reserve," and the signature, "A. W.," which the earlier editions contain. It has been pointed out that Hugh Macdonald is mistaken in assigning the essay to Blount.[4] The essay is addressed, as a letter, *to* Blount and differs considerably from the views that Blount held. Eugene Purpus has cited many contemporary notices that distinguished between A. W.'s views and Blount's. Purpus, however, is not satisfied with denying Blount's authorship of the essay. He also denies that Dryden could have written it. For this statement there is no evidence. He proceeds directly to his conclusion from the assumption that, "No one who examined the content or history of the piece would now claim the work for Dryden."[5] By the "history of the piece" he seems to mean its reception as a deistical work and its signature, "A. W." Purpus comes to the conclusion that A. W. was a man whose initials really were A. W. but he adds: "The full name of A. W. must, at least for the present, remain a mystery. There were at the time no similar works published under those initials or under any name for which those initials would stand; and a study of the biographical dictionaries and bibliographical indices reveals no likely candidate."[6] It must be remarked

3. See Eugene R. Purpus, "Some Notes on a Deistical Essay Attributed to Dryden," *PQ*, XXIX (1950), 347.

4. Macdonald, *John Dryden: A Bibliography*, p. 184; he gives no reason for his attribution; cf. Hutcheson, *Cherbury's "De Religione Laici,"* p. 58, n. 8 and Purpus, p. 347.

5. Purpus, p. 347.

6. Ibid., p. 349.

that this is odd because it is suggested in the essay that its author was a man of some reputation.[7]

If we are to go any further in solving the problem of Dryden and "A. W." it will be, it seems to me, by first examining the content of the essay more closely. The title of the 1745 edition informs the reader that the essay attempts "to prove that Natural Religion is alone necessary to Salvation, in Opposition to all Divine Revelation." The 1693 copy bears the title *Of Natural Religion, as opposed to Divine Revelation.* Here the sense of "as opposed to" can be "as distinguished from" divine revelation; yet it too carries a connotation of hostility which is not manifest in the essay itself. Near the end of the work we are told:

> It has been demanded of me, Whether I should be convinc'd of my Opinion, and admit of supernatural Religion, in case the Gospel (*i.e.*) a supernatural Religion had been promulgated to all the World? I answer'd, I should; and was contented that the whole stress of the Dispute should be terminated in that one Point. It was reply'd, That then if it could be proved that this [u]niversal Revelation was unnecessary, I ought to acquiesce; I granted that also.[8]

It seems probable that the bellicose title was the work of a second or third hand. In the essay as a whole, we must also note, there is evidence that the author was not a confirmed or conventional deist. His first principle is *"That there is one infinite, eternal God, Creator of all Things."* [9] Leland noted that several "of the deists would be far from agreeing

7. See *Oracles of Reason,* pp. 208–9. Harth, *Contexts of Dryden's Thought,* pp. 84 ff., has reported his discovery of an early manuscript copy of the essay in the Department of Printed Books of the British Museum.

8. *Oracles of Reason,* p. 208.

9. Ibid., p. 195.

with this writer" on such a view.[10] The second principle is
even more exceptional: *"That he governs the World by
Providence."* [11] The one principle which identifies most forms
of deism is the rejection of God's immanence or continued
activity in the universe.[12] A. W., whoever he was, was not an
orthodox deist.

Another suggestion of a date of composition far removed
from 1693 is the author's rejection of "Arguments" which
"Sir Ch. Wolsy calls Demonstrations to prove a Reveal'd
Religion." [13] A. W. is here referring to Sir Charles Wolseley's
The Reasonablenes of Scripture-Belief (London, 1672). To
reject Wolseley's arguments A. W. does not have to argue
against all possibility of divine authority for the Scriptures.
Wolseley's thesis is simply that the authority of Scripture can
be established by rational arguments. There is no record
of a second edition of Wolseley's work or any other evidence
of great popularity. It seems probable, therefore, that the
essay attributed to Dryden was first written down soon after
1672 when a reference to Wolseley would not have drawn a
blank response from the author's correspondent.

Nothing that we know of Dryden, or of the book, entirely
rules out the possibility that the eighteenth-century attribution may be sound. The "deistical" position of A. W. in or
around 1672 is very much like the deism which Dryden was
putting in the mouth of Montezuma in 1668 and St. Catherine
in 1670. It is the singular deism of an objective Christian
with universalist tendencies. It was no ordinary deist who
would propound his examples (where any place-name would
have done equally well) in terms of "going to Whitehall from
Coventgarden Church." [14] One is led to suspect that the es-

---

10. John Leland, *Principal Deistical Writers*, I, 46.
11. *Oracles of Reason*, p. 195.
12. See Hutcheson, p. 55.
13. *Oracles of Reason*, p. 204.
14. Ibid., p. 201. The passage is given below in full.

sayist's connection with the church as well as with Covent-
garden and Whitehall was more than casual. The author's
familiarity with Wolseley's work is also possibly suggestive.
Dryden, we know, spent part of at least one summer at
Wolseley's estate.[15] If Dryden did address such an essay to
Blount some years before 1682 there is no longer any need for
Scott's surprise at Blount's address of his own *Religio Laici* to
Dryden.

The essay contains some evidence of a prose style such
as we associate with Dryden. An example of this prose, which
also illustrates a use of light imagery which we have met
elsewhere in Dryden, follows:

> The next Objection against the Sufficiency of Natural
> Religion to Happiness eternal, is only a bare Affirmation
> of our Adversaries, That Natural Religion is but an
> imperfect Light, which God gives us so far, as that by
> improving[it, we may arrive at a Supernatur[a]l Knowl-
> edge. As suppose I were going to *Whitehall* from *Covent-
> garden* Church, and can then see only to the end of the
> *Strand* before me, but coming thither, am directed
> further.
>
> But I wholly deny any Natural Light can lead to a
> Supernatural; there is no proportion betwixt those two
> extreams: There is a Gulph betwixt. . . . And 'tis not
> so easy a passage as from *Covent-Garden* to *Whitehall;*
> 'tis rather from *Coventgarden* to some place beyond the
> *Cælum Empyræum,* and wholly out of the boundaries of
> Nature. Also to prove that God can reveal to me what
> is farther Necessary, when I have us'd my best Natural
> Endeavours, is only to prove that God is Omnipotent
> and Infinite; but proves not that 'tis necessary he should
> or will do it: for *a posse ad esse non valet Consequentia.*

15. See Osborn, *John Dryden: Facts and Problems,* pp. 200–01. It was
the summer of 1680.

I have already endeavoured to prove that it is not necessary he should reveal more; and therefore till that point
be determin'd . . . I humbly doubt and suspend my
Belief.[16]

To claim this for Dryden on the basis of style would require,
however, a considerable additional vivacity of tone, probably
more imagery and specific reference, and somewhat less
"method" (in the plodding sense of "method"). If the essay
were indeed Dryden's, *Religio Laici* would itself constitute
a fascinating act of revision.

The same quest for salvation of heathens which lies at
the intellectual center of both *Religio Laici* and A. W.'s
essay is also present in a third composition that requires some
bibliographical introduction, as it is little known. We have
already seen that Burthogge's *Causa Dei* is extremely close
to *Religio Laici*—both in the specialization of a tradition that
it represents and in specific parallels to Dryden's prefatory
history of Noah's revelation and the closely related exordium
image that is the foundation of the whole poem—in structure
as well as thought. It remains for us to point out that Burthogge wrote his book (1675), as he tells us, in answer to a
letter "from One from whom I . . . little expected it." [17]
Burthogge reprints the letter complaining that his last book,
Divine Goodness (London, 1670, 1671, and 1672), did not
account for the injustice of eternal punishment, especially
for heathens. The letter is signed "W. A." and Burthogge
suggests in the dedicatory epistle that W. A. is a person of
stature who wishes to remain truly anonymous—that is, that
the letters "W. A." are a complete fabrication. Here again
the biographical dictionaries and bibliographical indices offer no clues.

16. *Oracles of Reason,* pp. 201–02.
17. See Burthogge's Epistle Dedicatory (sig. A6r).

One cannot help being struck by the coincidence of two compositions of approximately the same date, with the same initials in reverse, with salvation for heathens as their main topic, and both carrying suggestions (from completely independent sources) of connections with Dryden. But this is all that one can at present say.

APPENDIX B

Religio Laici and Hamon L'Estrange's "Prerogatives" for the Veracity of Scripture

Phillip Harth has shown that, in composing many of his arguments in the first half of *Religio Laici,* Dryden consulted *The Reasonablenes of Scripture-Belief* (London, 1672) by Sir Charles Wolseley. But Harth has exaggerated Dryden's intellectual passivity by suggesting that Dryden used Wolseley's book "not only as the source of his arguments, but as the basis for the thought pattern in which he presents them." [1] In spite of striking and unmistakable echoes from Wolseley's treatise, it is impossible to agree that Dryden submitted absolutely to Wolseley's views of questions about which he himself had probably formulated his own opinions, and concerning which he could have found arguments in many other places and in other forms often more congenial to the special tendency of his own thought. This is not to say that he did not make extensive use of Wolseley's book; no doubt he did. But it is hard to believe, for example, that Dryden's forty-one lines of "proof" for the veracity of Scripture represent a mere abridgement, as Harth theorizes, of almost two hundred pages of Wolseley's polemics. [2] Dryden's use of *The Reasonablenes of Scripture-Belief* in the construction of his larger arguments in the poem was substantially limited by his conviction,

1. *Contexts of Dryden's Thought,* pp. 109–10. The material in this appendix has previously appeared in "New Light on Dryden's 'Religio Laici,'" *N&Q,* XVI (1969), 375–79.

2. Ibid., pp. 293–97

recorded in the Preface to *Religio Laici,* that one should not
and could not "prove Religion by Reason" (l. 89). Even
though he hoped that reason could somehow "apprehend" the
Scriptures "to be the word of God" he was not willing to
commit himself to a rational compulsion to accepting the
authority of the biblical text (l. 100). His hesitation on this
important point is reflected in the phrase he chose to intro-
duce the evidences of reason in his poem: "Proof needs not
here" (l. 126).

Dryden was not relying on Wolseley alone for his arguments
or his thought patterns. The nonproofs, as we might call them,
that he presents were available, for example, in a compact
list of only ten pages specifically enumerating them as nonproofs and explicitly addressing itself to the question of a
"necessary" minimum of divine truth (which we saw in chapter
6 is so crucial for Dryden's thinking in the poem). The list
appears in Hamon L'Estrange's *Considerations, upon Dr
Bayly's Parenthetical Interlocution; relating to the Churches
Power in deciding Controversies* (London, 1651), which a man
named Dryden bought at auction during the period of composition of *Religio Laici.*[3]

3. See Birrell, "John Dryden's Purchases," pp. 193–217. The auction of
1682, with which we are concerned, was patronized by many intellectual
notables, including Isaac Newton, Robert Hooke, Isaac Vossius, Henry
More, and John Locke. Pollard tells us that "the most interesting of
. . . early sales was that, on 15 May, 1682, of Richard Smith . . . who
had acquired and enlarged the collections of Humphrey Dyson. . . . The
Smith sale stands by itself." See *List of Catalogues of English Book Sales,
1676–1900, Now in the British Museum,* intro. Alfred W. Pollard (London, 1915), p. xi. John Lawler, *Book Auctions in England in the Seventeenth Century (1676–1700)* (London, 1898), pp. xxxvii–xxxviii, noted
that *"For variety and extent this library was one of the largest of any
private collection brought to the hammer in the seventeenth century."*
Macdonald originally excluded the possibility that the Dryden concerned could have been the poet, but he seems to have later altered
his opinion on this point (see Birrell, p. 193, n. 4). James M. Osborn has
questioned again whether it was really John Dryden the poet. His review
of Birrell's article, in *PQ,* XLI (1962), 580, is as follows: "Someone named

L'Estrange's exposition of the Anglican view is remarkable for the clarity it imposes upon opinions that are, in their very nature, ambivalent or subjectively balanced.

> I say, That the Scriptures are the word of God is a proposition, which must depend upon the evidence either of knowledge, or Faith. If of knowledge then it must be elicited, and extracted from the principles of natural reason. But all the reason in the world will never be able

---

Dryden purchased 146 books at the Digby sale, 19 April 1680, and the Richard Smith sale, 15 May 1682. There is no evidence that this was even one of the five contemporary John Drydens, for the Christian name never appears. Furthermore, most of the 146 books are tomes on obscure theological subjects; only about a dozen of the widely circulated titles can be shown to have been known to the poet." The coincidence of the 1682 purchases with the period of composition of *Religio Laici* does, however, add some credibility to Birrell's contention that it was the poet John Dryden who made the purchases. The close parallels between one of these obscure theological works and a part of the poem itself further suggest that Birrell's assumption may be correct, though Dryden may have come to this work in some other way. Ultimately, the parallels are mainly of interest to us for the context in which they help place Dryden's thought and the problem he faced.

L'Estrange was answering *Certamen Religiosum: Or, A Conference Between His late Majestie Charles King of England, and Henry late Marquess and Earl of Worcester, concerning Religion; at His Majesties being at Raglan Castle, 1646. Wherein the maine differences (now in Controversie) between the Papists and the Protestants is no lesse briefly then accuratly [sic] discuss'd and bandied. Now published for the worlds satisfaction of His Majesties constant affection to the Protestant Religion. By Tho: Baylie Doctor in Divinity and Sub-Deane of Wels* (London, 1649). The "Marquess" referred to was Henry, first marquis of Worcester (1577–1646) who, in the last months of his life, sent Bayly on a tour of the continent from which he returned a convert to Roman Catholicism. L'Estrange, as he tells the reader, doubted the authenticity of Bayly's record of the conference as well as Bayly's Protestant conviction. The exact extent of these doubts is not made clear. L'Estrange's answer to Bayly appeared as the second part of his *An Answer To the Marques of Worcester's Last Paper; to the Late King . . . . discussing briefly, the main Controversies between the English and the Romish Church* (London, 1651). Hamon L'Estrange (1605–60) was the brother of Roger L'Estrange (1616–1704).

to demonstrate, either that the Scriptures are the word
of God, or that they are not. Mistake me not, I do not
exclude reason, as a guide, nor place it so in the line of
incidence, as if it stood neuter, or indifferently inclined
to both the affirmative and negative; no, I hold vastly
otherwayes; Arguments she hath many, and ponderous to
perswade that the Scriptures are of Divine inspiration;
that they are not so, to diswade she hath and can frame
none. But yet those Arguments are but soluble, no
Demonstrations; for in Demonstrations the understanding is so clearly convinced by reason, that it can possibly
incline no other way then one, *Ea est vera Demonstratio
quæ cogit, non quæ persuadet:* . . . so that impossible
it is for us to *know* that the Scriptures are the word of
God. [pp. 85–86]

The poetic balance of reason and faith that is operative in
Dryden's phrases, "apprehend them to be the word of God"
and "Proof needs not here" can only be understood within the
context of a reading of the poem. But L'Estrange's discussion
is extremely valuable in spelling out for us the traditional
coherence of Dryden's shorthand expressions.

L'Estrange's introduction to the "Arguments" for faith in
Scripture is also useful for understanding Dryden's overall
procedure in the poem. Using the terminology of Anglican
orthodoxy, L'Estrange constructs a gradual approach—never
quite arriving at the destination—to reason-as-knowlege that is
in itself no mean rhetorical achievement:

> though to the members of the Church, the Authority of
> the Church be a vehement and strong motive, yet to
> Pagans and Infidels who will own no such thing as a
> Church, it is no motive at all; if they question the
> Scriptures Divinity studious either of cavil, or to be con-
> verted they must be refuted, or invited by arguments

drawn from reason, wherein they intercommune with us; and to speak truth, reason will carry them a very great way on towards, even to the very brink of Faith; reason will tell them that the Soul is immortal. . . . It will tell them, that God is their last home, . . . *yet how to come there is beyond the ken of Reason;* and . . . though Religion be the way to him, yet dim-sighted reason will never be able to find that way, till God himself reveals it; for . . . God himself is, and must be the Authour of that which brings us to him: and it were inconsistent with the Providence of the All-wise God, to withhold from man that means, without which impossible it is for man to attain that end for which he was created. [pp. 88–89]

"God," in other words (to quote from Dryden), "wou'd not leave Mankind without a way" (l. 296).

L'Estrange's last sentences of introduction to his "Arguments" for faith in Scripture tend to obliterate the distinction between plausibility and certainty:

Augustine chargeth it . . . upon the Pagan Gods as a grosse neglect, in not instructing of their worshippers in the way and means to happinesse. *To the care of the solicitous Gods, saith he, it did belong not to conceal from their worshippers the rudiments of living well, but to teach them by clear publication, also to convent and reprove offenders; by their Prophets to threaten open punishment to those who do ill, and to promise reward to those who live well.* Reason therefore will thus teach them [i.e. non-believers] the necessity of some conveyance from God of his revealed will, and that necessity will also infer the actual being of such a Revelation, considering that *Deus non deficit in necessariis, God is not wanting in affording what is necessary.* This necessity and being of Divine revelation once allowed, reason will make it further credible that the Scriptures now received and entertained amongst us Christians as the word of God, are indeed and in truth, that revealed will of God. [pp. 89–90]

Dryden might have been especially attracted to the framework of L'Estrange's list because it was a response to the argument (fideistic or merely High-Critical, as the case may be) that the Scriptures are too obscure to be reliable. L'Estrange gives the conventional Augustinian answer that "whatsoever is necessary for us to believe is there clear and manifest" but also acknowledges his adversary's stricture on this point: "But the Doct. saith, no man hath ever yet defin'd what are necessary and what not, what points are fundamental and what not." L'Estrange's answer touches on the most sensitive points in the orthodox Anglican argument, as Dryden read it in 1682 after the publication of Simon's *Critical History.* L'Estrange writes:

> Hath no man defin'd what is necessary, what is fundamental? Yes Doctor, *Learned Hooker* tells you it is the Doctrine which the Prophets and Apostles professe; the late Reverend *Arch-Bishop* tells you,[4] the Articles of the Creed which is but the summary of that Doctrine are such, and so is the belief of the Scriptures to be the word of God and infallible. [p. 82]

The drift of Bayly's questions inevitably leads L'Estrange to take up the crucial question of the authority of Scripture.

> The Doctor is now entered into a weighty point, and not more weighty then intricate, *viz.* how we are ascertained that the Scriptures are the word of God. The Doctor with the Church of *Rome,* derives that assurance from the Testimony and tradition of the Church, and

4. The "late Reverend Arch-Bishop" was William Laud (1573–1645). The "Articles of the Creed" referred to are the Thirty-nine Articles formulated in Elizabeth's reign.

her Testimony is indeed of all, sufficient to render us so
assured, if she be so infallible and in-erring as they
pretend; for our Faith, in this particular, cannot be
guided by any thing beneath infallible. This question
being so considerable, and of such concernment, it will
not I hope be thought amisse, if I spend a little the more
time about it. [p. 85]

The "time" which L'Estrange spends on this question develops arguments which are helpful in making us see that
another Anglican work, of a very different kind from *The
Reasonablenes of Scripture-Belief*, offered Dryden convenient
materials that in some cases resemble the larger meaning as
well as the individual verses of *Religio Laici* more closely
than Wolseley's arguments. The verses of Dryden's first "proof"
for the authority of the Book, for example, sound very much
like L'Estrange's first "Prerogative":

> First Antiquity, the Doctrine of them being far ancienter
> then all other Religions in the world, and almost as
> ancient as time itself . . . before the Floud, even in Para-
> dise it self, there was the doctrine of saving Truth first
> instituted. [pp. 90–91]

Dryden writes:

> Whether from length of *Time* its worth we draw,
> The *World* is scarce more *Ancient* than the *Law*:
> Heav'ns early Care prescrib'd for every Age;
> First, in the *Soul*, and after, in the *Page*.
>
> [ll. 134–37]

Or, to take another instance, the suggestion for using the
complex metaphor of Scripture growing in "Natures Soil"—
where it is "unfed"—is also present in the Prerogatives which
correspond to Dryden's lines 156–63:

> All Faiths *beside,* or did by *Arms* ascend;
> Or *Sense* indulg'd has made *Mankind* their *Friend:*

> This *onely* Doctrine does our *Lusts* oppose:
> Unfed by Natures Soil, in which it grows;
> Cross to our *Interests,* curbing Sense, and Sin;
> Oppress'd without, and undermin'd within,
> It thrives through pain; its own Tormentours tires;[5]
> And with a stubborn patience still aspires.

Speaking of the moral content of the Scriptures, L'Estrange tells us that

> 'tis not a doctrine of sensuality and dissolutenesse, not a doctrine of self-ends and by-respects, not a doctrine of worldly pomp and state, not a doctrine of wicked principles and discipline, but a doctrine of sobriety, and of self-denial, and of humility, and of virtue; a doctrine tending onely to God, and what is in order to him, which sequestreth the soul from all earthly imaginations and cogitations. . . . *The Romans often pruned and lopt its Professors off, and still the more they increased.* [pp. 91–3]

L'Estrange sums up:

> Reason cannot conclude lesse than . . . *This must be the Lord's doing.* . . . *The voice,* the Word *of God* it must be, *and not of man.* [p. 94]

Dryden concludes:

> To what can *Reason* such Effects assign
> Transcending *Nature,* but to *Laws Divine?*
> Which in that Sacred Volume are contain'd;
> Sufficient, clear, and for that use ordain'd.
>
> [ll. 164–67]

After the publication of Simon's *Critical History,* however, not every part of L'Estrange's introduction could be palatable

5. Harth, p. 144, n. 78 and p. 145, is surely correct in noting Wolseley's strong influence on ll. 157 and 162.

to Dryden. L'Estrange believed (as did Wolseley and many others)[6] that "the Scriptures now received and entertained amongst us Christians as the word of God, are indeed and in truth, that revealed will of God" (p. 90). This belief, as L'Estrange points out, was a central part of the Anglican definition of "necessary truths." It was a definition which Dryden, in spite of the great importance he himself attached to a minimum of "needfull" truths (cf. *Religio Laici*, l. 409), could not accept in 1682. He had to readjust his thinking if he was to accommodate the stress imposed by Simon's researches.

6. Cf. *The Reasonablenes of Scripture-Belief*, pp. 263–88 and Harth, pp. 294–95.

APPENDIX C

"Th' Abyss of Light"

The images in lines 66–67 of the First Part of *The Hind and the Panther,*

> Thy throne is darkness in th' abyss of light,
> A blaze of glory that forbids the sight,

probably possessed a special ambience for poets of the later seventeenth century. Norris of Bemerton's "Hymn to Darkness," which was published in the same year as *The Hind and the Panther,* informs us that

> Though light and glory be th' Almighty's throne,
> Darkness is His pavillion;[1]

Henry Vaughan wrote in "The Night"

> There is in God (some say)
> A deep, but dazling darkness;[2]

and in *Paradise Lost* God the Father is addressed as follows:

> Fountain of Light, thyself invisible
> Amidst the glorious brightness where thou sit'st
> Thron'd inaccessible . . .
> Dark with excessive bright thy skirts appear,
> Yet dazzle Heav'n.

[III, 375–81]

1. *John Norris of Bemerton: Selected Poems,* ed. J. R. Tutin (Hull, Eng., 1905), p. 44.

2. Cited from *The Works of Henry Vaughan,* ed. L. C. Martin (Oxford, 1957). Cf. Thomas Traherne, "The Anticipation," viii, 7–9; and Dryden, *To the Pious Memory of . . . Anne Killigrew,* l. 11, *Britannia Rediviva,* l. 226; and l. 82 of his translation of Ovid, *Metamorphoses,* xv.

It is impossible to say who influenced whom, but we can, at least, sketch the general sources and usages of these images.

It has been pointed out that Vaughan's lines, at least, probably derived directly from the mystical writings of Dionysius the Areopagite.[3] In his letter to Dorotheus the Deacon, Dionysius wrote,

> The divine darkness is the inaccessible light in which God is said to dwell. . . . He is invisible by reason of the abundant outpouring of supernatural light.[4]

Dryden's images, we note, are very similar.

Milton's lines and his general conception of a "vast immeasurable Abyss" (*Paradise Lost*, VII, 211)—where "length, breadth, highth, / And time and place are lost" (*Paradise Lost*, II, 893–94)—may also owe something to Dionysius, but his more immediate debt, as M. L. Bailey has shown, is to the German mystic Jakob Boehme, whose writings we considered before in relation to the ground of *Religio Laici*.[5] Boehme taught that God "is in himself the Abyss [or Chaos]. . . . He is the nothing and all things; and is one only will, in which lieth the world and whole creation." "God is to be considered, as to what he is, without nature and creature in himself, in a self-comprehensible Chaos, without ground, time, and place." [6] Charles Hotham, More's tutor at Cambridge, expounded Boehme's views by emphasizing the "light" which flows "through the circuit of the infinite Abysse": the "bottomlesse Immensurable," he wrote, is "the eternal habitation of the

3. See Martin, p. 750, and E. C. Pettet, *Of Paradise and Light* (Cambridge, 1960), p. 152, n. 1. For the relation of Dionysius to Milton, see D. C. Allen, "Milton and the Descent to Light," pp. 188 ff.

4. From the modern translation by A. B. Sharpe in his *Mysticism: Its True Nature and Value* (London, 1910), p. 228.

5. Margaret Lewis Bailey, *Milton and Jakob Boehme: A Study of German Mysticism in Seventeenth-Century England* (New York, 1914), p. 143.

6. Quoted by Bailey, p. 143.

Godhead." [7] Norris's affiliates in the Cambridge group seem to partake almost equally of Boehmistic and Dionysian influence in their use of abyss imagery. Peter Sterry tells us that the Spirit sits "recollected, and concentred in an Unfathom'd Depth of Glorious Life," [8] while John Smith goes back to those striking passages in Dionysius which had held a powerful fascination for Aquinas: the soul, Smith writes, is "swallowed up in the boundless Abyss of Divinity . . . that [divine darkness] which the Areopagite speaks of, which the higher our Minds soar into, the more incomprehensible they find it." [9] When we read such passages as the following in Boehme we cannot help wondering if Dryden's revision of the "ground" metaphor (comparable in many ways to Boehme's "Grund")[10] of *Religio Laici* to the "abyss" or "deep" (comparable to Boehme's "Ungrund" or "Abgrund") of *The Hind and the Panther* can have been without special intent.

> Into the Light which is extinguished in it [the soul] *cannot* demerse it self in its *own* ability.
>
> But into the *Cause* of the Light, wherein there is neither Evil nor Good, it *can* demerse it self: for *it self* is the Ground: now therefore if it demerseth it self and fall down from its Imagibility or Imagination in it self on to the Abysse; then it is *there* already.[11]

From this point of view, it may be that Dryden's launching into the "abyss" in *The Hind and the Panther* was the logical extension of his entrance into the "ground" in *Religio Laici*; the later poem thus became the second stage in a continuous quest for divine light.

7. *An Introduction to the Teutonick Philosophie* (London, 1650), pp. 34 and 40.

8. *The Rise, Race, and Royalty of the Kingdom of God in the Soul of Man* (London, 1683), p. 24.

9. *Select Discourses,* p. 125; cf. J. Durantel, *Saint Thomas et le Pseudo-Denis* (Paris, 1919), p. 269

10. Cf. my discussion of this point in chap. 6.

11. *Concerning the Election of Grace,* p. 172.

Index

Abbot, Robert, 202
Abrams, M. H., 57 n.
Absolon, 204
Abyss, 234, 242
Abyss of light, 228, 235, 237, 254–56 passim. *See also* Dryden: *The Hind and the Panther*; Cambridge Platonists; Boehme; Dionysius; Ground metaphor
Academics, the, 39
Achitophel, 182, 204, 215 n.
Adam, 87
Aesop, 226, 227
Alexander the Great, 164
Algebra, 129, 130, 130 n.
Allegory, 222, 226 n., 227, 233, 237. *See also* Fable
Allen, Don Cameron, 85 n., 182 n., 236, 255 n.
Allison, Anthony, 219 n.
All Soul's College, Oxford, 86 n., 182 n.
Anabaptism, 25 n., 216
Anamnesis, 99–100. *See also* Ground metaphor
Ancient of Days, 231, 236 n.
Andrewes, Lancelot, 63 n.
Angels, 221, 234. *See also* Guardian angels
Animals, allegorized: ape, 164; ass, 184 n.; bear, 169, 191, 198, 199, 204, 217, 227; boar, 169, 204, 217; capricorn, 198, 208, 231; daw, 166; dog, 166; dove, 184 n., 231, 232; eagle, 198, 204; elephant, 167; fowl, 199; fox, 169, 204, 205; goat, 198, 203, 205; hare, 217; horse, 166, 185 n.; leopard, 199, 203; lion, 170, 186, 187, 198, 199,

204, 205, 217, 229; mouse, 165, 166, 169; pigeon, 232, 233 n.; ram, 198, 231; raven, 184 n.; rhinoceros, 167; sheep, 213; swallow, 230, 231; vulture, 229; wolf, 168, 169, 178, 179, 191, 200, 201, 227, 233 n. *See also* Birds; Hind; Panther
Antichrist, 201–08 passim, 210, 212, 214–19 passim, 223, 229, 231, 232, 233
Apocalyptic exegesis, 201–16 passim, 202 n., 203 n., 206 n., 207 n., 218, 219, 230, 233, 234
Apollonius, 31, 32, 33
Aquinas. *See* Thomas Aquinas, Saint
Archilochus, 6
Archimedes, 15, 130, 130 n.
Arianism, 14 n.
Aristotle, 89, 114; alluded to, 105
Arius, 80, 123, 142, 142 n. *See also* Heresy
Armada, Spanish, 47 n.
Arminianism, 67, 216. *See also* Heresy
Arthur, King, 193
Articles of the Creed, 250, 250 n.
Aspinwall, William, 204
Assyrians, 213
Athanasian Creed, 12, 123, 123 n., 124
Athanasius, Saint, 7, 12, 14 n., 18, 82, 123, 123 n., 124, 142, 142 n., 153
Athenian, the, 82
Augustan poetry, 179, 191
Augustine, Saint, 66, 220, 249, 250